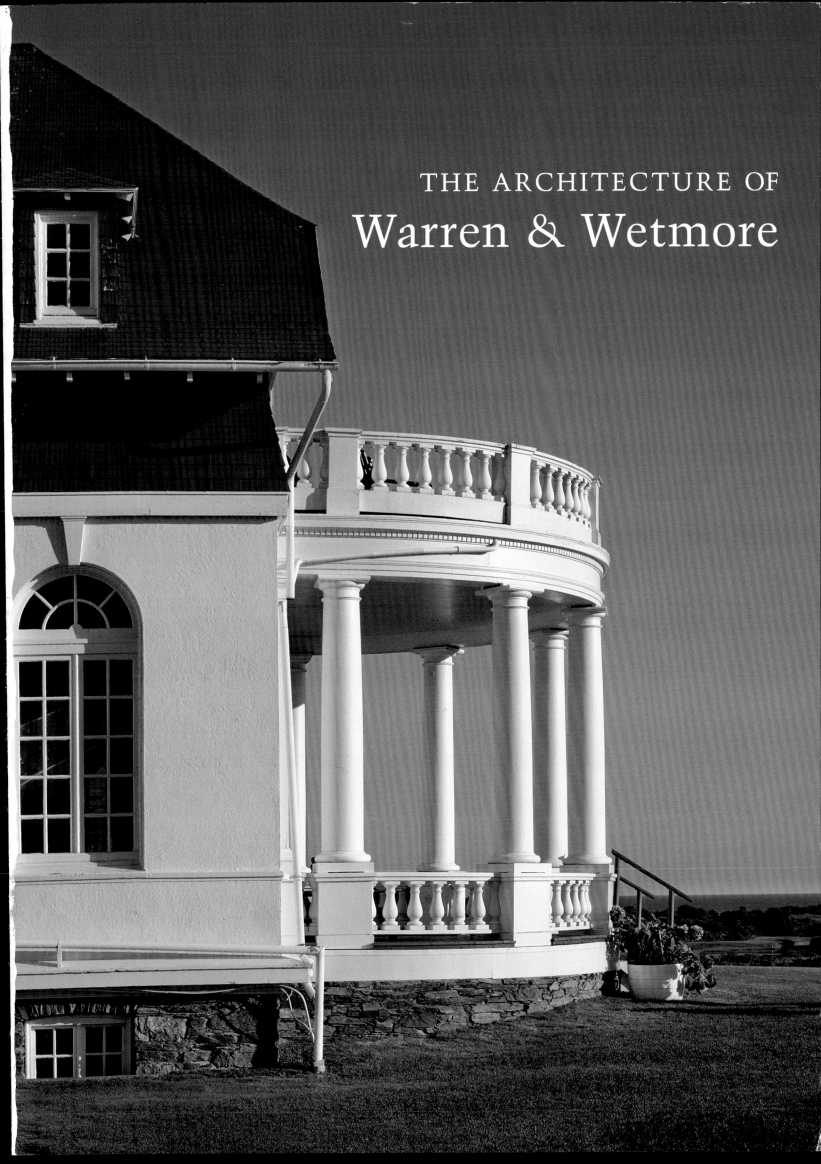

THE ARCHITECTURE OF
Warren & Wetmore

Newport Country Club

Newport, Rhode Island, 1894–95

Preceding page: East porch.

This page: Entrance facade.

Following pages: Oval salon.

New York Yacht Club

New York City, 1898–1901

Above left: Window detail.

*Above: Detail of gallery and ceiling,
model room.*

Opposite: Model room.

Court Tennis Court Building

Tuxedo Park, New York, 1899

Above: Entrance facade.

Left: Detail of carved brackets, entrance facade.

Opposite: Side porch.

William Starr Miller estate

*High Tide, Newport,
Rhode Island, 1900*

Above: View from Bailey's Beach.

James A. Burden Jr. house

New York City, 1902–5

Left: Reception room.

Opposite: Stair with murals by Hector d'Espouy.

Following pages: Ballroom.

Grand Central Terminal

New York City, 1904–13

Above left: Door detail, waiting room (now Vanderbilt Hall).

Above: Detail of chandelier and iron-work, main concourse.

Opposite: Main concourse.

Grand Central Terminal

New York City, 1904–13

Left: Ceiling detail.

Opposite: View looking east from Oyster Bar ramp.

Yonkers Station

Yonkers, New York, 1911

Above: Entrance facade.

*Right: Terra-cotta detail,
entrance facade.*

Westchester-Biltmore Country Club

Rye, New York, 1919–22

Left: Columns in the form of basket carriers supportng arcade, entrance facade.

Below: Entrance gallery.

Steinway Hall

New York City, 1923–25

Left: Detail of roofline.

Lower left: Barrel-vaulted corridor decorated with busts of the Steinways.

Opposite: Reception room.

Aeolian Building

New York City, 1925–27

Left: Detail of roofline.

New York Central Building

New York City, 1927–29

*Opposite: Detail of upper floors
and roofline.*

William K. Vanderbilt Jr. estate, Eagle's Nest

Centerport, New York, c. 1928

Opposite: View of bell tower from courtyard.

Right: View of south facade from boxwood garden.

Lower right: Boxwood garden with sundial.

William K. Vanderbilt Jr. estate, Eagle's Nest

Centerport, New York, c. 1928

Opposite: Main entrance.

Right: Library.

Lower right: Organ room with eighteenth-century Aubusson tapestry hiding a 2,000-pipe Aeolian organ.

University Library

Louvain, Belgium, 1922–28

Entrance facade.

University Library

Louvain, Belgium, 1922–28

Clockwise from lower left:

Roof detail, interior courtyard.

Cupola and gable with Allied symbols.

Bust of King Albert, entrance facade.

Bust of Cardinal Mercier by Pierre de Soete, side facade.

Opposite: Entrance arcade.

Following page: Main stair.

THE ARCHITECTURE OF
Warren & Wetmore

PETER PENNOYER AND ANNE WALKER

FOREWORD BY ROBERT A. M. STERN
NEW PHOTOGRAPHS BY JONATHAN WALLEN

W.W. NORTON & COMPANY
New York • London

For information about permission to reproduce selections
from this book, write to Permissions, W. W. Norton & Company, Inc.,
500 Fifth Avenue, New York, NY 10110

Manufacturing by Friesens
Book design by Abigail Sturges
Production manager: Leeann Graham

Library of Congress Cataloging-in-Publication Data

Pennoyer, Peter
   The architecture of Warren & Wetmore / Peter Pennoyer
   and Anne Walker; foreword by Robert A. M. Stern.
       p. cm.
   Includes bibliographical references and index.

   ISBN 0-393-73162-6
   1. Warren & Wetmore. 2. Architecture—United States—
   20th century. 3. Ecole nationale supérieure des beaux-arts (France)—
   Influence. I. Title: Architecture of Warren and Wetmore.
   II Walker, Anne. III. Title.

NA737.W34P46 2006
720′.92—dc22

2005048249

ISBN 0-393-73162-6

W. W. Norton & Company,
Inc. 500 Fifth Avenue, New York, N.Y. 10110

www.wwnorton.com

W. W. Norton & Company ltd., Castle House,
75/76 Wells Street, London W1T 3QT

0 9 8 7 6 5 4 3 2 1 0

Contents

Foreword

Peter Pennoyer and Anne Walker are leaders among a small but inspiring group of architects and scholars who are helping to rewrite the history of twentieth-century American architecture by bringing to our attention the accomplishments of long-overlooked figures—overlooked because they did not embrace stylistic modernism but instead preferred to work with traditional languages from the past, which they employed with amazing grace and considerable inventiveness. Much of this recent scholarship has concentrated on architects whose principal accomplishments were in the field of domestic architecture: David Adler, Mott Schmidt, and the firm of Delano and Aldrich, which was the subject of Pennoyer and Walker's previous book, come to mind. The literature covering the work of such firms has reinforced a view of traditional architecture that tends to confine it to the category of "refined taste" catering to escapist exurbanites who patronized disengaged architectural professionals unwilling to tackle the crucial problems of modernization and modernity. Such is hardly the case and no book better makes the point for the "relevance" of the work of American traditionalist architects than this one, documenting the partnership of Whitney Warren (1864–1943) and Charles Wetmore (1866–1941). As Pennoyer and Walker meticulously chronicle the work of this pair of highly professional, highly responsible, and highly successful architects, the crucial role of architectural traditionalism in shaping American life takes on a new dimension.

Warren and Wetmore were simply amazing in the range of the building types they took on, the ingenuity of their planning in response to new demands of the marketplace, and their ability to renew familiar forms. Though they designed notable New York townhouses and numerous country residences, it was the firm's larger-scale, more public work that put its achievements in a special category. Warren and Wetmore were classicists and traditionalists and among the most modern architects of their time. To understand what I mean by this, one has but to look beneath the dazzlingly accomplished surfaces of their work to discover buildings planned to meet the unprecedented needs of the new century, buildings perched atop underground railroad yards, buildings calibrated to serve American travelers on holiday in far-flung climates from Cuba to Colorado to Hawaii. Warren and Wetmore virtually invented the modern luxury resort hotel, perfected the grand apartment house, and transformed buildings for transportation into quintessential urban landmarks. Their numerous office buildings formed the fabric of Manhattan's Midtown and two of their skyline-defining skyscrapers—the Heckscher and the Con Edison towers—are among New York's most memorable icons.

First and foremost, most of us probably associate Warren and Wetmore with Grand Central Terminal, a project of immense complexity and sophistication involving the sometimes not entirely cordial collaboration of many architects and engineers. Reed and

Stem, architects who specialized in railroad stations, and William J. Wilgus, the New York Central's engineer, made very important contributions to this project. But it is Whitney Warren who gave the Terminal its final shape, creating the great limestone- and glass-clad volume that encompasses waiting rooms and the immensity of the Concourse which has become, in Philip Johnson's words, the American San Marco. And it was Whitney Warren who pushed through the Terminal's complement, the campanile-like New York Central tower astride the twin roadways of Park Avenue, realizing a vision of integrated multilevel traffic planning married to monumental urban form that is often miscredited to the modernist LeCorbusier, but was in fact derived from the early plans for Grand Central and its offshoot, Terminal City, which, in turn had their roots in the teachings of the Ecole des Beaux-Arts where Warren studied architecture and to whose planning principles he remained devoted throughout his career.

Though Warren and Wetmore's principal legacy is their large-scale urban and resort projects, Whitney Warren should also be remembered for his important contributions in support of France during the First World War and, most especially, for his University Library, Louvain, Belgium (1928), which replaced the fifteenth-century landmark destroyed by the Germans in 1914. Paid for by American citizens, the new building married a scholarly interpretation of late medieval and early Renaissance precedents in Flanders to the disciplined functional planning that was characteristic of the firm's work. The short life of the building—it was shelled by the Germans in May 1940, resulting in the loss of most of the building and all of its 700,000 books that had been gifts of Americans—is a too little remembered tragedy.

I salute Pennoyer and Walker for their scholarship and for their dedication. Now it remains for them and for others to go on with this project of historical retrieval: of the generation of Warren and Wetmore, which was also that of Frank Lloyd Wright, there remain many more important architects to be studied and written about: the partnership of John M. Carrère (1858–1911) and Thomas Hastings (1860–1929) comes immediately to mind, as well as the work of Cyrus L.W. Eidlitz (1853–1921), Henry J. Hardenbergh (1847–1918), and Bruce Price (1845–1903), among New York-based practitioners. And among younger architects also based in New York, are Harrie T. Lindeberg (1879–1959), Robert D. Kohn (1870–1953), Grosvenor Atterbury (1869–1956), and Guy Lowell (1870–1927), to name but four who also deserve the kind of serious scholarship that Pennoyer and Walker command. Other cities—for example, Boston, Chicago, and San Francisco—have their comparable talents awaiting scholarly recognition. There is much work to be done. The example of Pennoyer and Walker sets the bar appropriately high and invites others to take on this important job.

— Robert A. M. Stern

Introduction

In 1898 Whitney Warren (1864–1943) and Charles D. Wetmore (1866–1941) formed what was to become one of the most prolific and successful architectural practices in the history of America. The partners were fortunate to establish their firm in New York during the period known as the American Renaissance (1876–1917), an era of sweeping economic expansion fueled by the explosion in mercantile and industrial activity following the Civil War. At the turn of the twentieth century, nearly two-fifths of the shares listed on the New York Stock Exchange were associated with railroads. Because the banks and insurance concerns behind the industry shared board members with the railroad companies, the financial and industrial worlds were virtually interlaced.[1] As America was transformed by the telegraph, telephone, and railroads, cities grew substantially and flourished. New York City, the financial capital of the country, stood at the center of the thriving economy and provided fertile ground for the titans and robber barons of the day to impose their taste and ambitions. To celebrate the nation's wealth and its cultural coming of age, the period's leading citizens encouraged an architectural expression that conveyed a sense of permanence, sophistication, and opulence.

During the years leading up to the Great Depression, the flamboyant Beaux-Arts-trained Warren and his shrewd partner Wetmore grasped the stylistic requirements of their time to create a particular brand of architecture that reflected the cultural, social, and business aspirations of America's ruling class. Completing over three hundred major projects between 1898 and 1931, both individually and in association with the firm of Reed & Stem, the firm was responsible for shaping both the public and private worlds of its prominent clientele, from great railroad terminals, hotels, resorts, apartments, and houses to office towers (fig. I.1).

In 1893, five years prior to the formation of Warren and Wetmore's practice, Daniel H. Burnham (1846–1912), as master planner, had organized the World's Columbian Exposition in Chicago, creating a powerful and influential image indicative of America's emerging affluence and culture (fig. I.2). As a collaboration of the period's most talented architects and artists, the fair presented a monumental plaster and paint vision of a grand classical civic center composed of exposition buildings designed by Richard Morris Hunt (1828–1895), Charles McKim (1847–1919), Robert Peabody (1845–1917), Louis Sullivan (1856–1924), George B. Post (1837–1913), and Burnham's associate Charles Atwood (1848–1895), among others. The buildings were organized around a great artificial lagoon with Republic, personified as a classically draped figure of a handsome woman holding aloft a scepter and an orb supporting an eagle, rising at the center.[2] Enhanced with landscape design by Frederick Law Olmsted (1822–1903) and sculpture by Daniel Chester French (1850–1931), Burnham's spectacle evoked a classical grandeur unsurpassed in America, the reverberations of which were felt throughout the architectural world. Many of the collaborating architects had trained at

I.1. Built projects. Rendering by Vernon Howe Bailey. Warren & Wetmore Collection, Avery Architectural and Fine Arts Library, Columbia University.

the Ecole des Beaux-Arts and had drawn from what they had learned in Paris to skillfully reinvent the classical ideal as an American phenomenon. The emerging City Beautiful movement, which sought to impose the same principals of beauty and order upon the built environment, developed as Americans embraced new ways to communicate the country's progress and growth. In 1898, when Warren and Wetmore set out, the level of private wealth soared, unleashing clients' desires and expectations. Classical and French styles were the preferred modes of expression.

Like many of those involved in the exposition's design, Warren had also studied at the Ecole des Beaux-Arts. In the 1890s, the handful of architectural schools that existed in this country focused on technical issues rather than the connection between architecture and the arts. Aspiring American architects followed the example of Richard Morris Hunt, a towering figure in the nascent profession, who had been the first American to study in Paris (from 1846 to 1855). At the Ecole, students received a rigorous education rooted in the principles of classicism. Free to students who could pass the rigorous entrance examinations, the school offered instruction in geometry, mathematics, stereotomy (the study of the geometry of stone cutting), and other technical subjects. In addition, each student enrolled in an atelier—the critical and defining feature of the school's rigid architectural program.[3] Under the direction of the *patron*—typically a practicing architect—students were confronted with complex design problems, often on a civic scale, for which they were allowed a limited period to make basic decisions—the *parti*. The Beaux-Arts method stressed the organization of spaces and functions required by the program around major and minor axes. As a result, the elevations and sections were a clear and legible reflection of the program within. Once the *patron* approved the *parti*, students developed the scheme into a complete design, rendered in pen, ink, and watercolor. The competitive yet convivial atmosphere inspired the students as they competed within their ateliers for the approval of the *patron* and in school-wide competitions for mentions and prizes. Accumulating the requisite number of mentions for a diploma took anywhere from six to ten years; however, the Americans who attended before 1900 often ended their studies before graduating, satisfied with the core training in architecture and the prestige of being considered an *ancien éleve*.[4]

During the last forty years of the nineteenth century, American students were also exposed to different design ideologies and interpretations of the classical tradition. Charles Garnier (1825–1898), winner of the Grand Prix de Rome (1848), was the period's leading advocate of academic classicism. His influential design for the Paris Opera House (1861–75) exemplified the pictorial approach to architecture emblematic of the Beaux-Arts. Rather than representing one pure historical style, Garnier's building interpreted a number of different influences, including Roman, Greek, and Renaissance precedents, and combined arched openings, lintel openings, paired columns, and bull's-eye windows. The Opera supported an elaborate program of sculpture, from busts of great composers in history to huge figures of winged victory breaking the skyline. Ingeniously, Garnier organized the building's complex program into a robust, almost baroque, form that articulated its purpose and its principal rooms legibly on the facade. Eugène Emmanuel Viollet-le-Duc (1814–1879), a competitor for the Opera House commission, spearheaded the search for a more rationalist approach toward design. Fascinated by the structural basis of the Gothic, Viollet-le-Duc relished the architectural potential of iron and the beauty inherent in revealed structure and advocated the elaborate decoration of even the simplest parts of buildings: nails, rivets, and collars.

American students emerged from the intense and competitive French system with strong professional training with which to develop a personal style at home. As Whitney Warren commented, "Architecture is always an evolution. Of course, we use old styles; we can't invent a new one, we can only evolve a new one. So we are taking the best elements in the old styles, and we are attempting to produce from them what is suggested and demanded by our present conditions—a new and American style."[5]

Among Warren and Wetmore's generation, the search for such a style produced a variety of approaches. McKim, Mead & White, the country's most productive and important practice, established a more academic reading of classical vocabulary. With Thomas Hastings (1860–1929), John Russell Pope (1874–1937), and Ernest Flagg (1857–1947), they embraced scientific eclecticism—an overt reliance on historical models and styles—and looked to such sources as Paul Letarouilly's *Les Edifices de Rome Moderne*, a two-volume compendium of plans, sections, and details. The "western architects," attempting to avoid having their work measured against the canons of classicism, searched for a more original paradigm of revealed structure. Of this group, Louis Sullivan (1856–1924) stood out in solving the particularly American problem of the skyscraper without resorting to any styles then in vogue. His buildings were simple forms with incised decoration in repeating patterns of geometric and organic forms that replaced traditional ornament.

Warren & Wetmore was devoted to Beaux-Arts classicism, as taught in Paris, a style that came to be known as "modern French" when translated into American practice. Howard Greenley, the architect, observed that Whitney Warren adhered "to the standards of the best periods of French architecture. Completely familiar with the idiom of such masters as François Mansart, Louis Le Vau, François Blondel and Ange-Jacques Gabriel, he adapted their vocabulary, in new and imaginative ways, to the requirements of the age. Any review of [Warren's] work . . . would be incomplete if it did not . . . include a reference to his notable

I.2. Columbian Exposition in Chicago, 1893. Prints and Photographs Division, Library of Congress, #9749.

interior decorative compositions [in which] the treatment of the detail displays even greater refinement and delicacy than is to be found in the traditional French prototypes."[6] The philosophy of the firm remained grounded by the core tenet of the Ecole: A clear and legible plan would give rise to clear and legible elevations and sections. Like Garnier, Warren & Wetmore embraced the Ecole's emphasis on joining all three divisions of the Beaux-Arts—architecture, painting, and sculpture. However, the firm often took the Beaux-Arts principles one step further to create buildings in which the arts were fused so entirely that the physical boundaries of sculpture and architecture were blurred. Some of the firm's greatest works, including Warren's florid clubhouse for the New York Yacht Club (1898–1901), were so imaginative that they escaped easy analysis. In 1901 a typically enthusiastic critic found much to praise in the club's design but seemed embarrassed by its excess, asking, "Surely this is not a legitimate architectural design?"[7]

While the firm's work expressed an energy and extraordinary emphasis on detail, the partners also broadened their scope and were successful in filtering their idealism about the future of the American city into larger and more ambitious urban schemes. Inspired by years spent in Europe, Warren sought to impose an ordered beauty onto New York's streetscape. The firm's celebrated design for Grand Central Terminal and Terminal City, the twentieth century's first great building venture, created a civic scale evocative of the streets of Paris in mid-town Manhattan where each building, from elegant apartment house to office building, participated to create a monumental and harmonious effect. Within the contours of a career that included both commercial and residential commissions, Warren & Wetmore's devotion to Beaux-Arts principles instilled its impressive body of work with a distinctly rich and memorable character.

CHAPTER ONE

Background and Beginnings

On his seventy-fourth birthday, Whitney Warren declared, "I don't believe there was ever any one else who got as much fun out of life as I did" (fig. 1.1).[1] Born into privilege and affluence, Warren was a bold and imaginative thinker with a sense of adventure and purpose. His father, George Henry Warren (1823–1892), a lawyer from Troy, New York, was an influential financier and director of the Union Trust Company. His mother, née Mary Caroline Whitney Phoenix (1832–1901), descended from two distinguished New York families. Warren's grandfather, Hon. Jonas Phillips Phoenix and his great-grandfather, Stephen Whitney, had been successful merchants and public-spirited citizens; J. Phillips Phoenix served in Congress and the New York State Assembly. During the 1860s, the Warrens moved to New York City from Troy where generations of the Warren family had prospered in commerce.[2] In Troy the Warrens were also important architectural patrons, having commissioned Alexander Jackson Davis to design a villa in the family compound on top of Mount Ida and a Gothic Revival stone church, the Church of the Holy Cross (1843). In addition, they commissioned a Gothic Revival family chapel and vault (1860), designed by Henry Dudley, in Troy's Oakwood Cemetery.[3] Due to the Phoenix family connections, the couple was immediately accepted into the insular world of New York society. As a member of Ward MacAllister's exclusive Patriarchs Club and one of Mrs. Astor's Four Hundred, George Henry Warren bore the imprint of prominence.

The Warrens were a large and close-knit family. One of eight children, Whitney was born at his parents' house at 145 Madison Avenue and raised in New York City and Troy.[4] Like others in their set, his parents migrated to Europe for the season, sometimes leaving "little Whitney" in the care of his maternal grandmother, who lived in New York and at Glenwood, the Phoenixes' country seat in Hudson, New York.[5] In 1881 George Henry Warren purchased and renovated a villa at 68 Narragansett Avenue in Newport, Rhode Island, establishing the family's longtime association with the fashionable summer enclave.[6]

Both Whitney Warren's father and his grandfather, Nathan Warren, were musically inclined. Nathan Warren was considered a noted composer; George Henry Warren, a guiding force behind the founding of the Metropolitan Opera, moonlighted as organist at St. Thomas's Church on Fifth Avenue.[7] From an early age, Whitney Warren gravitated toward art—an interest nurtured by his mother. As he recalled, "I wanted to be a painter and drew instinctively. . . . My mother, who greatly encouraged me in my desire for an artistic career, felt that I should master drawing before devoting myself to painting. I attempted this and came to want to know something about architecture, since an interest in drawing naturally leads on to this field. I found architectural drawing intensely absorbing and determined to become an architect."[8] After being schooled by private tutors, Warren enrolled in Columbia University's School of Architecture, class of 1886.

Like many of his peers, Warren found the program uninspiring and remained only briefly. The architecture school, established in 1881, was small and in its formative years. Because it was incorporated into the university's School of Mines, its curriculum focused on practical rather than artistic issues. At the age of twenty, after marrying Charlotte Tooker, also of New York and Newport, Warren left for Europe. In 1884 he arrived in Paris to begin working toward admission to the Ecole des Beaux-Arts, the preeminent course of study for an aspiring American architect.

Warren's ten-year Parisian sojourn provided the direction that would shape his life and give his artistic pursuit purpose. He entered the Ecole in 1887 and studied in the atelier of Honoré Daumet and Charles Louis Girault, a studio favored by Americans (fig. 1.2).[9]

1.1. Portrait of Whitney Warren at James Hazen Hyde's Ball, Sherry's Restaurant, January 31, 1905. Museum of the City of New York, Byron Collection, #93.1.1.9545.

Honoré Daumet, who won the Grand Prix de Rome in 1855, was one of the Ecole's most respected *patrons*. Since establishing his atelier in 1860, Daumet had drawn such architects as Charles McKim, Robert Peabody, and Francis Ward Chandler. During the 1880s and 1890s, Richard Morris Hunt's sons (Richard Howland Hunt and Joseph Howland Hunt), Samuel Breck P. Trowbridge, Austin W. Lord, Joseph McGuire, and Joseph H. Freedlander also chose Daumet as their *patron*. As the heart of the Beaux-Arts system, the atelier offered a challenging environment that was altogether lacking at American schools. Because advancement was based on obtaining the necessary academic points and honorable mentions in competitions, the system promoted creativity and generated an intense camaraderie among its students. In their respective ateliers, students competed with the other studios monthly on *projets* that were then judged by the school. Foreign students were not eligible for the Prix de Rome, the Ecole's highest honor; however, ateliers with a history of winning the prize were sought after. The Daumet–Girault atelier was particularly successful, winning the award eight times between the years of 1860 and 1907.[10]

Although Warren won few awards, he flourished in the Beaux-Arts system. In 1891 he advanced to the first class; however, he returned to the United States in 1894 without his diploma.[11] Nonetheless, Warren came into his own in Paris. Possesing an "ineffable sense of humor, he was keenly alive to the lighter and more amusing side of existence" and enjoyed a "jolly rollicking, carefree youth" amidst artistic Americans and Europeans.[12] He took pleasure in the social whirl of the city and his apartment was considered a rendezvous for artists and musicians of all kinds. While Warren relished the life and freedom of Paris, he also

1.2. Daumet–Girault atelier
at the Ecole des Beaux-Arts.
Whitney Warren on far right,
second row. Warren & Wetmore
Collection, Avery Architectural and
Fine Arts Library, Columbia
University.

1.3 (opposite). Whitney Warren,
plans, elevation and section of
the tower in Chiaravalle,
Milanese, Italy, September 25,
1887. Graphite; brush and red
and brown watercolor on cream,
heavy wove paper, 12 ⁵⁄₁₆ x 9 ⅜ in.
(313 x 238 mm). Cooper-Hewitt,
National Design Museum,
Smithsonian Institution. Gift of
Mrs. William Greenough, 1943-51-5.
Photo: Matt Flynn.

earned the respect of his *patrons* and was elected into the prestigious Academy of Fine Arts at the Institut de France in 1909. Because the academy consisted of only forty academicians, including eight architects and ten corresponding members (foreigners), it was a particularly impressive distinction.[13]

Like all Beaux-Arts–trained architects of his generation, Warren learned his art by sketching and painting. On travels through Holland, northern France, Germany, and Italy, he filled sketchbook after sketchbook with contemplative and carefully rendered drawings and watercolors. Though familiar with the key monuments of Europe, Warren seemed more interested in ordinary structures and began building a visual library of details that would become part of his architectural vocabulary. His quick sketches included notations on color and materials and focused on details such as eaves, chimneys, and paving patterns. Warren felt strongly that a foundation in drawing was imperative for an architect—"that it ought to be a pleasure and a pastime—both freehand and mechanical"—and his drawings expressed an experimental and romantic quality that would feed his later work.[14] His fascination with towers and campaniles, as seen in his watercolor of the Tower in Chiaravalle (1889), and his interest in vernacular buildings types, such as sheds and barns from the Black Forest, would form an important ingredient of Warren & Wetmore's architecture (figs. 1.3, 1.4).[15]

Paris—its streets, its buildings, and its atmosphere—captured Warren's soul and never diminished in his imagination. While living abroad, the young architect grew into a true cosmopolite and an ardent Francophile, assuming the French manner and style of dress.

Scale = 0.005 = 1. = 1/200 ex.

Torre de Chiaravalle N.
du 13 siècle -
Note Probably built by
the same man who built
St Gottardo at Milan.

Sept 25th 1889 P.

W. W.

Plans -

Coupe.

13

Steeple of
Village church—

House in Gaggenau—

little roof dormer—

the letters simply thick wire
gilded—

shingle

Bell cupola—
even more top
heavy than this—
very pretty—

Gaggenau—
Sept 18th 1887

Very pretty form of gables—
overhang in both sheds
is at least 3 ft.

Black Forest Sketches—
Sept 18th 1887

1.4 (opposite). Whitney Warren, Black Forest Sketches, plate 47 from the Album "Whitney Warren Original Sketches," September 18, 1887, Graphite on cream wove paper, 12 ⁵/₁₆ x 9 ³/₈ in. (311 x 238 mm). Cooper-Hewitt, National Design Museum, Smithsonian Institution. Gift of Mrs. William Greenough, 1943-51-127. Photo: Matt Flynn.

1.5 (above). Newport Country Club, Newport, Rhode Island. Newport Historical Society.

Throughout his life, he would wear an unvarying costume of blue shirt, white silk scarf, white double-breasted waistcoat, dark suit, opera cloak, broad-rimmed black hat, and later, a gold-tipped cane. With his piercing eyes, aristocratic features, and full head of sandy-colored hair, Warren made a strong impression. As Lawrence White, son of Warren's great friend Stanford White, commented: "He was an absolutely fantastic person just to look at. He was very handsome. . . . He carried himself and acted exactly as if he was a French aristocrat before the Revolution. He wore very peculiar clothes, but got away with it."[16]

Immediately upon his return from Paris in 1894, Warren won the commission for the Newport Country Club (fig. 1.5). One of the first country clubs in America, it was organized in 1893 by a group of wealthy Newporters headed by Theodore Havemeyer. In 1894, Havemeyer and his friends, Cornelius Vanderbilt, Perry Belmont, John Jacob Astor, Robert Goelet (Warren's brother-in-law), Oliver H. P. Belmont, Edward Berwind, Ogden Goelet, Frederick Vanderbilt, and William K. Vanderbilt, among others, formed a syndicate, purchased land on a high promontory just outside Newport, and held an open competition for a clubhouse. That Warren won, against some of the more established practices of the day, including the Boston firm of Peabody & Stearns, was an extraordinary accomplishment for a young architect.[17] His Y-shaped wood and shingle building straddled the top of a ridge overlooking the original nine-hole golf course and gave the impression of a stone Beaux-Arts pavilion (fig. 1.6). A colossal pedimented frontispiece marked the entrance to the clubhouse, and symmetrical wings, which were slightly lower, reached out to the landscape with half-round columned porches on either end.

The procession through the building demonstrated Warren's mastery of architecture as sculpture to create emotional effect. A relatively compact stair hall at the entrance led to an oval salon that soared up two levels into the mansard roof (fig. 1.7). The surfaces not given over to overscaled sculptural details—wave-like brackets and free-carved garlands—were mirrored, and an arcaded balcony supported yet another layer of ornament beneath the shallow dome. At night the room completely dematerialized as the brackets, leaves, garlands, and masks were animated by the flickering gaslight and reflected in the multiple mirrors. Beyond, caryatids supported a colonnaded piazza, and a terrace, roughly twice the size of the salon, extended toward the golf course (fig. 1.8). In an era when leisure sports were capturing the American imagination, the clubhouse quickly became a popular haunt for Warren's Newport friends and colleagues and was singled out as "supreme in magnificence among golf clubs, not only in America, but in the world."[18]

Following the triumph of the Newport Country Club, Warren tried to win commissions but was unsuccessful in channeling his unabashed creativity into a steady job. Although his sketchbooks include designs for a series of houses for prominent Newport friends, including a colorful scheme for Oliver Belmont's monkey house, it appears that none of them was actually built (fig. 1.9). And while his competition entries were impressive, none took first place. In 1894 Warren's exuberant French design for the Baltimore Courthouse was recognized as one of the ten best designs submitted, and his 1897 Beaux-Arts scheme for the New York Public Library was chosen as one of the top twelve contenders out of the eighty-eight entries.[19] Warren's inability to settle into his profession concerned his wife. In 1895, writing to her husband's close friend and mentor Stanford White, she pleaded, "can you 'pull any wires' to help Whitney to be asked to make plans for the proposed circus—he has been very anxious for a year . . . and last evening at dinner he heard several men had already made plans for it. I think it would be a splendid thing for Whitney if he could build it. . . . He knows nothing of my writing this and would not like it if he did—that you are such a good friend to him, that I always think of you instinctively in connection to him."[20] In response, White wrote, "I think you are right and that all Whitney wants to make him happier is work. He is certainly full of ability and somehow or other should buckle down to regular work."[21]

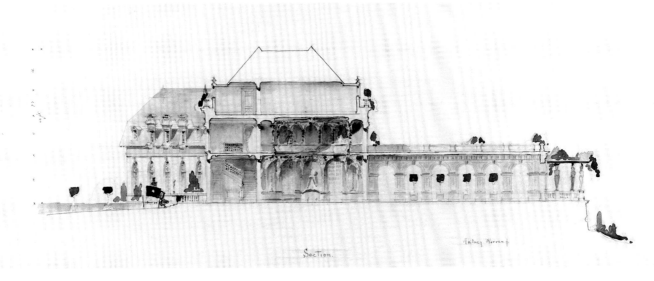

Section.

With help from White, Warren took an apartment in the tower at Madison Square Garden, the occupants of which were an interesting coterie of artists and free thinkers, including inventor Peter Cooper Hewitt, sculptor Daniel Chester French, and Warren's sister, Harriet Louise (1854–1912), a painter married to real estate baron Robert Goelet (1841–1899).[22] Unlike many Americans, Warren did not narrow his horizons upon his return to the United States but maintained a wide circle of friends that included society members and artists, both American and European. With White, Warren shared a penchant for mischief and self-indulgence. Wine and champagne flowed liberally at the exotic revelries and extravagant twelve-course dinner parties that filled the men's social calendar. One notorious stag party organized by White and financier Henry Poor in 1895 at the studio of White's client, photographer James Breese, was featured in *The New York Times* as the "Pie Girl Dinner" and drew the company of Warren, Charles McKim, William Mead, Charles Dana Gibson, Nicola Tesla, Cooper Hewitt, J. Alden Weir, and Willard Metcalf, to name a few. Catered by Sherry's, New York's most lavish restaurant, the soiree included the usual pleasures: blondes pouring white wine, brunettes pouring red, banjo music, and course upon course of rich food. But the press was less blasé about the sixteen-year-old girl who popped out of a giant pie of feathers to dance for the men. This was the sort of bacchanal that White, Warren, and those in their circle relished. As close friends, Warren and White mulled over the social scene while trading information about silk shirts and Parisian boot makers for architectural tips, such as how far a shop window could project. Whitney always signed his letters to White with a flourish: Bibi or Bébé la Poupette.

From 1896 to 1898 Warren worked intermittently in the offices of McKim, Mead & White as a draftsman while he tried to pull in his own commissions (fig. 1.10). Part of the legacy of an education at the Ecole was membership in the close group of practitioners who supported each other even in fostering the independent careers of talented employees. However, Warren was not a standard employee and was unlisted in the firm's roster. There seemed to be no question that Warren would strike out on his own rather than apprentice at a larger firm, and White encouraged this move. Warren seemed unembarrassed to ask White

1.10. Whitney Warren, elevation for proposed house for George Eustis, n.d. Photostat (of a wash drawing) on white wove paper, 4 7/16 x 8 1/4 in. (113 x 210 mm). Cooper-Hewitt, National Design Museum, Smithsonian Institution. Gift of Mrs. William Greenhough, 1943-51-374. Photo: Matt Flynn.

for help, even pleading, "I am very much behind on my competition—can you lend me a chap to block out a perspective and another to finish up plans?"[23] When he won the commission for the New York Yacht Club in 1898, Warren was working out of McKim, Mead & White's offices. It was at this point that he paired with lawyer Charles Delevan Wetmore for whom he had designed a house.[24] Warren, impressed by his client's artistic abilities, persuaded the young and capable lawyer, who moved in the same social circles, to alter the course of his career and to go into business with him.

Like Warren, Charles Wetmore came from a wealthy family prominent in business and civic life. Born in Elmira, New York, Wetmore was the son of Charles Canvass Wetmore (1829–1867) of Warren, Pennsylvania, and Rosalia Elona Hall (1838–1912) of Busti, New York. Wetmore's father, a civil engineer and shrewd businessman, amassed a considerable fortune during his short lifetime. In addition to holding one of the largest contracts on the Philadelphia & Erie Railroad, he was a pioneering figure in the development of Western Pennsylvania's oil lands and an investor in a thriving lumber company on the Allegheny River. Wetmore's grandfathers, Hon. Lansing Wetmore and Chapin Hall, both had served in Congress and were leaders in the business and industry of Warren County, Pennsylvania; Lansing Wetmore had been an original stockholder in the Philadelphia & Erie Railroad. Soon after Wetmore's birth, his father died in a wagon accident; Rosalia Wetmore, a wealthy widow, then married Alba Morgan Kent, who had been a proprietor of one of her father's many businesses, and moved to an Italianate mansion in Jamestown, New York.[25]

After attending public schools in western New York, Wetmore entered Harvard College in 1885 and subsequently graduated from Harvard Law School in 1892. Actively involved in college life, he joined the Sparring Association, the Art Club, and the Republican Club as well as several of Harvard's all-important social clubs: the Institute of 1770, D.K.E., and the Hasty Pudding Club. Wetmore was not one to be turned down. When he was not invited to join the Porcellian, Harvard's most exclusive club, he helped establish the Fly Club.[26] Later, in law school, he was a member of The Pow Wow, Harvard's top law club, and the social organization, Choate Chapter.

In Cambridge Wetmore's interest in real estate and his aggressive business instincts emerged. In 1892 he began buying property along Mt. Auburn Street, between Harvard Yard and the river, to construct rental housing for wealthy college students. His first venture, Claverly Hall, was designed by Cambridge architect George Fogerty and completed in 1893. Its immediate success prompted Wetmore to finance a second dormitory, Apley Court, designed by John Edward Howe. Wetmore's developments attracted the sons of millionaires, who were drawn from the antiquated Harvard college dormitories to the luxurious new quarters in what came to be called the "Gold Coast." Other investors soon discovered the profitable potential of the glorified dormitories. In 1897 Claverly Hall's light was threatened by plans for a new dormitory, Randolph Hall, to be built by Archibald Coolidge, a professor at the college. To deter its construction, Wetmore secretly purchased land opposite Coolidge's site and commissioned plans for a ten-story building that would, in turn, block Randolph Hall's light. Wetmore threatened to go ahead with the building if plans for Randolph Hall went forward. Finding no other option, Coolidge was forced to acquiesce to Wetmore's conditions: to buy Wetmore's land across the street at his price and to build Randolph with a setback that would allow Claverly unimpeded light.[27]

According to his son-in-law Edward Weeks, editor of the *Atlantic Monthly*, Wetmore was "passionately devoted to Harvard" and "believed that the presidency of Harvard was second only to the presidency of the United States."[28] However, Wetmore's loyalty to the college did not deter his improving its campus for financial benefit. In 1898 he designed and built the sumptuous Tudor style Westmorly Hall, the second wing of which was constructed in 1902 (fig. 1.11). A brick Tudor building with a profusion of limestone trim, it was derided in the architectural press as "a little exaggerated beyond what would have occurred in the Tudor work, on which the design is based." Critics also felt that "the building [gave] rather the impression of an apartment house than a dormitory for a great university."[29]

The interiors, however, were sumptuously fitted with all the makings of a modern social club—gym, handball courts, showers, telephones, and fireplaces. Of most interest were the elaborate indoor/outdoor swimming pool with treillage, topiaries, and fireplaces and William K. Vanderbilt Jr.'s lavishly furnished oak-paneled suite (figs. 1.12, 1.13). Wetmore also attempted to convince the school in 1909 to buy property below Mt. Auburn Street and across the river for a secondary campus. His ambitious Beaux-Arts plan, which included a formal park, a collection of uniformly designed dormitories, a grand bridge on axis, and a stadium on the opposite bank of the river anticipated the development of the Harvard Business School site and Soldier's Field.[30]

After graduation from law school, Wetmore moved to New York and joined the offices of Carter & Ledyard as a trial lawyer. On the side, he invested in real estate. One of his first acquisitions was Holworthy Chambers, a four-story building of bachelor apartments at 152 Madison Avenue, where Wetmore kept rooms. In addition, he formed City Real Property with Edmund L. Baylies, a real estate lawyer also at Carter & Ledyard, and began investing in other properties in New York. Wetmore continued to work in law until 1898, but his career was prematurely curtailed by partial deafness. As a result, he was easily convinced to try a second career that incorporated his love of buildings and real estate. In 1898 Wetmore joined forces with Warren, who was fresh from winning the commission for the New York Yacht Club.

From the outset, Warren and Wetmore were successful in drawing commissions from the elite circles in which they moved (fig. 1.14). Most clients were active in business and club life, and many were heirs to fortunes only conceivable at the height of the Gilded Age. The partners set up an office at 3 East 33rd Street and took on Whitney's brother Lloyd

1.12. William K. Vanderbilt Jr.'s room at Harvard, c. 1899. Suffolk County Vanderbilt Museum.

1.13 (following pages). Westmorly Hall. Swimming Pool. Warren & Wetmore Collection, Avery Architectural and Fine Arts Library, Columbia University.

Warren (1868–1922) and Cambridge architect John Howe (1863–1908) as associates. In the early 1900s L. Henry Morgan briefly became a partner, and the firm was renamed Warren, Wetmore & Morgan for a short time. With its success, the firm grew into a large practice with several associates and a sizable staff of draftsmen.[31] During the 1910s the firm relocated to 16 East 47th Street, an office located in Warren & Wetmore's Ritz-Carlton Hotel. Over time, the assembled talent of the firm included Emmanuel Louis Masqueray (1861–1917), Leonard Schultze (1877–1951), Morris Lapidus (1902–2001), Sylvan Bien (1893–1959), and Ronald H. Pearce (1887–1962). Until Warren's retirement in 1931, Warren and Wetmore continued as partners; Wetmore remained with the firm until the mid-1930s.[32] After retiring, Warren served as director of the Beaux-Arts Institute of Design, a position he had held since 1922, and worked from his studio in the organization's building on East 44th Street.[33] The firm of Warren & Wetmore operated into the 1950s under the direction of Patrick Corry (1876–1962), formerly New York Central's superintendent of construction, and Julian Holland (1888–1961), a Brooklyn-born architect and longtime associate of the firm.[34]

Warren was a passive investor in some real-estate ventures; Wetmore was the business mind of the firm who continually invested in property, including several of Warren & Wetmore's projects, and served as a director on such boards as the Windsor Trust Company and Bethlehem Associates. Though contributing little of the design sense of the firm, Wetmore appears to have been critical to its financial success. Warren would later say, "I owe [Wetmore] everything . . . in my career such as it has been . . . he has been the force which I did not have in myself to keep me at my task—and I—a very trying personage, impossible, not altogether selfish, but *impossible.*"[35] Unlike Wetmore, Warren could never "take things

easily."[36] He claimed his "greatest fault [was] being too serious" but declared, "if I have any virtue to counterbalance it, it is enthusiasm."[37]

Although Warren saw his enthusiasm as a virtue, his tendency to get carried away was almost fatal to his partnership because it led to a five-year hiatus from his practice. In a radical move Warren relocated to Paris in 1914, where he worked tirelessly for the cause of the Allied Forces through the end of the war in 1918. For Warren, France represented more than a great culture and the nation that had given him his architectural education. He saw the country as the epitome of a mature, civilized society and was so disturbed by the threat posed by the Germans that he left for Europe just days after war broke out. While his involvement in politics had been minimal to that point, Warren forged a position for himself as an American–French press liaison and lectured as an advocate of American participation on the Allied side. In addition, he dedicated his energies toward such aid societies as the Red Cross Commission, American Clearing House, and the Secours National and, after the war, remained active in political issues, championing Italy's presence in the Adriatic. Warren's vital role in the war effort eventually led to what would become his most prized commission, the reconstruction of the university library (1922–28) in the devastated town of Louvain, Belgium.

In their heyday, the two men made a formidable pair. The flamboyant and charismatic Warren was a bold individualist with little patience for charlatanism (fig. 1.16). Headstrong and mercurial, he was often guided by emotion and quick to react. In Newport, for example, he would assault a photographer whom he believed had invaded his wife's privacy at Bailey's Beach.[38] Yet he also carried himself with a cool self-absorption that produced a certain awe among his colleagues. Reflecting on Warren's life, architect Howard Greenley would write: "There was a certain definite splendor about the man himself, in his appearance and carriage that one instinctively recognized. There was also about him that indefinable quality of radiance that one felt was so inherently a part of the rare distinction of his thought and of his person. To the unprejudiced mind he can be considered as the personification of what is implied by the 'grand manner.'. . . It was, so to speak, a fundamental quality in the man, and the essence of his whole personality."[39]

Charles Wetmore (fig. 1.15), as Edward Weeks recalled,

was very sure of himself and very stylish. His complexion was florid (so . . . was his temper), his fine white hair was brushed back above his ears and with his high-ridged aristocratic nose, thin lips and light blue eyes he was clearly one who enjoyed authority. . . . Never had I encountered such a combination of intelligence, will power, and contentiousness as when I tried to hold my end up against Mr. Wetmore. He was an implacable Republican and twitted me about my admiration for Woodrow Wilson; he had no use for contemporary writing, seldom read a book, was a stickler for facts, and depending on how sure he was, would bet me five or ten dollars that I was wrong. . . . On anything having to do with building or finance, he was sharp as a buzz saw. . . . To him a challenge was the quickest way to test a man, and he once admitted that his closest friends were those he had angered at the outset. He had achieved renown in his field without a degree in architecture and he scorned Who's Who and jury awards—"Who are they to judge me?" was his attitude."[40]

Like most men in their circle, Warren and Wetmore held multiple club memberships. Both were members of the Knickerbocker and the Racquet and Tennis Clubs; Wetmore belonged to the University, Harvard, and Meadowbrook Clubs and was president of the interclub backgammon league; Warren joined the South Side Sportman's Club, Fencers Club, and the Coffee House, an informal club of writers, artists, and architects.[41] Conspicuously missing on both men's resumes, however, was membership in the Century Association, the oldest of New York's arts-oriented social

1.14. Whitney Warren aboard William K. Vanderbilt Jr.'s yacht, Tarantula, 1912. Suffolk County Vanderbilt Museum.

1.15 (above). Charles D. Wetmore. Edward Weeks, *My Green Age* (Boston: Little, Brown & Company, 1973).

1.16 (left). Whitney Warren. Warren & Wetmore Collection, Avery Architectural and Fine Arts Library, Columbia University.

organizations. An amateur athlete, Warren was in tip-top shape and cared tremendously about his physique. He was considered one of Newport's strongest tennis players and golfers; as a fencer and boxer, he trained regularly with Artie McGovern, later coach to Babe Ruth and golfer Gene Sarazen. Warren's ambitious twelve-mile swim from Bailey's Beach to Narragansett Pier made the front page of *The New York Times* in 1910.[42]

Warren, a devoted husband and father, was close to his wife Charlotte (1864–1951) and their three children, Charlotte (1885–1957), Whitney Jr. (1898–1986), and Gabrielle (1895–1971).[43] Yet, as a man easily enchanted by beauty and charm, he was also a philanderer. For many years he carried on a passionate affair with the glamorous French actress and singer Cécile Sorel of the Comédié Française, who was once likened to "one of the prints of duchesses which illustrate[d] the rare editions of Thackeray's works."[44] In 1946, Sorel would publish her memoirs, *Les Belles Heures de ma Vie*, which included explicit passages about her relationship with the architect. When the actress appeared in engagements during New York's 1926 theater season, Warren took on the role of concerned lover. He was known to have burst into rehearsal to demand improvements to the stage set and decorations. In her memoirs, Sorel included a full-page portrait of the architect with the torrid caption, "Mon Aigle Américain" (my American eagle).

Warren had an eye for beauty and, as a rich man, he could afford to surround himself with rare and beautiful things.[45] His home, first an apartment in Carlton House, the residential wing of the firm's Ritz-Carlton, and later in 280 Park Avenue, designed by Warren & Wetmore in 1920, was brimming with Louis XV and Italian Renaissance furniture, sixteenth and seventeenth-century sculpture, paintings by Sargent, Italian majolica, and antique tapestries and lace. As the Parke–Bernet catalogue, published in 1943 when Warren's estate was auctioned, would note, "[Warren] was only secondarily interested in condition, and would buy a shard if he saw beauty in its texture or coloring . . . [his] collection has been filtered through the selectivity of a learned taste."[46] Warren's studio, or "Cloister," as he called it, was decorated with busts, globes, and tapestries. His library of over two hundred fifty vol-

umes included works by Paul Letarouilly, Palladio, Viollet-le-Duc, Inigo Jones, and Vitruvius and books on Colonial, Spanish, Gothic, and Italian architecture, Roman and Byzantine art, Chinese ornament, and furniture.[47]

Wetmore, a longtime bachelor, married Sara Thomson Watriss in 1917 after her divorce from Frederick Watriss, a lawyer prominent in the social life of Long Island's North Shore. After they wed, Wetmore adopted Sara's son William, whom he treated, by all accounts, as his own. At their brownstone at 8 West 53rd Street, the Wetmores lived in a residential pocket off the growing Fifth Avenue shopping district in a neighborhood dominated by John D. Rockefeller. Eschewing fashionable resorts such as Newport, Wetmore and his family, which also included two stepdaughters, opted for Long Point, a house on the banks of Lake Chautauqua in western New York, where Wetmore had picnicked as a child (fig. 1.17).[48] Warren and his family enjoyed the summer months in the vigorously social Newport from their house on Clay Street, which was near his siblings' homes: Ochre Point (the Robert Goelets), High Tide (the William Starr Millers), and Seafield (the George Henry Warren Jrs.).

Never to forget his debt to France, Warren devoted much of his time to furthering architectural education in the United States after the Beaux-Arts model. With Thomas Hastings and Ernest Flagg, among others, Warren helped establish the Society of Beaux-Arts Architects in 1894. In his words, "not only did we want to keep the old crowd together with all its joyous memories; we wished also to continue our teachings and traditions, to keep the flame alive and to hand on the torch to those who were to come after us in our own country."[49] Many of the society's charter members, in addition to Warren, were alumni of the Daumet–Girault atelier: Emile Baumgarten, John P. Benson, George Cary, Austin W. Lord, Joseph H. McGuire, and Samuel Breck P. Trowbridge.

At the turn of the twentieth century, a boom in building activity swelled the demand for competent designers. With American architectural schools in their infancy, it was widely believed that the best professional education could only be acquired in France. But such study was a luxury available only to a comparatively small number of aspiring architects. Warren and his colleagues attempted to introduce French methods into American practice by setting up office ateliers, establishing educational programs, and recreating the competitive and convivial atmosphere of the Ecole. As a motivating force, Warren served as president and vice-president and on the society's education committee.

In 1916 Whitney Warren's younger brother Lloyd (1868–1922) incorporated the Beaux-Arts Institute of Design, an accredited program born out of the society's informal ateliers. Having chosen architecture as his vocation, Lloyd Warren followed his brother's footsteps to Paris and studied in the Daumet–Girault atelier at the Ecole under its succeeding *patron* Pierre Esquié. According to one source, "the two were inseparable, and the same taste in music and art furnished occasion for as a fine a companionship in ideas as is possible to conceive."[50] After receiving his diploma in 1900, Warren worked at his brother's firm for several years before leaving his position as partner to head the society and broaden its educational reach. Together, the brothers funded the Warren Prize, to be awarded for the best solutions to a planning problem, and Lloyd Warren instituted the prestigious Paris Prize, whose winner passed directly into the first class at the Ecole. After Lloyd's untimely death in 1922, Whitney continued to exert his influence and play a central role in the organization to support, but never take credit for, his brother's initiative.[51] Whitney filled his brother's position as director of the Beaux-Arts Institute of Design and as chairman of the American committee at the Fontainebleau School of Fine Arts, an intensive summer program developed for American students in 1923 to experience the French method and culture without spending years studying in Paris.[52]

Whitney Warren's most vibrant contribution to the Society of Beaux-Arts Architects was the annual Beaux-Arts Ball, a fundraiser to develop the Beaux-Arts Institute of Design's educational programs. The lavish costume ball, first held in January 1913, was a phenomenal success and immediately became a mainstay in the city's social season. As honorary chairman, Warren presided over the fantastic spectacle whose glamorous, sometimes outlandish, themes revolved around historical settings and events. In 1914, the grand ballroom of the Hotel Astor was transformed into "Paris: La Ville Lumière"; in 1928, the theme was North Africa during the French occupation. The riotous "Fête in the Garden of Versailles" was held in 1926. As Louis XIV, Whitney Warren held center court dressed in a magnificent costume of satin and jewels; *The New York Times* would proclaim in a headline, "Whitney Warren as King."[53] Although the ball remained popular in the 1930s, historical subjects were abandoned for more abstract themes: "Fête Moderne"(1931) and "Fête de Rayon Fantastique" (1936). When Warren retired as acting director of the Beaux-Arts Institute in 1937, his fabulous balls, which had become a New York institution, came to an end.

For an American, Whitney Warren accumulated an impressive list of honors from the other side of the Atlantic: Royal Academy of San Luc, Rome; Institut de France; Société Centrale des Architects Français; Société des Artists Français; and Grand Cordon of the Order of the Crown of Belgium. In 1913 he received an honorary master's degree of art from Harvard, his partner's alma mater, and in 1917, the Medal of Honor from the New York Chapter of the American Institute of Architects for his firm's work, his personal contribution to architectural education, and his efforts to better the relations between the United States and France.

Warren and Wetmore attempted to shun publicity throughout their tenure; however, they unfailingly seemed to raise controversy by the very nature of their personalities. During the 1910s and 1920s, the office became the focus of two major lawsuits and, for a period, found its way into the pages of *The New York Times* almost daily. In 1916 the firm was charged with violating its contract with Reed & Stem in their association on the design of Grand Central Terminal. The five-year lawsuit resulted in Warren's expulsion from the American Institute of Architecture and the firm's paying out $500,000 in damages. In 1928 a highly publicized debate over the balustrade inscription of Warren's new library in Louvain, Belgium, instigated riots in the town and turned into a three-year suit over the rights of an artist. The headstrong and passionate Warren and the unflappable Wetmore formed a dynamic team that was self-confident and resolute in its convictions. In both cases the partners stood their ground, despite heavy opposition. Yet controversy never permanently scarred the flourishing practice but only added to the aura of drama surrounding the colorful pair. Although the effects of scandal would subside, Warren & Wetmore's inspiring catalogue of work would make a lasting impression.[54]

CHAPTER TWO

Early Projects: 1898–1904

THE NEW YORK YACHT CLUB

Four years after returning from Paris, Warren won his first major commission in New York City: the design for the New York Yacht Club.[1] By 1898, the Yacht Club, founded in 1844, had outgrown its rented rooms in a house at 67 Madison Avenue, and the governors desired a larger building with all the accoutrements of a modern social club. A committee for the "New Club House" was charged with the task of finding an architect for the New York Yacht Club's fifth city home, to be built on West 44th Street on a 75-foot lot donated by the commodore of the club, J. Pierpont Morgan, whose sole condition was that the new building fill out the street front. Nearly one dozen architects were invited to submit plans; this list was whittled down to seven: Howard, Cauldwell & Morgan; R. H. Robertson; H. Edwards Ficken; Clinton & Russell; Peabody & Stearns; George A. Freeman; and Whitney Warren.[2] The building committee enlisted Professor William R. Ware of Columbia University to guide the competition. As an educator, Ware (1826–1914) had headed the first American school of architecture at the Massachusetts Institute of Technology for fourteen years before establishing the architecture department at Columbia's School of Mines in 1881.

Despite Ware's lukewarm endorsement of Warren's design, the committee pronounced it the winning scheme by February 1899. At that time, Warren was working out of the offices of McKim, Mead & White at 160 Fifth Avenue. Competition guidelines had called for a design that was "dignified and simple, suited to the character of the club, without conspicuous ornamentation," and along those lines, Ware had recommended the more restrained entries of Howard, Cauldwell & Morgan and Clinton & Russell.[3] Warren's design, in contrast, presented a modern French facade made riotous by an outpouring of sculptural ornament embodying nautical forms and details. In coming to his solution, Warren "carefully considered the object of [the] particular club and its cause for existence." As part of his competition entry, he wrote, "This being a Club with the special object—the furtherance of naval architecture from an amateur point of view, I consider that externally and internally the arrangements should be such as to place that object in evidence, and not to retire it and make the Club House appear that of an ordinary social institution."[4] In other words, Warren not only disapproved of the club's suggestion of restraint but also advocated an explicitly representational approach. While his description detailed a reasoned rationale for a nautical club, in Warren's hands it became a mandate for a scenographic style that would become his signature. With its design, Warren established himself as the master of fusing art and architecture to express a building's position and purpose. On the building's monumental limestone facade, Warren designed the *piano nobile* as three enormous arched windows anchored by extending bays expressed as sterns of Spanish galleons. The street elevation came alive with

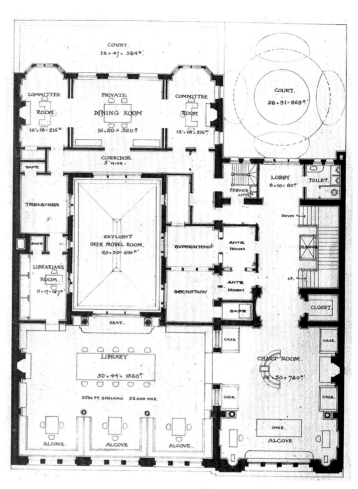

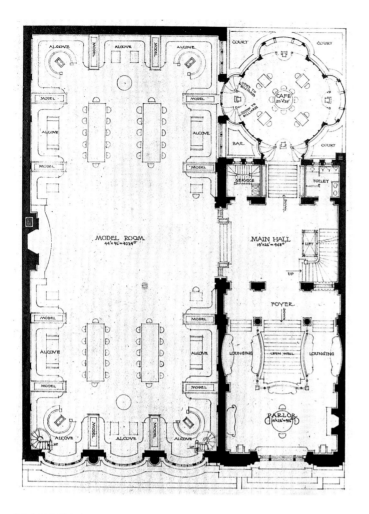

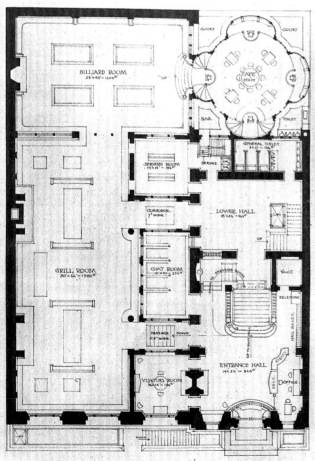

*2.2 (clockwise from bottom left).
New York Yacht Club. Entrance,
first, and third floor plans.*
Warren & Wetmore Collection, Avery
Architectural and Fine Arts Library,
Columbia University.

2.3. New York Yacht Club. Entrance hall. The Architectural Review 6 (April 1899).

jumping sea creatures, twisting seaweed, and watery stone wakes that seemed to drip off the facade of the six-story building (fig. 2.1).

Unlike most of his competitors, Warren produced an asymmetrical scheme with the entrance of the club at the east side of the facade and the three bays of the model room occupying the remaining 45 feet and reaching back through the depth of the 100-foot lot (fig. 2.2). From the street-level entrance lobby, a flight of stone steps drew members up to the *piano nobile* (fig. 2.3). At the landing, Warren shifted the primary axis, pulling members into the double-height model room, the club's principal space and location of its extensive collection of boat models, which was displayed on brackets mounted on the walls (fig. 2.4). For Warren, it was imperative to locate the model room on the front of the building because "the room [was] essentially 'The Club'" and "to place it where there would be any effort to reach it, as [he was] concerned, would be fatal."[5] Warren tempered the overwhelming scale of the space by dividing the room into alcoves with furniture (fig. 2.5). His bold Caen stone mantel, dripping with carved seaweed and coiling with sea serpents, commanded the room. Painted moldings, undulating brackets, robust wood details, and a colorful Tiffany glass skylight reinforced Warren's aquatic fantasy (fig. 2.6); even the cast-iron balustrades dripped with gilded sea grass. The design's voluptuous quality left the press wondering if Warren had not crossed the line that defined architecture. One critic, writing for *The Architectural Review*, was ambivalent: "While there was some semblance of reserve in the exterior in this most interesting building, there is little of this quality visible so far as the interior is concerned." He complained of "the riot of swags and spinach, icicles and exotic vegetation that is in progress in the chimney-piece of the model room, [which] takes away one's breath."[6]

The clubhouse also included a billiards room, bar, library, chart room, bedrooms, and a grill-room emulating the 'tween decks of a wooden ship (fig. 2.7). Warren's café or palm room, a circular space with a domed glass ceiling and treillage, was located between the first and second floors and connected the *piano nobile* with the public spaces below (fig. 2.8). In the tradition of roof gardens, Warren also incorporated a terrace on the fourth floor, where the three bedroom floors were set back. In the tradition of architect as decorator, the firm specified palms, shrubbery, awnings, and trellises and designed much of the furniture and even light fixtures.

As an avid student of naval architecture and yachting, Warren grounded his exuberant architectural fantasy in nautical history. His library included a number of texts on navigation, naval architecture, and ship construction, with illustrations and plans. He also owned a unique collection of ship drawings that he used as inspiration for the design.[7] Warren's uncle, Lloyd Phoenix, to whom he was close, had served twice as commodore of the New York Yacht Club (1886–1888) and was a leading spirit in American yachting. And Warren's European sketchbooks, which included romantic drawings of sailboats against shorelines

2.4. New York Yacht Club. Warren's competition entry of model room. The Architectural Review 6 (April 1899): pl. 23.

2.5. *New York Yacht Club.*
Window niche in model room,
2005. Photo: Jonathan Wallen.

2.6. *New York Yacht Club.*
Brackets in model room, 2005.
Photo: Jonathan Wallen.

and detailed sketches of rigging, masts, and hardware, reflected a deep fascination with boats. As he recalled: "I have always been fond of ships because they seem to me to be things appearing to have a soul. To be sure it is the soul of the thing that guides them. It is probably for that reason unconsciously and undoubtedly that the sailor becomes so devoted to his ship to the point of rather than forsake her in time of distress to die with her. She symbolizes that which we would idealize in a woman."[8]

During the competition, Warren was without an office or staff of his own and unequipped to handle the practical aspects of such a large commission. In support of his friend, Stanford White offered his firm, should Warren win the commission, to associate with the fledgling architect in carrying out the business end of the work. In a letter from

2.7 *(following pages). New York*
Yacht Club. Dining room.
Museum of the City of New York,
Wurts Collection, #116895.

lawyer Lewis Cass Ledyard on behalf of White to the club's building committee, White asked that his gesture be kept hidden from Warren through the competition.[9] Because Warren formed a practice with Wetmore soon after winning the commission, he did not need White's assistance. By 1900, the firm had established offices at 3 East 33rd Street and taken on Warren's brother Lloyd as a partner.

Stanford White did, however, act as a critic and advisor throughout the Yacht Club's construction. He was especially helpful in the decorating phase, recommending marble workers and painters and specifying tapestries. In one letter, Warren solicited White's help "in making the Yacht Club presentable when the moment comes. . . . I am worried that it will look bare and cheerless."[10] And in later correspondence, White reassured Wetmore that the bold scheme would be embraced by members: "The subduing of the parti-colored scheme to a simpler one of brown and gold can be so quickly and easily done, should the club desire it, that your one course is to carry out the original color scheme of the room to completion. Anything bold and original, and different from that which people are accustomed to, is always apt at first to shock, not only laymen, but also professional judges, and it is only after the first surprise is over that a calm judgment can be taken; and I feel that in the end the club will never wish the change to be made." He feared, however, that the skylight was not "up to the artistic character [and might] injure it."[11]

The Yacht Club opened on January 19, 1901, to much fanfare. Reviews of the design were mixed, but there was no doubt that Warren's building was sensational. One critic for *The Architectural Review* admired Warren's "frank acceptance of an unsymmetrical parti, and its frank expression in the exterior," his "well-composed facade" and his "somewhat ostentatious but ingenious" display of nautical forms and symbols.[12] *The Sun* called the building the "finest town house of any yacht club in the world," and *The New York Times* heralded it as "unique" and "magnificent."[13] Warren's design won a silver medal at the 1900 Exposition Universelle in Paris.

Though the Yacht Club was the firm's first commission, the building exhibited many of the qualities that would characterize its later work. Warren had spent more than ten years honing his skills and was not one to hold back his artistic sensibilities. The Yacht Club established an approach to design that was bold and voluptuous, rich in color and texture, with a generous use of architectural sculpture. Warren's rooms were often outfitted with several shades and varieties of stone, and his full-blown architectural details and moldings were sculpture in their own right. Sculpturally curved rooms and often, circular spaces, such as the palm room, and oval rooms were a theme in his plans. Though Warren developed his rational plans, he sometimes took them one step further by incorporating surprising axis shifts or diagonals.

COURT TENNIS COURT BUILDINGS

The New York Yacht Club led to a number of commissions for sports buildings, beginning with the Tuxedo Tennis and Racquet Club. Since 1886, Tuxedo Park had been an important center of activity for high society during the fall and winter months. Tobacco heir Pierre Lorillard had formed the exclusive sporting community after he abandoned his Newport cottage, The Breakers, for the relative obscurity of the Ramapo Hills north of New York City. Lorillard commissioned Bruce Price to design and plan the park on 5,000 acres of family land; by 1886 a number of houses and a 100-room clubhouse had been built within the gates of the lakeside colony. Both Warren and Wetmore socialized with the Tuxedo set, and Warren was briefly a member of the club, as were his father and brothers.

Located adjacent to Price's clubhouse, Warren & Wetmore's tennis building (1899) housed one of the few court tennis courts in the country (fig. 2.9). Court tennis, from which

2.8. New York Yacht Club. Palm room. Wurts Brothers, Prints and Photographs Division, Library of Congress, #9749.

2.9 (following pages). Court Tennis Court Building, Tuxedo Park, New York. Warren & Wetmore Collection, Avery Architectural and Fine Arts Library, Columbia University.

2.10. *Court Tennis Court Building. Interior, 2004. Originally the arched windows were open.* Photo: Jonathan Wallen.

2.11. *Court Tennis Court Building. Plan.* Warren & Wetmore Collection, Avery Architectural and Fine Arts Library, Columbia University.

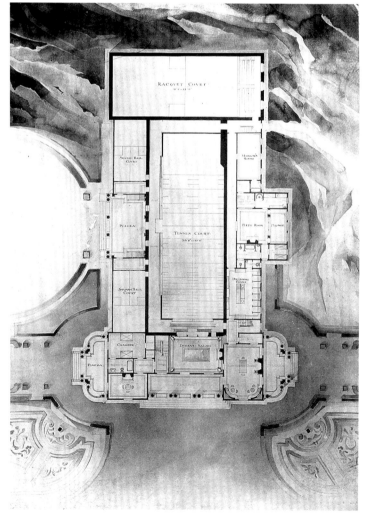

modern tennis descended, was also known as "royal tennis" and had been popular among the French and English ruling classes for centuries. Often equated with the game of chess, the sport required strategy, quick judgment, and good hand–eye coordination to win. A standard court consisted of a hard-walled room with various openings and a roofed shed, or penthouse, running along the end walls and one side wall (fig. 2.10). The game, governed by a complicated set of rules, revolved around laying down "chases." By placing the ball into certain areas of the court or penthouse or into the holes in the wall, the final decision of a point could be deferred to a chase in which the opponent's play was limited. Though introduced in the United States in 1876, court tennis had a limited following, in part because it required special courts that were expensive to build. As an avid tennis player and member of the Newport Casino—home to the second court in the country—Warren knew the sport well; in Paris the game was widely recognized. In fact, Warren entered a set of plans of Tuxedo's court building into the 1901 Exposition in Paris.

Tuxedo's court, the sixth to be built in the United States and Warren & Wetmore's fourth commission as a firm, was constructed at a cost of $80,000, largely raised by sports enthusiast Thomas Suffern Tailer and fellow Tuxedo members Oliver Harriman and Richard Mortimer.[14] The white stucco pavilion, visible from the lake, screened a shingled, gabled structure with a glass-paneled roof containing the court tennis court, two courts for squash, and one for racquets (1902), a faster version of squash using a hard ball (fig. 2.11). Warren & Wetmore animated the symmetrical pavilion with treillage, eyebrow dormers, Ionic columns, and exposed rafter tails. Compared to the Yacht Club, the design appeared pared down; however, brackets supporting the balconies—robustly carved with rams' heads, fruit swags, and acanthus leaves—had the same animated and sculptural quality.

Warren & Wetmore's practice flourished as court tennis continued to draw enthusiasts during the first decade of the twentieth century. In 1902 the firm was commissioned to design a court for the Myopia Hunt Club in South Hamilton, Massachusetts.[15] Home to the country's oldest polo field and third-oldest golf course, the club drew many members with Harvard connections. Thirty members raised $30,000 for the building, and Warren & Wetmore donated its services, designing a simple brick Georgian structure outfitted with a court tennis court, a squash court, locker rooms, and spectator's gallery. In the same year Warren & Wetmore also designed a court in the fashionable winter resort of Aiken, South Carolina, for William C. Whitney and his friends, modeled on the Myopia design.[16]

HOUSES AND ESTATES

The success of the Yacht Club and the Tuxedo Tennis and Racquet Club brought Warren & Wetmore a flood of residential commissions in the country and the city. Like their more established colleagues and competitors, Carrère & Hastings and McKim, Mead & White, Warren & Wetmore attracted clients from New York's highest circles of wealth and prestige. With the level of private wealth at its peak, clients lavished incredible fortunes on their homes.

Warren & Wetmore moved freely between styles and boldly incorporated a variety of elements and inspirations into its residential architecture. This range may have been attributable to the differing tastes and predilections of the partners. Warren leaned toward European inspiration, from urbane Parisian examples to the bucolic and provincial styles of northern Europe, whereas Wetmore, schooled among the brick colonial buildings of Harvard, seemed inclined toward a simpler, more American architecture, as exemplified by his design for a large wood colonial revival house for William Harrison Allen (c. 1898) in Warren, Pennsylvania, with shutters, gambrel roof, and dormer windows.[17] Although Wetmore was considered an able designer, it was Warren whose talents established the firm's reputation. Warren embraced color and texture and transformed his encounters with European architecture, meticulously recorded in sketchbooks, into three-dimensional collages. This approach

2.12. Henry Winthrop Munroe estate, Crow's Nest, Tuxedo Park, New York. Courtesy of the Tuxedo Historical Society.

gave rise to a collection of imaginative and original country houses and outbuildings that, although elegant and luxurious, were not always thoroughly coherent.

Around the time of the Tuxedo Tennis and Racquet Club's completion, Warren & Wetmore embarked on two house projects in Tuxedo Park. Henry Whitney Munroe's Crow's Nest (c. 1900) was the firm's eighth commission (fig. 2.12).[18] The Harvard-educated Munroe (1860–1920) was director of the New York branch of John Munroe & Co., a well-known French banking house founded by his parents. Like Warren, Munroe had strong ties to France, and these ties were reflected in the design of Crow's Nest, a picturesque château executed in native fieldstone and brick with a steeply hipped and flared roof, exaggerated rafter tails, multiple chimneys, and dormers capped with copper cresting. The elegant central turret and oval conservatory enclosed with treillage added sophistication and complexity to the scheme, but Warren & Wetmore's underlying plan was comparatively straightforward (fig. 2.13). The entrance, set at the center of the L-shaped house, opened into a large oval hall with a fireplace and curving stair (fig. 2.14). Radiating off the hall were the main entertaining rooms, all with views of Tuxedo Lake (fig. 2.15). The generously proportioned rooms, with arching French doors, windows embellished with over-scaled plaster swags and keystones, and delicate hardware imported from France, showcased Warren's command of the Louis XIV style. The confidence of the design and that of the adjacent carriage house was striking (fig. 2.16).

On a smaller scale, Warren & Wetmore designed a shingled weekend cottage, Tuck's Eden (c. 1900), for Amos Tuck French (1863–1941). French, a Harvard graduate, member of the New York Stock Exchange, and vice-president and director of the Manhattan Trust Company, came from a family embedded in Tuxedo and Newport society; his sister Elsie married Alfred Gwynne Vanderbilt, the wealthiest Vanderbilt of their generation. Tuck's Eden, built high on an overlook, was a plain three-story shingled box with ample windows, dentillated cornices, and spandrel panels (fig. 2.17).[19] Like Warren's design for the Newport Country Club, the

2.13 (left). Crow's Nest. Conservatory. Warren & Wetmore Collection, Avery Architectural and Fine Arts Library, Columbia University.

2.14 (below left). Crow's Nest. Stair hall. Warren & Wetmore Collection, Avery Architectural and Fine Arts Library, Columbia University.

2.15 (below). Crow's Nest. First and second floor plans. Warren & Wetmore Collection, Avery Architectural and Fine Arts Library, Columbia University.

2.16 (following pages). Crow's Nest. Carriage house. Warren & Wetmore Collection, Avery Architectural and Fine Arts Library, Columbia University.

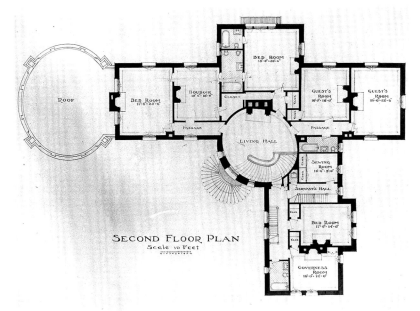

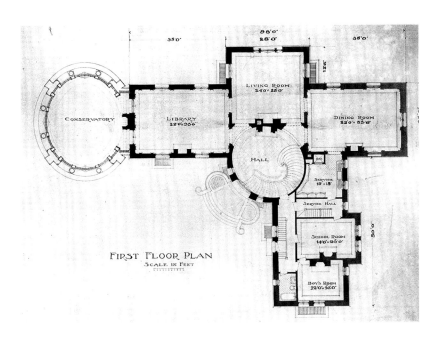

robust French details and formal symmetry gave the impression of a stone house; however, elements such as the oversized Palladian window with floridly carved garlands and half-timbered wing gave the design a more whimsical, somewhat disjointed quality. Here was an example of the challenges posed by Warren's tendency to draw from many sources without an entirely successful strategy for making one coherent work of architecture.

Warren designed his one Newport cottage in 1900 for his sister Edith (1866–1933) and her husband, William Starr Miller (1857–1935), a Harvard-educated capitalist and industrialist.[20] Their house, High Tide, occupied an elevated lot overlooking Bailey's Beach and Almy Pond. It had spectacular views of the ocean and other Newport cottages, including Warren's brother George Henry Jr.'s rambling villa Seafield. With its multigabled roof, chimneys, and L-shaped plan, High Tide resembled the Munroe House; however, the stucco and wood construction gave the house a light and airy quality more suitable to its seaside perch. In his plan, Warren exploited the views and incorporated a circular reception room, a diagonal axis through the corner of the building, and an ample servants' wing. From the exterior, High Tide, which was built into the sloping land of the site, appeared vast, yet the delicate detailing of the interior architecture and Ogden Codman's decoration gave the rooms an intimate scale. Because the Millers had only one daughter, the house contained just three master bedrooms, but it had more than ten rooms for servants.

Around 1904 Warren & Wetmore also designed large estates in Jericho, on the North Shore of Long Island, for Ralph J. Preston (1864–1919) and Joseph Sampson Stevens (1867–1935). Preston, a wealthy lawyer, commissioned a large brick Georgian-style house with French windows, a heavy classical balustrade, and hipped roofs.[21] Unlike Warren & Wetmore's earlier houses in Tuxedo, the Preston estate, Ivy Hall, was surrounded by extensive property and included a series of outbuildings—a gatehouse, stable, carriage house, and farm buildings. A symmetrical block, the house connected to an arcaded conservatory and one-story pavilion (fig. 2.18). Warren & Wetmore carved a double-height porch out of the rear

facade on axis with the entrance vestibule and stair hall that overlooked the gardens. Embellished with a full-blown Ionic portico, it enclosed a double-story paneled glass window that lit the stair hall behind it. The scale of the portico, with its colossal marble columns, dwarfed the wings of the house—an unfortunate juxtaposition emphasized by the treatment of the pilasters and rustication in brick.

Joseph Sampson Steven's neighboring estate, Kirby Hill, was set on a 148-acre property located near the Meadow Brook Club where Stevens, a club champion, rode into history as one of the era's best polo players. During the Spanish-American War, he was one of Theodore Roosevelt's Rough Riders; as a descendant of Albert Gallatin, he came from a wealthy family with ties to French royalty. Like the Preston estate, Kirby Hill was a large brick house; however, Warren & Wetmore used a simpler Georgian idiom. The entertaining rooms, carried out in Georgian and Elizabethan styles, were contained within the central block, and a servants' wing with twelve bedrooms extended out at a 45-degree angle (fig. 2.19). Warren & Wetmore oriented their design to exploit light and views and worked with Umberto Innocenti in carrying out Kirby Hill's gardens.[22]

Warren & Wetmore's outbuildings at Harbor Hill, Clarence H. Mackay's 648-acre compound in Roslyn, and Idle Hour, William K. Vanderbilt's estate in Oakdale, were among the firm's most elaborate and successful designs. Clarence Mackay (1874–1938) was one of the era's richest men. His inherited

2.20 (above). Clarence Mackay estate, Harbor Hill, Roslyn, New York. Carriage house. Warren & Wetmore Collection, Avery Architectural and Fine Arts Library, Columbia University.

2.21 (opposite top). Harbor Hill. Stables. Warren & Wetmore Collection, Avery Architectural and Fine Arts Library, Columbia University.

2.22 (opposite middle left). Harbor Hill. Dairyman's cottage. Warren & Wetmore Collection, Avery Architectural and Fine Arts Library, Columbia University.

2.23 (opposite middle right). Harbor Hill. Spectator's gallery, court tennis court building. Warren & Wetmore Collection, Avery Architectural and Fine Arts Library, Columbia University.

2.24 (opposite bottom). Harbor Hill. Court tennis court building. Warren & Wetmore Collection, Avery Architectural and Fine Arts Library, Columbia University.

wealth—his father's Comstock Lode silver fortune—was substantial, and as founder of the Postal Telegraph Cable Company and the Commercial Cable Company with James Gordon Bennett Jr., he had multiplied his inheritance. Harbor Hill, the most celebrated estate on the North Shore, designed by Stanford White in 1899–1902, was a palatial château modeled after François Mansart's Château de Maisons-Laffitte. However, Mackay's wife, Katherine Duer Mackay, both headstrong and spendthrift, controlled the house project and clashed with its willful architect.

In 1902, after the completion of the main house and gatehouse, the Mackays turned to Warren & Wetmore to design the various outbuildings on the property.[23] Set on one of the highest points in Long Island, Harbor Hill was a world unto itself. The firm's carriage house and stable, located on a rise near the main house, was so grand that it rivaled White's elaborate design (fig. 2.20). It was not uncommon for outbuildings to be flamboyant or daring; some of the stiffest and most predictable mansions of the period were graced with imaginative designs for gatehouses and stables, such as Warren & Wetmore's U-shaped building, accessed through an allée of trees and formal court. Its design showcased Warren's propensity for drama. Not only was the scale of the building impressive but its architecture verged on the fantastic. In picturesque fashion, Warren & Wetmore expressed the roofline as a rhythm of crested dormers, arched entryways, and round turrets, and included a miniature campanile at center. In contrast to the carriage house, Warren & Wetmore designed the estate's kennels, polo pony stable, farm buildings, and cottages in an informal Stick style that fit naturally into the rural landscape designed by Guy Lowell (figs. 2.21, 2.22). The firm's Tudor-style court tennis court building (1906), one of the few private court tennis buildings in the country, only furthered the broad range of Harbor Hill's architecture inspired by formal French examples as well as the more provincial styles of northern France (fig. 2.24). Its spectators' gallery, with beamed ceiling, crystal chandeliers, and massive stone mantel, celebrated the Mackays' extravagant tastes (fig. 2.23).

Similarly, William K. Vanderbilt's countryseat, Idle Hour, reflected the extraordinary wealth of its owner. In 1879 Richard Morris Hunt designed a vast Stick-style house for the family that overlooked the Great South Bay and the Connetquot River. The undeveloped

2.25. William K. Vanderbilt Sr. estate, Idle Hour, Oakdale, New York. Sculptor Sylvain Salières in front of tennis court wing. Warren & Wetmore Collection, Avery Architectural and Fine Arts Library, Columbia University.

region of Long Island near Islip and Oakdale became popular in the 1870s when the South Side Sportsmen's Club, an exclusive hunting and fishing concern, began drawing members of New York society. When Hunt's Idle Hour was destroyed by fire in 1899, Vanderbilt (1849–1920) was spending most of his time in either Newport or France. However, since he had recently replaced his brother, Cornelius II, as head of the Vanderbilt railroad companies, a country estate near the city seemed appropriate, so Vanderbilt quickly turned to Hunt's son, Richard Howland Hunt, to rebuild the house; the second Idle Hour was a huge L-shaped Beaux-Arts mansion with neo-Flemish flourishes and a palm garden connected diagonally by cloisters on axis with the main house.

Vanderbilt began expanding the estate immediately after it was completed. In 1902 he commissioned Warren & Wetmore to design a twelve-bedroom bachelors' wing and indoor tennis court.[24] The facades of the building, adjoining the far side of the palm court, blended with the brick and limestone exterior of Hunt's design and incorporated French sculptor Sylvain Salières's giant urns into the garden terrace (fig. 2.25). Inside, however, Warren indulged in architectural fantasy, creating the interior equivalent of a folly overlooking the court (fig. 2.29). From an arcaded gallery adjoining the bachelors annex, spectators could watch tennis on the glass-roofed clay court below. The heavily rusticated stone of the gallery wall, exuberantly carved with atlantes and fanciful over-door sculpture and painted with scrolling frescoes, created a sculptural backdrop so surprising and original that it overwhelmed the vast open space of the court. For an ancillary building, the scale and energy of the architecture were tremendous. At the same time the wing was constructed, the palm garden—the entrance to the court— was transformed into an exotic Turkish harem, festooned with silk tents and colorful ornaments (fig. 2.26).

2.26. Idle Hour. Lounge. Warren & Wetmore Collection, Avery Architectural and Fine Arts Library, Columbia University.

50

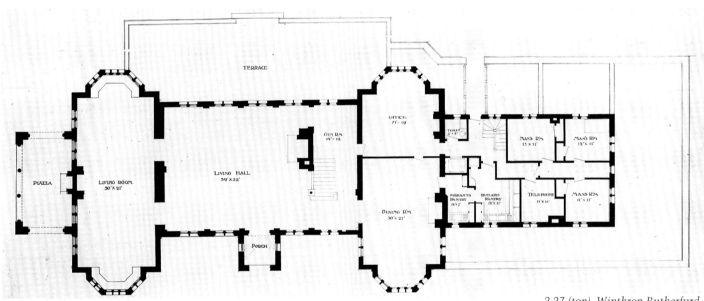

2.27 (top). Winthrop Rutherfurd estate, Rutherfurd House, Allamuchy, New Jersey. Warren & Wetmore Collection, Avery Architectural and Fine Arts Library, Columbia University.

2.28 (above). Rutherfurd House. First floor plan. Warren & Wetmore Collection, Avery Architectural and Fine Arts Library, Columbia University.

2.29 (following pages). Idle Hour. Tennis court wing. Warren & Wetmore Collection, Avery Architectural and Fine Arts Library, Columbia University.

In 1902 Warren & Wetmore also designed Winthrop Rutherfurd's Tudor-style estate, Rutherfurd House, in Allamuchy, New Jersey (fig. 2.27). During the 1890s, Rutherfurd's romance with Consuelo Vanderbilt, William K.'s daughter, had been successfully dashed by her brash and domineering mother, Alva Smith Vanderbilt.[25] Rutherfurd (1862–1944), a descendant of Peter Stuyvesant and John Winthrop, went on to marry Alice Morton, the daughter of Vice-President Levi Morton, in 1902, and later, in 1920, a widower, he married Lucy Mercer, made famous by her affair with Franklin Delano Roosevelt. As one of the largest houses the firm would design, Rutherfurd House was formal and imposing (fig. 2.28). With its axial plan and symmetrical facades, the design was rational and straightforward; however, the many windows and chimneys, balustrades, and cresting gave the brick and limestone mansion a picturesque appearance.[26] In addition to Rutherfurd's 1,000-acre New

2.30 (top). Moses Taylor estate, Annandale Farm, Mount Kisco, New York. Warren & Wetmore Collection, Avery Architectural and Fine Arts Library, Columbia University.

2.31 (above). Annandale Farm. Entrance hall. Warren & Wetmore Collection, Avery Architectural and Fine Arts Library, Columbia University.

Jersey farm, he also owned considerable property in New York and an estate in Aiken, South Carolina.

Like New Jersey and the North Shore, Westchester was emerging as a popular location for affluent New Yorkers to establish a second or third home. In 1900 Moses Taylor V commissioned Warren & Wetmore to design several buildings at Annandale Farm, his 500-acre Mount Kisco property (fig. 2.30). Taylor (1871–1928), active in banking, railroads, and iron and steel industries, inherited $7 million from his father, H. A. C. Taylor, a Lackawanna Steel magnate who had commissioned two of McKim, Mead & White's seminal Georgian-inspired houses in New York and Newport in the 1880s and 1890s. Like his father, Moses Taylor gravitated toward an architecture of elegant simplicity. Clean Georgian lines defined Warren & Wetmore's two-story wood house, but European flourishes, such as French windows, pilasters, attic balustrade, oculi, and an arching cornice, added a layer of sophistication to the design. Inside, the main hall that extended through the center block was articulated by paneled wainscoting that framed a large central fireplace and Ionic columns that marked the entrance vestibule (fig. 2.31). At Annandale, Taylor employed up to forty people; the working farm also included a series of outbuildings, garages, and kennels, carried out by the firm in field-stone and wood.[27]

Wampus Farm, John T. Magee's estate in Mount Kisco, was one of the firm's most eclectic and bizarre designs (fig. 2.34). Because the imposing white house was built into a slope, the front of the house stood one story taller than the rear. A three-story pavilion with a cornice and balustrade supported by an Ionic colonnade marked the main entrance and obscured the servants' quarters in the attic (fig. 2.32). On the symmetrical wings extending to either

2.32 (left). John Magee estate, Wampus Farm, Mount Kisco, New York. Detail of entrance facade. Mattie Edwards Hewitt Collection. New York State Historical Association, Cooperstown, NY.

2.33 (below). Wampus Farm. Garden facade. Mattie Edwards Hewitt Collection. New York State Historical Association, Cooperstown, NY.

2.34 (following pages). Wampus Farm. Entrance facade. Warren & Wetmore Collection, Avery Architectural and Fine Arts Library, Columbia University.

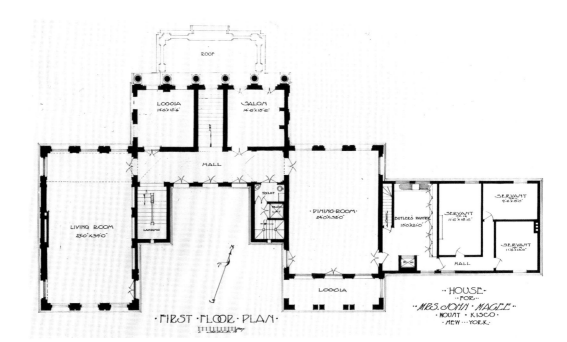

2.35. *Wampus Farm. First floor plan.* Warren & Wetmore Collection, Avery Architectural and Fine Arts Library, Columbia University.

2.36. *Wampus Farm. Dining room.* Warren & Wetmore Collection, Avery Architectural and Fine Arts Library, Columbia University.

2.37. *Wampus Farm. Pool and trellis.* Mattie Edwards Hewitt Collection, New York State Historical Association, Cooperstown, NY.

2.38. Fifth Avenue. Looking north from 77th Street, c. 1910. Collection of The New-York Historical Society, #54029.

side, Warren & Wetmore interspersed large panels of applied treillage between the double-height windows. As the ivy matured, it remained contained within the panels, lending color and texture to the facades and virtually growing into the design.

Compared with the grand scale of the front of the house, the garden facade was diminutive (fig. 2.33). A peculiar medley of Tudor style and formal classicism, it consisted of two pavilions that hugged a half-timber overhang with a tile roof and painted brackets. The critical lines of the architecture—stringcourses, rooflines, and eaves—collided in unexpected ways, and the ivy and trelliswork engulfed the facade. The bizarre yet compelling approach demonstrated Warren's inclination toward scenographic effect, even at the expense of the rigor in architectural form.

At Wampus Farm, Warren & Wetmore's huge panels of glass in the wings were essentially a modern concept (fig. 2.35). Inside, the double-height windows and high ceilings rendered the rooms airy and bright. However, no space was left for an appropriate cornice between the tops of the windows and the ceiling; between the windows, segments of wall were treated as independent panels (fig. 2.36). Warren & Wetmore also designed a series of

2.39. *832–34 Fifth Avenue, New York City (second house from right).* Milstein Division of United States History, Local History, and Genealogy, The New York Public Library, Astor, Lenox, and Tilden Foundations.

outbuildings with applied treillage set within Ellen Shipman's extensive gardens (fig. 2.37).[28]

Compared to its country houses, which were seldom fully coherent designs, Warren & Wetmore's city houses exhibited a consistent modern French approach. As society had fled the encroaching business district by relocating uptown, the streets between Fifth and Madison Avenues from the 50s to the 90s became a residential enclave for the very rich. The building boom of the 1880s and early 1890s left a formidable imprint of elaborate châteaux and mansions lining Fifth Avenue (fig. 2.38). Although the economic recession of 1893 reduced the amount of construction, building activity recommenced at a furious pace after 1900. In 1901 and 1902, over two hundred dwellings were constructed in the fashionable residential district.[29]

As construction renewed, architectural tastes began to move away from the flamboyant compositions of Richard Morris Hunt and C. P. H. Gilbert. John Carrère and Thomas Hastings formed their practice in 1885 after working in the offices of McKim, Mead & White. Their pioneering interpretations of the French baroque and *regénce* styles generated well-ordered designs—such as residences for H. T. Sloane at 9 East 72nd Street (1893) and E. K. Dunham at 35 East 68th Street (1899)—and influenced the architects who followed to adopt a freer reading of European precedent. Although some found the more animated manifestations of the style excessive and dubbed it "cartouche architecture," the modern French grew in popularity among clients, architects, and speculative builders.[30]

Because most of Fifth Avenue was developed by the time Warren & Wetmore formed, the

2.40 (above left). 9–11 East 84th Street, New York City, c. 1940. Municipal Archives, Department of Records and Information Services, City of New York.

2.41 (above right). Francis K. Pendleton house, 7 East 86th Street, New York City. Warren & Wetmore Collection, Avery Architectural and Fine Arts Library, Columbia University.

firm executed only a handful of residences there but designed many more that were located just two steps off the main thoroughfare, where they enjoyed oblique views of the park. Property on or near Fifth Avenue was in such demand that builders could construct expensive homes from architects' plans and turn them for great profit. In 1901 the firm designed a pair of five-story houses for builders John T. and James A. Farley at 832–34 Fifth Avenue at a cost of $500,000 (fig. 2.39). William Guggenheim and Frank Jay Gould, son of financier and railroad baron Jay Gould, later occupied the 70-foot-wide speculative houses.[31] Similar in plan and elevation, each was comprised of a triple-bay and a consistent cornice. Their steeply pitched mansard roofs, bull's-eye dormers, and balconies were French in spirit, and although the pair presented a uniform facade to the street, each was marked by individual ornament at the cornice and base.

The firm went on to design a smaller set of speculative houses in 1901 at 9–11 East 84th Street (fig. 2.40). As it had done at 832–34 Fifth Avenue, Warren & Wetmore subtly distinguished the pair of limestone modern French dwellings with robust ornament but maintained uniform cornice heights and architectural order that recreated the typical composition of the nineteenth-century Parisian streetscape. Number eleven, the slightly more elaborate of the two, had a bowed front and curved balcony at the fourth floor; Francis de R. Wissmann, a real estate investor and agent, lived there until 1906, when the Sands family purchased the house. City Real Property, Wetmore and Edmund Baylies's development company, built number nine, which eventually was sold to Mary Bishop and her brother, Ogden Mills Bishop.[32]

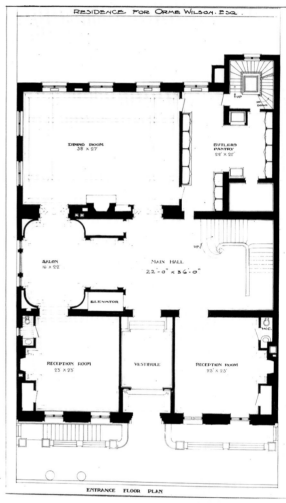

RESIDENCE FOR ORME WILSON ESQ.

DINING ROOM
38 × 27

BUTLERS
PANTRY
28' × 21'

SALON
16 × 22

MAIN HALL
22'-0" × 36'-0"

ELEVATOR

RECEPTION ROOM
23 × 23

VESTIBULE

RECEPTION ROOM
23 × 23

W.C.

ENTRANCE FLOOR PLAN

2.42 (above left). M. Orme Wilson house, 3 East 64th Street, New York City. Museum of the City of New York, Wurts Collection, #110449.

2.43 (above right). Wilson house. Entrance floor plan. Warren & Wetmore Collection, Avery Architectural and Fine Arts Library, Columbia University.

Warren & Wetmore's best house designs were private commissions. In 1900 Francis Key Pendleton (1850–1930), a lawyer who would become a state supreme court justice, commissioned a house at 7 East 86th Street (fig. 2.41). For Pendleton, Warren & Wetmore produced a red-brick and stone tripartite design with a limestone base, heavy balustrade, steep mansard roof, bull's-eye windows, and decorative consoles at the attic story. The architects distinguished the facade with three arched French windows, which expressed the *piano nobile*, set within a Doric colonnade. All of the main rooms spanned the 25-foot width of the house and opened to a square stair hall that rose through the center of the building. While the brick on the exterior created an austerity often associated with more American styles, Warren & Wetmore inventively balanced the design with French details.[33]

Construction on Warren & Wetmore's largest house in New York also began in 1900. Mr. and Mrs. M. Orme Wilson's limestone mansion at 3 East 64th Street, located on a triple lot, was 65 feet wide. Orme Wilson (1861–1926), the son of Richard T. Wilson, came from a prominent southern family that had done famously well by marriage. Wilson's sisters married Cornelius Vanderbilt III and Ogden Goelet, and in 1884, Wilson, who had joined his father's banking business, wed Caroline Astor (1862–1948), granddaughter of the first John Jacob Astor and daughter of the period's most influential social arbiter, Mrs. Astor of "the 400." Ten years after the couple's elaborate wedding in the Astors' private art gallery at 350 Fifth Avenue, Mrs. Wilson bought land on 64th Street and later commissioned Warren & Wetmore to design a substantial modern French mansion (fig. 2.42). A master of composi-

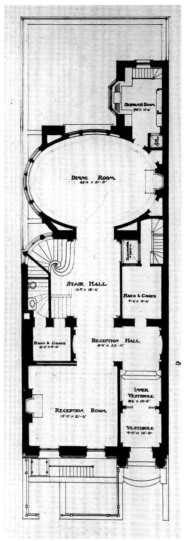

2.44 (far left). Mrs. Sidney Dillon Ripley house, 16 East 79th Street, New York City. Warren & Wetmore Collection, Avery Architectural and Fine Arts Library, Columbia University.

2.45 (near left). Ripley house. First-floor plan. Warren & Wetmore Collection, Avery Architectural and Fine Arts Library, Columbia University.

tion, Warren incorporated a smooth facade that created a taut surface to juxtapose the exuberant foliate keystones and sculptural details at the front door, windows, and balustrade. Warren's concave recessed arched windows at the piano nobile balanced the more sculptural bull's-eye dormers and cresting along the blue slate mansard.

Like many of the Gilded Age mansions, Warren & Wetmore designed the house for grand-scale entertaining. The Wilsons were well known for their lavish balls and musical events. On the entrance level of their house, the architects included two reception rooms, a Louis XVI-style dining room, small salon, and spectacular stone stair hall; on the second floor they located a wood-paneled library, a third reception room, salon, and sizable ballroom (fig. 2.43). For decoration, the Wilsons used H. Nelson, a Parisian firm well regarded by New Yorkers. H. Nelson's *Devis Approximatif des Travaux* from 1900 detailed everything from elements of the interior architecture, such as boiseries, mantelpieces, and hardware, to decorations that included brocade curtains with tassels, carpets, furniture, tapestries, sculpture, and mirrors.[34]

In contrast to the modern French exuberance of the Wilson house, Mr. and Mrs. Sidney Dillon Ripley's brick and limestone townhouse at 16 East 79th Street from 1901 reflected the more restrained quality of an English terrace house (figs. 2.44, 2.45). Ripley (1863–1905), treasurer and director of the Equitable Life Assurance Society, was an avid horseman and devoted member of the Meadow Brook Club; he had inherited millions from his grandfather, Sidney Dillon, builder of the Union Pacific Railroad. Mrs. Ripley, née Mary B. Hyde, was the sister of James Hazen Hyde of the Equitable Life fortune. For the Ripleys, Warren & Wetmore

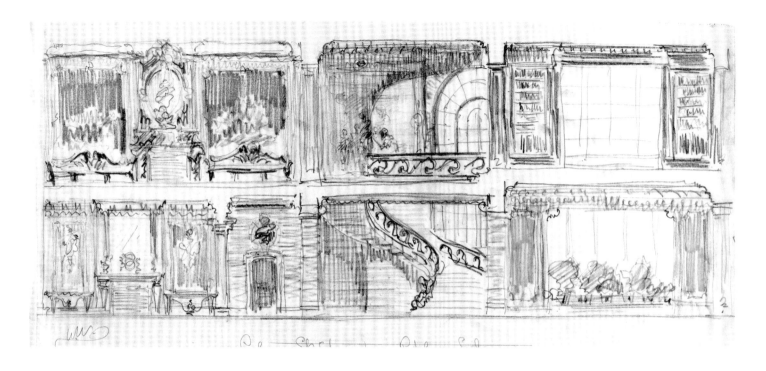

2.46. Whitney Warren, color sketch for Ripley scheme, n.d. Graphite; red, blue, green, and yellow crayon on tracing paper, mounted on off-white laid paper, 9 ³/₁₆ x 19 ¾ in. (233 x 489 mm). Cooper-Hewitt, National Design Museum, Smithsonian Institution. Gift of Mrs. William Greenough, 1943-51-420. Photo: Matt Flynn.

2.47 (above). Ripley house. Reception room. Warren & Wetmore Collection, Avery Architectural and Fine Arts Library, Columbia University.

2.48 (right). Ripley house. Dining room. Warren & Wetmore Collection, Avery Architectural and Fine Arts Library, Columbia University.

2.49 (above). Ripley house. Salon.
Warren & Wetmore Collection, Avery
Architectural and Fine Arts Library,
Columbia University.

2.50 (right). Ripley house. Stair. Warren
& Wetmore Collection, Avery Architectural
and Fine Arts Library, Columbia University.

produced a 35-foot wide house with a heavily rusticated limestone base and an entrance portico and detailed the upper section of the house, laid in Flemish bond, with limestone window surrounds, band course, cornice balustrade, and urns. Although the exterior of the house presented a more subdued front than Warren & Wetmore's more typical designs, the brick bond pattern gave the facade a subtle and pleasing depth. The interiors, however, recreated the atmosphere of a Parisian hôtel particulier with a voluptuously curving stair that rose through the center of the house, overscaled details, elaborate plasterwork and mirrors in the reception room and salon, and oval-paneled dining room. Louis XV furniture, art, sculpture, and tapestries enhanced the European atmosphere (figs. 2.46–2.50).[35]

Warren & Wetmore's houses for Frederick Edey, George Henry Warren Jr., and Robert Livingston Beeckman exhibited the firm's preference for designing in variations of the modern French mode.[36] Edey was a banker and member of the New York Stock Exchange and his wife, a leader in the women's suffrage movement. In designing their limestone house at 10 West 56th Street (1901), Warren & Wetmore distinguished the slender building with a large sculptural Palladian window, a central shell motif, and bull's-eye windows on either side of the front door (fig. 2.51). For its 1902 house for Warren's older brother, George Henry Warren Jr. (1855–1943), at 924 Fifth Avenue, the firm produced a more austere design with spandrel panels, swags, window enframements, and a Parisian glass and iron entrance canopy (fig. 2.52). In contrast to the restraint of the facades, Warren & Wetmore's interiors were rich in color, carving, and mural art (figs. 2.54–2.55). Livingston Beeckman's house at 854 Fifth

2.52 (above left). George Henry Warren house, 924 Fifth Avenue, New York City. Architecture 11 (May 1905): pl. 91.

2.53 (above right). R. Livingston Beeckman house, 854 Fifth Avenue, New York City, c. 1910. Milstein Division of United States History, Local History, and Genealogy, The New York Public Library, Astor, Lenox, and Tilden Foundations.

2.54 (left). George Henry Warren house. Sitting room, 1935. Gottscho-Schleisner Collection, Prints and Photographs Division, Library of Congress, #6679.

2.55 (following pages). George Henry Warren house. Living room, 1935. Gottscho-Schleisner Collection, Prints and Photographs Division, Library of Congress, #6679.

Avenue (1903) had a double-bay composition and steep copper mansard with cresting and both round-arch and bull's-eye dormers (fig. 2.53). Beeckman (1866–1935), a member of the New York Stock Exchange, became Governor of Rhode Island in 1915; he was also the director of the Newport Trust Company for whom Warren & Wetmore designed a bank building in 1928.

In lavishing money on architecture, clients did not stop with their houses. Warren & Wetmore's city carriage houses and stables demonstrated the suitability of the modern French style to the equestrian building. For Augustus van Horne Stuyvesant (1838–1918), the firm designed a monumental brick and limestone stable at 33 West 44th Street (1902) with a deeply rusticated base and concave entry recess, rigorously carved tympanum, clock, and oversized lanterns set on either side of the door (figs. 2.56, 2.57). The architects enlivened the plain brick facade of banker James Henry Smith's stable at 133–35 West 55th Street (1904) with geometric limestone details, varied window sizes and patterns, a massive entry, and cornice (fig. 2.58).[37] Its vaulting ceilings, skylights, topiaries, and wood-paneled harness room were emblematic of the sophistication and luxury that the firm brought to its service buildings (figs. 2.59, 2.60).

Mr. and Mrs. James A. Burden Jr.'s 1902 mansion stood as the pinnacle of the firm's city house designs (fig. 2.61). In 1895, Burden (1871–1932), heir to the Burden Ironworks in Troy, New York, married Florence Adele Sloane (1873–1960) at her family's baronial country cottage, Elm Court, in Lenox, Massachusetts. As a wedding present, the bride's parents, Emily Vanderbilt and William D. Sloane, commissioned Warren & Wetmore to design a house for

2.58 (left). James Henry Smith carriage house, 133–35 West 55th Street, New York City. Warren & Wetmore Collection, Avery Architectural and Fine Arts Library, Columbia University.

2.59 (below left). Smith carriage house. Stalls. Warren & Wetmore Collection, Avery Architectural and Fine Arts Library, Columbia University.

2.60 (below). Smith carriage house. Bridle room. Warren & Wetmore Collection, Avery Architectural and Fine Arts Library, Columbia University.

the young couple at 7 East 91st Street, on land purchased from Andrew Carnegie. At the same time, the Sloanes also purchased the lot at 9 East 91st Street to build a house for Mrs. Burden's sister, Emily Hammond; this house was designed by Carrère & Hastings and completed in 1906. In designing the Burden house, the architects adroitly combined the massing and simplicity of an Italian palazzo with the sculptural quality and detail of a Parisian *hôtel*. While the architects kept the ornament on the exterior to a minimum, the stonework gave the facades a robust depth and texture. On the third floor Warren & Wetmore expressed the immense scale of the *belle étage* with three colossal arched windows set within sculptural recessed niches; the square windows of the family's private living quarters on the second floor were interspersed between massive carved brackets supporting the balcony and ironwork above. Like a palazzo, the house had a muscularly rusticated base and flat roof, but it also had a modillioned cornice and rooftop balustrade more characteristic of French design.

The New York Times proclaimed that "so perfectly is the French idea carried out at the Burden residence that the only way one can enter is through a courtyard, separated from the street by heavy doors."[38] In true French manner, Warren & Wetmore situated the main entrance to the house through a small garden that adjoined the Hammond house next door. Heavy wooden doors at the street revealed a porte-cochère that led back to the canopied entrance to the house to the west; the driveway then curved back out to the street through the garden to the east (fig. 2.62).[39]

The central axis of the Burdens' house ran parallel to the street, and the voluptuous oval stair hall was aligned with the main entrance on the east side of the building. The architects located the billiards room, reception room, and James Burden's office—known as the "bearskin room"—on the first floor and the Burdens' apartments on the second story (figs. 2.63, 2.64). The important entertaining spaces on the third floor were accessed by a sweep-

2.61. James A. Burden Jr. house, 7 East 91st Street, New York City. Architecture 11 (May 1905): pl. 90.

2.62 (opposite top). Burden house. Porte-cochère, 2004. Photo: Jonathan Wallen.

2.63 (opposite bottom, left to right). Burden house. First, entresol, and second floor plans. Warren & Wetmore Collection, Avery Architectural and Fine Arts Library, Columbia University.

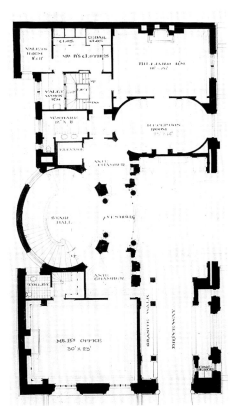

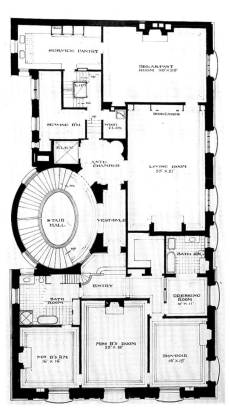

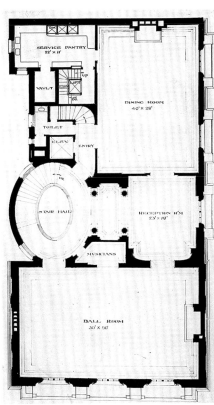

ing stair of Hautville marble with "tread so low and wide that one ascends without being conscious of any effort."[40] The stair was crowned with a stained-glass skylight and Hector d'Espouy's colorful mural depicting the arts (fig. 2.65).

The architects kept the Burdens' spacious entertaining rooms separate from the family's living quarters. According to Edith Wharton and Ogden Codman Jr.'s *The Decoration of Houses*, "Gala rooms are meant for general entertainments, never for any assemblage small or informal enough to be conveniently accommodated in the ordinary living-rooms of the house; therefore to fulfill their purpose they must be large, very high-studded, and not over-crowded with furniture, while the walls and ceiling—the only parts of a crowded room that can be seen—must be decorated with greater elaboration than would be pleasing or appropriate in other rooms."[41] Although furnishings were sparse, Warren & Wetmore created a riot of color and decoration in the double-height ballroom, designed in the style of Louis XIV's Galeries des Glaces (fig. 2.66). Violet-gray marble columns, deep green marble panels overlaid with gilt trophies of musical instruments, giant glass doors and panels, crystal chandeliers, and herringbone floors recalled the atmosphere of a Parisian *hôtel particulier* and made a suitable backdrop for the Burdens' many parties and balls. The gilded swags, shells, crown and tiara motifs at the cornice, a Louis XIV tapestry, and the rose-colored marble mantel of cascading flowers and fruits added a burst of color to the opulent space. With its arched white plaster ceiling carved with groupings of putti, flowers, fruit, shields, and helmets, the firm created a spectacle for all guests to see. Warren & Wetmore carried the magnificent finishes through the dining room with Campan vert marble walls, the French gray reception room, and stair hall with gilded Ionic columns and intricate wrought-iron balustrade. These materials and the crafts and arts they represented were essential in bringing to life the form of a fully developed Beaux-Arts–style room. Here, the Burdens enjoyed the American equivalent of the life of European royalty.[42]

2.65. *Burden house. Reception room to stair hall.* Warren & Wetmore Collection, Avery Architectural and Fine Arts Library, Columbia University.

2.66. *Burden house. Ballroom.* Warren & Wetmore Collection, Avery Architectural and Fine Arts Library, Columbia University.

OFFICE BUILDINGS

As Warren & Wetmore forged a name for itself through its residential commissions, the firm began to develop a reputation for commercial work.[43] At the turn of the twentieth century, American architects were in the process of adapting architectural language and forms to the new problem of the tall office structure. Warren & Wetmore's first commercial venture in New York, a building for the banking company Kean, Van Cortlandt & Company at 28–30 Pine Street, followed the typical classical arrangement of base, shaft, and capital used by firms specializing in commercial design, such as Carrère & Hastings and Clinton & Russell.[44] The twelve-story midblock structure, designed in 1902, consisted of a heavy limestone base with bold Ionic pilasters, which supported a plain brick shaft punctuated by three bays of iron-clad windows (fig. 2.67). Great brackets and a gabled cornice crowned the building. Although critic Barr Ferree found the design "an honest effort to apply Beaux Arts ideas to the high building," he also noted that it was "lacking in interest" and that the "ornamental enrichment of the lower stories [was] heavy and large" and "more rigorous by far than that which any French architect would produce."[45]

COMPETITIONS AND UNREALIZED PROJECTS

Following the completion of the New York Yacht Club, Warren went on to prepare a design for J. P. Morgan's library, planned for 36th Street and Madison Avenue (fig. 2.68).[46] Warren's 1900 scheme detailed a richly sculpted pavilion with a large circular hall, off of which radiated subsidiary rooms for reading and offices. The design recalled the energy of the Yacht Club yet involved a simple underlying geometry. In fact, Warren's compass circles that ruled the principal outlines, proportions, and rooms of the pavilion all radiated from a well-worn point in the center of the plan—still visible in the original drawing (fig. 2.69).

By the time Morgan decided to move forward with the project in 1902, he had become one of the most important patrons of the new American Academy in Rome, the brainchild of Charles McKim. Morgan's endorsement of the academy coincided with the decision to award the commission for his library to McKim. Perhaps Morgan felt

2.67. Kean, Van Courtland Company Building, 28–30 Pine Street, New York City. Warren & Wetmore Collection, Avery Architectural and Fine Arts Library, Columbia University.

that McKim's more academic and correct classical vocabulary would be more appropriate for his important collections of books.

While Warren's proposal for the Morgan Library showed his ability to fuse architecture and sculpture, his competition entry for the campus at the University of California in Berkeley displayed his desire to design on a grand scale (fig. 2.70). In 1898 the university held a major international competition to find a campus architect. Phoebe Hearst, the widow of mining and real estate scion Senator George Hearst, funded the effort as a memorial to her late husband. One hundred entrants were asked to design a master plan for the university that reflected the assumption that time and resources were unlimited. Among the eleven finalists, Warren & Wetmore produced a grandiose modern French scheme that revolved around a massive oval arena reminiscent of a Roman coliseum; secondary buildings formed a uniform wall around an open green.[47] The awe-inspiring monumentality of the campus plan and the sculptural richness of the Morgan Library scheme were the defining qualities that would shape the firm's most successful and compelling work.

2.68. *Whitney Warren, proposal for the J. Pierpont Morgan Library, New York; front elevation, 1900. Graphite on cream wove paper, 19 ¹/₈ x 29 ¹/₈ in. (485 x 740 mm).* Cooper-Hewitt, National Design Museum, Smithsonian Institution. Gift of Mrs. William Greenough, 1943-51-332.

2.69 *(right). Whitney Warren, sketch plan for the library museum for J. P. Morgan, c.1900. Graphite; pen and black ink; brush and blue and yellow watercolor; red and green crayon on tracing paper, mounted on white laid paper, 12 ? x 17 in. (324 x 432 mm).* Cooper-Hewitt, National Design Museum, Smithsonian Institution. Gift of Mrs. William Greenough, 1943-51-334. Photo: Matt Flynn.

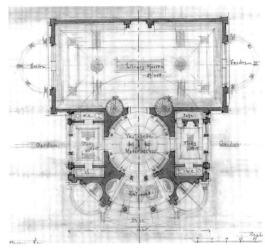

2.70 *(below). Competition entry for the University of California, Berkeley.* Warren & Wetmore Collection, Avery Architectural and Fine Arts Library, Columbia University.

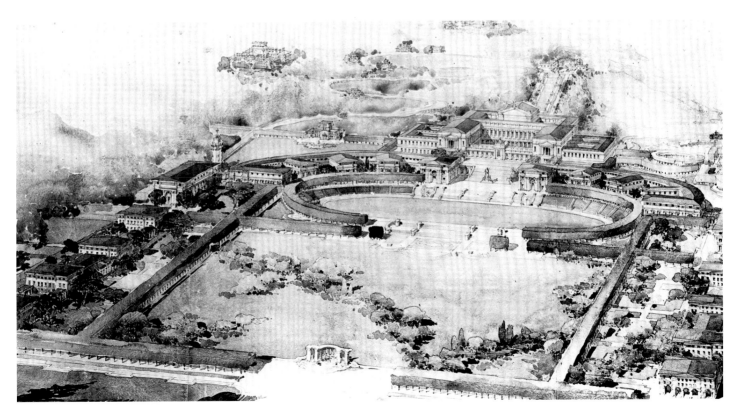

CHAPTER THREE

The Grand Central Years: 1904–1914

In 1904 Warren & Wetmore sought the commission for the Grand Central Terminal complex, the era's largest building venture and city improvement. Up to that point, the firm had primarily brought in residential commissions, but involvement on the terminal design and a series of opportunities—many in conjunction with the railroad—transformed the practice. Over the following ten years, as the design and construction of the highly publicized, world-famous building was carried out, Warren & Wetmore's reputation grew significantly and its architectural range expanded. Although the firm continued to design the occasional house or estate building for friends and family, larger commercial projects in New York and terminals, hotels, offices, and ancillary buildings for the railroads became its bread and butter.

While the New York Central and Hudson River Railroad's ambitious building campaign extended well into the 1920s, the work completed during the first decade of the ongoing project was the product of collaboration between two firms: Warren & Wetmore and Reed & Stem. As the associated architects worked on the numerous railroad commissions from shared space at 314 Madison Avenue, Warren & Wetmore also focused on its own projects from its office at 3 East 33rd Street. So as the firm built its reputation as a railroad architect in tandem with the more experienced firm of Reed & Stem, it worked separately on store and hotel designs, forging relationships with some of the country's leading hotel chains and securing future commissions.[1]

An admirer of the grand urban planning of Baron Haussmann in Paris, Warren longed to bring order and beauty to the streets of his native city and envisioned a New York of tree-lined boulevards and axial gateways. In 1903 Mayor Seth Low, who was instrumental in creating the municipal Art Commission, organized the New York City Improvement Commission, and George McClellan, the succeeding mayor, appointed prominent artists, politicians, and businessmen, including Francis Pendleton, Daniel S. Lamont, Harry Payne Whitney, Daniel C. French, and Whitney Warren, to the advisory committee. With the goal of transforming New York into "one of the great metropolitan cities of the world," the commission devised a plan for grouping buildings, laying out parks and boulevards, and improving the waterfront.[2] The commission's aesthetically based final report (1907) reflected little concern for economics and transportation with its presentation of renderings of spacious plazas and radiating boulevards connecting key buildings, city entries, and parks. The keynote of the plan—the broadening of 59th Street—created a monumental axis between the Queensboro Bridge, Central Park, and a projected Hudson River bridge. In concept, the comprehensive scheme gave New York a certain monumentality and grandeur—qualities that Warren, whose ideas the commission respected, encouraged and felt New York lacked.[3] Although little of the plan was implemented, it did prompt the firm's modern French design for the Chelsea Piers (1907–10), an important city improvement on the Hudson River, which

embraced the ideals of the City Beautiful movement, and presaged the George Washington Bridge, eventually built further uptown.

However, it was Grand Central Terminal and the surrounding buildings—a pocket of cohesive design in midtown Manhattan—that embodied New York's greatest example of City Beautiful principles and planning. Warren once stated that he "believe[d] in the moral effect of the cultivation of the aesthetic sense."[4] In his designs he set out to create an aesthetic response through beauty and order; in no other project was this concept more highly developed than in the Grand Central complex. The prosperity of the period, coupled with the extensive building activity, burgeoning travel, and railroad industries, created the perfect milieu within which Warren & Wetmore imprinted the streets of New York with its aesthetic sensibilities.

GRAND CENTRAL AND TERMINAL CITY: 1904–1914

> "In ancient times the entrance to the city was through an opening in the walls or fortifications. This portal was usually decorated and elaborated into an Arch of Triumph, erected to some naval or military victory, or to the glory of some great personage. The city-of-today has no wall surrounding that may serve, by elaboration, as a pretext to such glorification, but nonetheless, the gateway must exist, and in the case of New York and other cities, it is through a tunnel which discharges the human flow in the very center of town. Such is the Grand Central Terminal."
>
> — WHITNEY WARREN, "Apologia"

Shortly after the Civil War, shipping magnate Commodore Cornelius Vanderbilt (1794–1877) had amalgamated the great transportation empire, the New York Central and Hudson River Railroad. In 1871 he commissioned John B. Snook, architect of the fashionable A. T. Stewart Department Store, to design Grand Central Depot at 42nd Street. After the commodore's death in 1877, his son, William H. Vanderbilt (1821–1885), took over as director of the company and augmented the family fortune considerably. William's eldest son, Cornelius II, succeeded his father in 1885 and William K., the second son, replaced Cornelius as director after his brother's death in 1899. By this time, Snook's French Renaissance fifteen-track terminal, with its great arched iron-truss train shed, was overwhelmed by the volume of trains. Although architect Bradford Gilbert enlarged the building in 1899 and Samuel Huckel Jr. renovated the interiors one year later, the phenomenal growth within the railroads soon necessitated a new terminal to accommodate the rising number of travelers. Across town, Pennsylvania Railroad Company's president, Alexander Cassatt, was working to extend his railroad lines into New York City. In 1901 Cassatt announced plans to build Hudson and East River tunnels to create access to the city—an engineering feat made possible by the revolutionizing development of electric power and locomotives.

Before the turn of the twentieth century, New York's trains operated by steam power and ran in open tracks along Park Avenue—which was, as a result, rendered unattractive and undesirable by the fumes and noise. Cutting through the center of Manhattan island, the railroad created a distinct divide between the city's most exclusive residential enclaves, which sprang up to the west, and the factories and slaughterhouses, which were relegated to the east. William J. Wilgus (1865–1949), New York Central's chief engineer and vice-president, recognized the benefits of electric power for trains—a concept that had been publicly introduced at the Paris Exposition of 1900—and had been contemplating the switch since meeting Frank J. Sprague (1857–1934), a leader in the fields of science, electrification, and motors, in 1899.[5] For the exposition, the Paris and Orleans Railroad set an influential standard by using third-rail electric current and constructing two miles of underground service between the Gare d'Austerlitz and Victor Laloux's Gare d'Orsay. Although plans to electrify New York Central's tracks were underway, it was not until 1902, when seventeen passengers died in a fatal accident in the Park Avenue tunnel, that the New York Central Railroad seriously reevaluated its facility. Due to bad visibility and dangerous conditions, an incoming commuter train failed to halt at its signal inside the tunnel and collided with a stopped train. The accident drove the state to prohibit steam engines below the Harlem River after 1908 and prompted the railroad company to commit to a grand scale redevelopment plan incorporating the cleaner and safer electric system. Wilgus laid out a conceptual plan for a new terminal, its tracks, and the surrounding buildings. His guidelines, which were presented to New York Central's president, William H. Newman, in late 1902, would shape the ultimate success of the vast undertaking.[6]

The establishment of an "air rights" district over a system of buried tracks was central to Wilgus's plan. Because electric power did not require open rail yards, trains could be depressed and the land above freed for more profitable enterprises. Wilgus envisioned a complete transformation around 42nd Street—a picture that included two levels of fixed tracks underground, restored cross streets on Park Avenue north of 45th Street, and revenue-producing buildings, including a hotel on Madison Avenue, on the newly vacant lots. Wilgus's scheme, which enabled the railroad company to recoup a portion of the project's enormous expense, also proposed extending Park Avenue below 45th Street to create a continuous thoroughfare connecting Park Avenue to Fourth Avenue. His suggestion to use stairs or ramps to access the trains would become an important guideline in defining the terminal's spatial flow.

Upon approval of Wilgus's plan, the company held a competition. Four architects and firms were invited to participate: Chicago's Daniel H. Burnham; Stanford White of McKim, Mead & White (Charles McKim was occupied with the design of Pennsylvania Station); Samuel Huckel Jr. of Philadelphia, designer of the existing station's 1900 renovations; and Charles Reed of Reed & Stem from St. Paul, Minnesota. Of the surviving plans, both those of Reed & Stem and McKim, Mead & White reflected the influence of Beaux-Arts planning and the City Beautiful movement. In his entry, White ran Park Avenue through a fourteen-story terminal building and included an epic sixty-story campanile modeled after Seville Cathedral's Giralda Tower (fig. 3.1). Reed & Stem's scheme detailed a twenty-two-story hotel above the terminal and a line of buildings and civic institutions—a Court of Honor—that created an impressive northern approach (fig. 3.2). However, Reed & Stem's idea of elevating the driveways around the building and connecting them to the south by a bridge over 42nd Street took Wilgus's vision one step further than its competitors' designs. Reed & Stem's broad ramps, which moved traffic through the terminal, added a level of sophistication to the firm's submission.

While nepotism may have played a role in Reed & Stem's victory—Wilgus's wife, May, was Charles Reed's sister—it was also clear that Reed & Stem's scheme offered the most viable and creative solution. Reed, a graduate of the Massachusetts Institute of Technology, was an experienced railroad architect who had worked for several lines throughout the country. He had joined Allen Stem, an architect from Ohio, to form a successful practice in St. Paul in 1891. In the Grand Central commission, however, Reed & Stem's triumph would be short-lived. In the fall of 1903, soon after the firm had won the commission, Whitney Warren approached Wilgus to express his desire to prepare plans for the terminal building. Although the project's architects had been selected, President Newman thought it wise to let Warren & Wetmore submit plans because the firm's principals were well acquainted with some of the company's directors, particularly William K. Vanderbilt, the chief executive.[7] Warren & Wetmore's proposal presented a compact modern French building with a tripartite entry facade, paired columns, and sculptural groups (figs. 3.3, 3.4). Even though Warren & Wetmore's plans did not include the ideas developed by Reed & Stem, such as ramps and viaducts, Vanderbilt endorsed aspects of Warren's aesthetic treatment of the building and added the firm to the team of architects.

In February 1904 Reed & Stem and Warren & Wetmore were named the Associated Architects of Grand Central Terminal and an employment agreement was drawn up with the railroad company, with Charles Reed designated as chief executive. The Associated Architects had its own accounts, employees, and office, as noted, located at 314 Madison

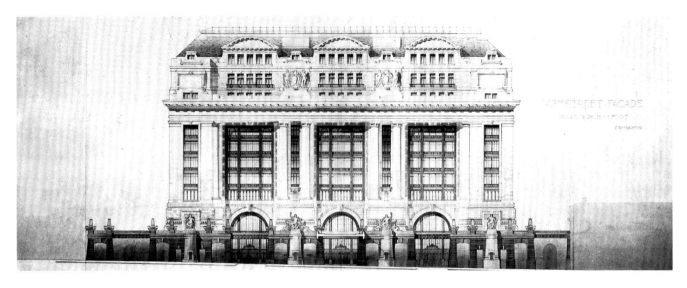

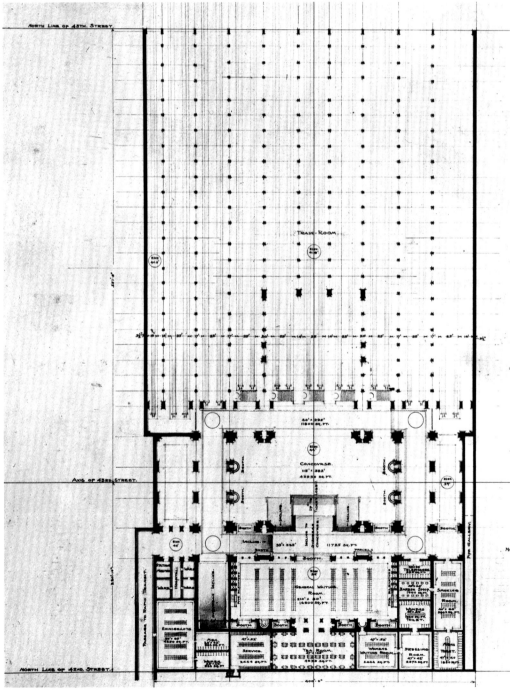

3.3. *Warren & Wetmore's 1903 proposal for Grand Central Terminal. 42nd Street facade.* Warren & Wetmore Collection, Avery Architectural and Fine Arts Library, Columbia University.

3.4. *Warren & Wetmore's 1903 plan for Grand Central Terminal.* Warren & Wetmore Collection, Avery Architectural and Fine Arts Library, Columbia University.

3.5. Excavations for Grand Central Terminal, 1908.
Detroit Publishing Co., Prints and Photographs Division, Library of Congress, #6676.

Avenue.[8] Leonard Schultze, who went on to form a successful practice with Spencer Fullerton Weaver in 1921, was put in charge of the design department.[9]

Demolition and excavation based on Reed & Stem's plans had already begun in 1903 (fig. 3.5). By that time, New York Central had bought up all of the land bounded by 42nd and 50th Streets between Lexington and Madison Avenues, which would form Wilgus's "air rights" district once it was cleared, excavated, and redeveloped.[10] Over the ensuing years, two hundred buildings were razed within the area and three million cubic yards of material were carved out of Manhattan's bedrock and removed to make way for Wilgus's sophisticated double-level track system, whose upper level was to be 20 feet below the existing track, and the bottom tier, 25 feet lower. The use of 118,600 tons of steel to construct the roof of the lower level and the cross streets and Park Avenue viaducts above restored street patterns. Amazingly, train service continued to operate from a temporary terminal located on Lexington Avenue throughout the demolition and construction phase. Three distinct sections, excavated by some 2,000 men, were successively finished before the next one was started—a method that isolated the work area and freed space for train service to continue.[11] In September 1906 the first electric train departed the terminal, and by 1907, the conversion to electric power by a direct-current third rail was complete.[12]

While work was underway, the Associated Architects continued to refine and reconcile the various aspects of the terminal's scheme. From the outset, Warren & Wetmore's addition to the equation was a source of controversy within the design team. Not only did Wilgus dislike the manner in which Warren & Wetmore had joined the project; he also strongly disapproved of the firm's radical changes to the scheme—particularly its elimination of the elevated, circumferential driveways, 42nd Street viaduct, and interior ramps—the keynotes of Reed & Stem's design. For the most part, Wilgus found Warren & Wetmore's suggestions counterproductive and was appalled by the firm's proposal to lower the tracks further—an

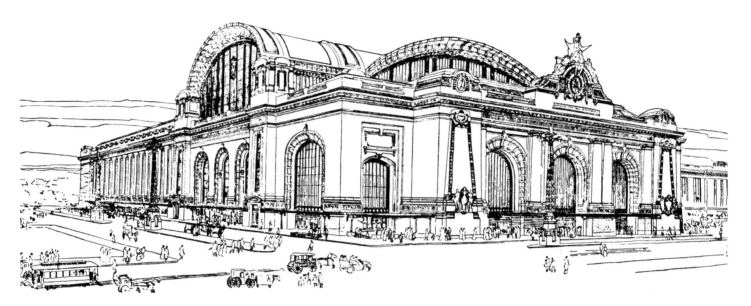

3.6. Rendering of Grand Central Terminal, 1904. The Inland Architect and News Record 44 (December 1904): 39.

3.7 (opposite top). Rendering of Grand Central Terminal, 1910. Warren & Wetmore Collection, Avery Architectural and Fine Arts Library, Columbia University.

3.8 (opposite middle). Whitney Warren, design for Grand Central Terminal, New York City. Facade, 1910. Pen and black ink, graphite on cream tracing paper, 10 x 12 ¹⁵/₁₆ in. (254 x 328 mm). Cooper-Hewitt, National Design Museum, Smithsonian Institution. Gift of Mrs. William Greenough, 1943-51-13. Photo: Matt Flynn.

3.9 (opposite bottom). Grand Central Terminal. Preliminary 42nd Street elevation with Whitney Warren's written notes. Collection of The New-York Historical Society, #58229.

3.10 (following pages). Grand Central Terminal. Corner of 42nd Street and Vanderbilt Avenue, New York City. Warren & Wetmore Collection, Avery Architectural and Fine Arts Library, Columbia University.

expensive change—to relocate the waiting room. Between 1904 and 1909, Warren & Wetmore effectively transformed Reed & Stem's vision into their own by removing the Court of Honor and reducing the height of the twenty-two-story terminal to create a low-lying monumental edifice (fig. 3.6). Its changes to the interior were similarly sweeping. In Warren's hands, Reed & Stem's narrow concourse became the terminal's centerpiece, inspired by Victor Laloux's Gare d'Orsay. Though Warren & Wetmore's design moved forward, some—including Wilgus—found it laced with arrogance.

In 1907 Wilgus left his position at New York Central in defeat to form his own practice; however, after his departure, the railroad ultimately returned to the important planning aspects of Reed & Stem's design that had since been eliminated.[13] The New York, New Haven and Hartford Railroad operated its service out of the terminal and was to share one-third of the cost of its construction. Unwilling to carry the cost of Warren & Wetmore's more expensive proposal, the company rejected the firm's changes. As described by Kurt C. Schlichting in Grand Central Terminal: Railroads, Engineering, and Architecture in New York City, an emergency meeting was called in 1909 to settle the question of what form the building would take. Board members William K. Vanderbilt and William H. Newman represented New York Central, and J. P. Morgan, William Rockefeller, and Lewis Cass Ledyard represented the New Haven line, among others. To compensate for the absence of Reed & Stem's income-producing terminal building, Rockefeller suggested that Warren's plans incorporate foundations capable of carrying a high-rise structure to be built in the future and Ledyard moved to restore Reed & Stem's circumferential driveways. The final plans, filed on January 13, 1911, were a synthesis of Reed's practical planning and Warren & Wetmore's architectural genius (figs. 3.7–3.9).[14]

Two years later, at midnight on February 1, 1913, the terminal officially opened. The years of labor, disagreement, and revision had yielded a highly sophisticated design. Reed & Stem's planning and spatial organization and Warren & Wetmore's artistic handling of the complex had created a unique composition. Like many of his colleagues trained in the Beaux-Arts, Warren felt strongly that "architecture being a reasoned art, for any specified purpose there should be precedent and tradition—every motive and element should have its reason for being, and in all compositions, no matter how simple, the elements must explain themselves and justify their presence."[15] Much in the manner of European monuments, Warren's heroic structure, which straddled Park Avenue, created an impressive vista from the approaching streets, and its definitive southern facade and three great round-arch windows formed a modern-day portal to the city.[16]

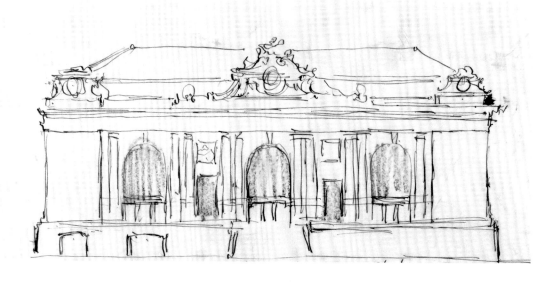

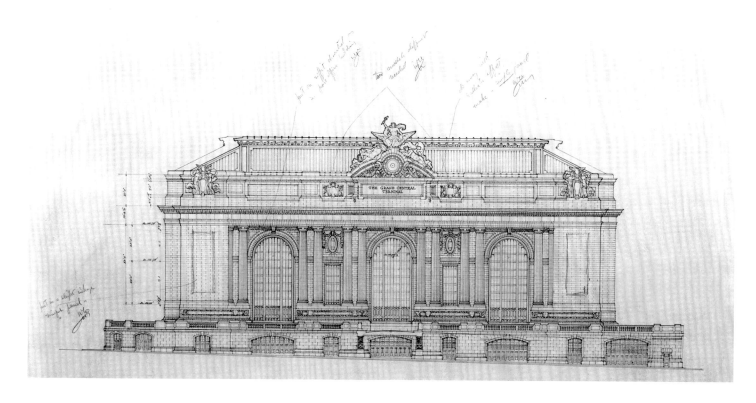

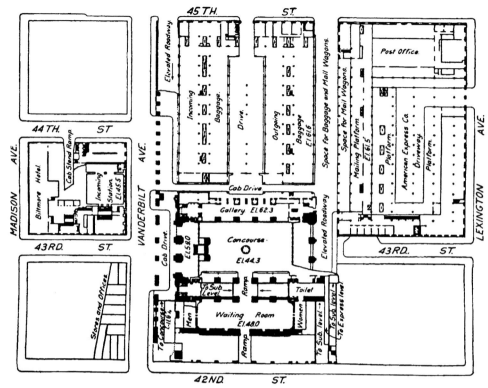

3.11. *Grand Central Terminal. Plan of street level.* John A. Droege, *Passenger Terminals and Trains* (New York: McGraw-Hill, 1916): 165.

17

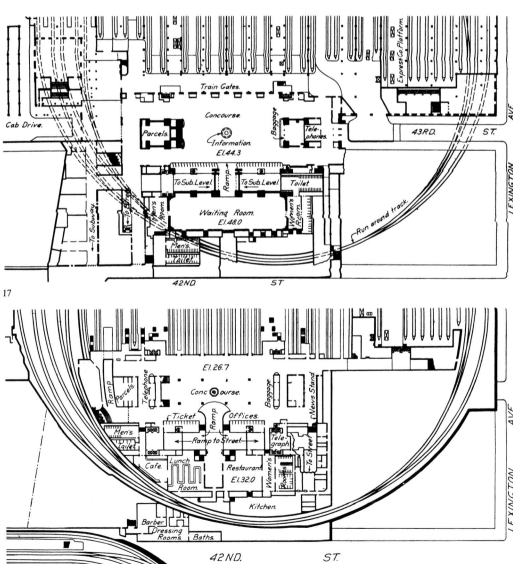

3.12. *Grand Central Terminal. Plan of express and suburban levels.* John A. Droege, *Passenger Terminals and Trains* (New York: McGraw-Hill, 1916): 166–67.

Labels within the illustration: CAB DRIVE · EXPRESS CONCOURSE · EXPRESS TRAIN ROOM · SUBURBAN CONCOURSE · RAMP FROM SUBURBAN TRAINS · SUBURBAN TRAIN ROOM · MAIN WAITING ROOM · SUBURBAN RAMP · RESTAURANT · TO ALL SUBWAYS · TO 42ND STREET · INTERBORO SUBWAY · TO INCOMING STATION AND STREET · HUDSON & MANHATTAN TUNNEL · BELMONT TUNNEL · EXPRESS TRAIN

3.13. Grand Central Terminal. Section. Warren & Wetmore Collection, Avery Architectural and Fine Arts Library, Columbia University.

The terminal building complex stretched from 42nd to 45th Street and included a post office and office space on Lexington Avenue, built over the now-below-grade rail yards (fig. 3.10). At the intersection of 42nd Street and Park Avenue lay the primary axis through the terminal, where Warren's symbolic portal dominated the center of the south facade. Jules-Alexis Coutan's 40-foot-wide sculptural group, expressive of, in Warren's words, the "glory of commerce as typified by Mercury, supported by moral and mental energy—Hercules and Minerva," embraced a gilded clock, faced with colored Tiffany glass, at the center of the composition.[17] The qualities of Progress, and Mental and Physical Force—emblematic of New York Central's growing transportation empire—stood tall above the terminal's broad cornice and copper roofline. Completed one year after the terminal opened, the sculptural group was carved in situ by William Bradley from a clay maquette (one-fourth scale) sent from Coutan's Paris atelier.[18] In addition to the three windows, Warren embellished the southern facade with pairs of engaged fluted columns, bull's-eye windows, and isolated bursts of sculptural detail. Theodore Starrett, writing for *Architecture and Building*, described Warren & Wetmore's carvings as springing "from original sources, namely the brain of the designer," but felt their exuberance created "a beautiful contrast with the plain surrounding walls."[19] Another critic deemed the design "so very un-American, with its big arches, its pylons and blank wall spaces, so very European on the other hand, and so much like a Beaux-Arts *projet* that it has rather caught the popular fancy."[20]

The terminal ushered in a "new era in the vertical building of railroads." *Real Estate Record and Builder's Guide* emphatically declared that "modern terminals in great cities must be below the street level thereafter."[21] Up to the early twentieth century, massive train sheds had formed the basis of railroad architecture, but with the electrification of lines and depression of tracks— as exemplified by Victor Laloux's Gare d'Orsay (1900)—the design emphasis shifted. In the United States architects would follow the model set by Grand Central Terminal by placing tracks underground and replacing the train shed with the concourse as the monumental focus.

Within Grand Central, the Associated Architects created three stations, each with separate baggage checking, ticketing facilities, and information booths, and successfully funneled circulation through a series of axially aligned spaces to the sublevel tracks (figs. 3.11, 3.12). Reed & Stem's inventive ramps, which guided travelers and commuters up and down

3.14 (following pages). Grand Central Terminal. Waiting room. Detroit Publishing Co., Prints and Photographs Division, Library of Congress, #8503.

3.15. Grand Central Terminal. Tracks. Warren & Wetmore Collection, Avery Architectural and Fine Arts Library, Columbia University.

through the building, set Grand Central Terminal apart as the first stairless railway station in history (fig. 3.13).[22] From the 42nd Street entrance, travelers passed through the grand 40-foot-tall waiting room, which was furnished with heavy oak benches and capable of accommodating five thousand people (fig. 3.14). With its walls of simulated Caen stone (a mixture of crushed limestone, Portland cement, lime, sand, and plaster that created the appearance of limestone), bronze-colored ceiling, ornamental cornices, and multitiered nickel and gold plated chandeliers, the soaring space created an impressive entry point from which traffic flowed down a gentle slope, enclosed by 8-foot walls, to the expansive express concourse. Against the north wall of the concourse, a series of ramps led down to the long-distance trains and platforms (fig. 3.15). The terminal's Incoming Station, located in an annexed area underneath the western edge of Vanderbilt Avenue, was separated from the main concourse and possessed immediate access to the street and the hotel to be built overhead. From the express level, a set of ramps descended beneath the bridge between the waiting room and concourse to the suburban concourse and restaurant directly below, where twenty-five additional tracks serviced the commuter lines (fig. 3.16). Looped tracks, which continued underneath the southern portion of the terminal to the storage yards at the easterly side, enabled passengers to disembark on one side and the trains to move around to the outbound side without having to back out—an innovation that substantially increased arrivals and departures. The Beaux-Arts tenets of rational organization and defined spatial flow fueled the building's efficiency. By separating the stations and incorporating ramps, the Associated Architects successfully isolated each type of traveler and eased traffic and congestion within the terminal.

The sheer size and striking decor of the express concourse embodied the spirit of a great urban entryway (fig. 3.17). At 120 feet wide, 273 feet long, and 125 feet high, the hall—which extended transversely through the building—was "the largest of its kind in the world."[23] As the terminal's centerpiece, it was grandly appointed with marble ticket booths, Tennessee marble floors, bronze light fixtures, and walls of simulated Caen stone trimmed with Botticino marble. Warren's barrel-vaulted ceiling hovered dramatically overhead. A striking

3.16. *Grand Central Terminal. Suburban concourse.* Detroit Publishing Co., Prints and Photographs Division, Library of Congress, #8503.

shade of cerulean blue, it glimmered with gold-leaf constellations and stars illuminated by tiny electric lights. Warren had conceived of the mural with his friend and colleague Paul César Helleu (1859–1927), a Beaux-Arts graduate and accomplished French painter and dry-point etcher; Beaux-Arts trained architects and muralists J. Monroe Hewlett and Charles Basing carried out their vision.[24] French artist Sylvain Salières, who worked on the terminal for five years, was responsible for the sculptural decoration throughout the building (fig. 3.18).[25] His elaborate plaster-cast ornament of winged locomotives and globes set within the lunettes at ceiling level expressed themes of transportation and travel (fig. 3.19). Throughout the interiors, Warren & Wetmore restricted sculptural ornament to key features of the design, which rendered it more powerful in the context of the strong, simple lines of architecture (fig. 3.20).

By encasing the building's steel structure, capable of bearing the weight of a twenty-story tower (never built), in colossal piers, the architects created an elegant support for the heavy bracketed entablature and celestial ceiling. An eight-story office tower anchored each corner of the terminal, and glass passageways, set between the inner and outer glazing of the giant round arched windows to the east and west, connected the separate buildings. Though most of the terminal's steel structure was obscured behind the large expanses of imitation Caen stone, the architects exposed iron throughout the building to express its role in the structure, including many elements at the ground level, such as the marquee at the corner of 42nd Street and Vanderbilt Avenue and the brackets framing the vehicular drive on Vanderbilt Avenue (fig. 3.21). Placed where the span of construction would seem implausible in stone, the steel celebrated the potential of exposed structure with complex curves and patterns of rivets that recalled the train sheds of Paris and the lessons of the French architect Viollet-le-Duc. Similarly, the green-grey ironwork incorporated into the great windows of the concourse and waiting room combined the practical and artistic properties of steel.

The terminal's grand interior spaces unfolded sequentially and, despite their overpowering size, were not overwhelming. Vistas were revealed as one moved through the building;

3.17 (following pages). *Grand Central Terminal. Express concourse.* Detroit Publishing Co., Prints and Photographs Division, Library of Congress, #6676.

3.18. *Grand Central Terminal.
Sylvain Salières.* Warren &
Wetmore Collection, Avery
Architectural and Fine Arts Library,
Columbia University.

3.19. *Grand Central Terminal.
Lunette detail, 2005.* Photo:
Jonathan Wallen.

3.20 (far left). Grand Central Terminal. Detail in express concourse, 2005. Photo: Jonathan Wallen).

3.21 (near left). Grand Central Terminal. Iron detail, 2005. Photo: Jonathan Wallen.

side aisles with descending ramps and galleries created lofty axes elegantly decorated with square skylights and exquisite acorn-shaped chandeliers. As noted by the *Real Estate Record and Builder's Guide*, "the bigness of the room neither startles or repels. Attention is held by pleasing vistas, the rich texture of Botticino marble, the warmth of color, the artistic directness with which utilities are fitted to their purpose. The succession of impressions created enables one to apprehend the room less as an embodiment of the abstract idea of space than as a panorama, elementally simple, but full of diversified concrete meaning and interest."[26] In the suburban-level restaurant carved into the curve of the looping tracks, the architects used a lightweight vaulting system developed by the prominent Catalonian-born, New York-based craftsman Rafael Guastavino (fig. 3.22). The textured herringbone pattern of the unadorned terra-cotta tiles created an intimate, cave-like space that was considered one of the most advanced structural features in the terminal's design.[27]

The building was immediately hailed as a landmark. Compared to the Pennsylvania Railroad Company's station, completed two years earlier, Grand Central Terminal presented a compact and creative interpretation of the building type. Charles McKim's impressive terminal at 34th Street (1902–1911), the design of which was adapted from the Baths of Caracalla, offered a grand and scholarly rendition of the Roman prototype. While both buildings were architecturally distinct, Warren & Wetmore strayed from iconic reading, using terra cotta, sculpture, and mural art to original effect, and Reed & Stem moved travelers efficiently through the space with its innovative ramps. As one critic noted, the planning features of the building worked to advantage: "from the standpoint of ingenious solution of a tremendous problem, the Grand Central is easily the better. . . . Considering circulation alone, in the Grand Central it is compact and easy. . . . In the Pennsylvania Station, the lines of circulation are long and there are many flights of steps, some them merely to gain interesting architectural effect."[28]

The construction of the terminal, auxiliary buildings, and the underground system of tracks was the century's first important undertaking, and Grand Central Terminal, the most publicized building project of the period, vaulted its architects into the national spotlight. However, despite the fact that Reed & Stem had initially won the commission and had been working on the project for eight years, Warren & Wetmore was more assertive in taking credit for the design and claiming the honors.

3.22 (following pages). Grand Central Terminal. Restaurant. Detroit Publishing Co., Prints and Photographs Division, Library of Congress, #6676.

Charles Wetmore's illicit maneuvering after the death of Charles Reed, the executive head of the Associated Architects, in 1911 was the first act that would push his firm's name forward. Four days after Reed's death, Wetmore sent New York Central's president William Newman a new contract that "intended to follow the old form in all particulars, except that Warren & Wetmore [would be] the architects."[29] Upon receipt of Wetmore's letter, the railroad company cancelled the old contract and signed the new one, substituting Warren & Wetmore as architects. Stem, who was attending Reed's interment in Rochester, New York, at the time was kept unaware of the new contract that eliminated his firm from the partnership. As a result, Warren & Wetmore assumed sole ownership of the design of the project, and Reed & Stem's contributions were obscured. In 1911, in an article entitled "Buildings in New York City that are Looked upon as Monuments to the Genius of the Architects," *The Wall Street Journal* did not refer once to Reed & Stem:

> Grand Central Terminal is the first important opportunity the Warren brothers have had. In their careers, they refute the assertion that rich men's sons are idlers. They are the sons of George Henry Warren of Newport and New York, one of the very rich men of the United States. Both Whitney Warren and his brother Lloyd were ambitious to make careers for themselves which were not dependent on their father's money. It may be said that the close intimacy established between them and William K. Vanderbilt is reflected in the acceptance of their designs. Mr. Vanderbilt however, is not the man to accept designs of magnitude, involving great cost, simply on the grounds of personal friendship. . . . Now that the plans have been, the critics say that his confidence has been fully justified.[30]

Not content to be marginalized, Stem, in an attempt to set the record straight, brought suit against the firm in the Supreme Court of New York County for betraying the trust and confidence of the partnership. His associate, Alfred Fellheimer, published *Inception and Creation of the Grand Central Terminal* (1913), which clearly outlined the project's time line and the contributions of those involved. The lawsuit, which came to trial in 1916 after the terminal's completion, extended into the 1920s. Because Warren & Wetmore had reworked the contract, the firm continued to earn money by completing projects the Associated Architects had begun together, including branch stations in Westchester, several office buildings, infrastructure, and the Biltmore Hotel—Wilgus's Madison Avenue hotel located over the Incoming Station. In addition, Warren & Wetmore continued to operate from the shared office, which had since moved to 70 East 45th Street, and to utilize the Associated Architects' joint staff in carrying out the incomplete work.

By 1916 Warren had relocated to Paris and Wetmore was left to sort out the consequences of the trial. Harold Swain, the plaintiff's attorney, claimed that Wetmore was reckless and uncooperative throughout his testimony and adopted "an attitude of brazen self assurance, indicating that he was answerable to no one for his actions."[31] No one, however, was more caustic in his criticism than William Wilgus. Having been wary of Warren & Wetmore from the start, he found the firm's conduct abominable and spent the next decade calling attention to what he described as "the moral turpitude which marked the course of Warren & Wetmore in their entire relation to the Grand Central Station architecture."[32] In 1916 the Supreme Court of New York State decreed that Warren & Wetmore had taken for themselves "not only financial reward which it was their duty to take for the Associated Architects, but also to a large extent the credit for the masterful work of their deceased partner Reed" and had violated the trust and fiduciary agreement between the partners.[33]

Because he was in Paris, Warren's role in the Grand Central suit was limited. The records suggest that it was Wetmore alone who engineered the secret contract and was uncooperative during the trial.[34] After the 1916 ruling, Warren & Wetmore doggedly appealed the decision through two more courts, both of which held in Stem's favor. In one letter to Wilgus, Swain noted that "a determined effort was made on the part of Warren & Wetmore

3.23. *Terminal City. Rendering by Vernon Howe Bailey, 1913.* Detroit Publishing Co., Prints and Photographs Division, Library of Congress, #6676.

to escape from the obligation of the judgment, which on the appeals, they resisted so earnestly."[35] However, Warren & Wetmore managed to whittle down the punitive damages and in the end paid Stem $500,000—his share of the profits that had accrued since the cancellation of the original employment contract. Warren was expelled from the American Institute of Architects on May 3, 1920. This sorry outcome did not, however, alter the fact that Warren had been the genius behind Grand Central's bold architectural expression.

By 1913 Wilgus's vision of a terminal city had begun to materialize (fig. 3.23).[36] In addition to the terminal proper, the Associated Architects designed several buildings in the 42nd Street area as part of the complex. By the time the main building was complete, half of New York Central's air rights had been improved or were scheduled for development. Early buildings such as the Grand Central Palace, Post Office, and Adams Express Company Building were located on Lexington Avenue on land that had been excavated during the first phase of construction. The Associated Architects' powerhouse on 50th Street, with its two massive smokestacks (1912), supplied live steam, electricity, hot water, and compressed air to the railroad and all of the buildings within the air-rights district, facilitating the area's rapid transformation (fig. 3.24). Because it was the most utilitarian building in Terminal City, the architects exposed all of the structural steel bracing in front of the plane of the bricks walls. The pair of square towers that fronted a pair of round smoke stacks framed the building's central bay, creating an astonishing three-part composition in which all forms were supported by exposed steel skeletons.

This first wave of construction was integrally connected to the terminal. Composed of brick, limestone, and granite, the buildings—with the exception of the Grand Central Palace—

3.24. New York Central Power House, 100 East 50th Street, New York City, located between the Adams Express Company Building (left) and Railroad Y.M.C.A. (right). Warren & Wetmore Collection, Avery Architectural and Fine Arts Library, Columbia University.

were consistent in height and cohesive in design. The Grand Central Post Office Annex (1906–9), the first building to be completed after Warren & Wetmore's revised plans, also contained office space and reflected the terminal in detail. The window bays had geometrically patterned and riveted frames that recalled Warren's use of exposed steel in the terminal's design (fig. 3.25).[37] However, the building formed only half of the intended structure originally designed for the east side of the Terminal City. The office block between 44th and 45th Streets, distinguished by an end pavilion, colossal columns, and cartouches at the attic story, was to have mirrored an identical wing to the south. Smaller buildings to the north and south as well as a projected twelve-story rooftop addition were never constructed. Grand Central leased space to the postal service at street level, and the railroad kept offices on the upper floors and maintained tracks directly below. Because the building lacked a basement, the mechanical systems were located on the fifth floor behind the heavy entablature and cornice.[38]

The Grand Central Palace, located two blocks north of the post office on Lexington Avenue, was completed in 1911 and leased by the Merchants and Manufacturers Exchange as exhibition space (fig. 3.26). The lower floors contained an open four-story hall, divided by great Corinthian columns carrying heavy ceiling panels, and the upper stories held additional office space. Differentiated by a double-height Palladian arcade and deep cornice at the attic level, the brick facades were punctuated with strips of windows and massive four-story fluted Doric columns that marked the entrance to the exhibition hall. The Adams Express Company Building on the west side of Lexington Avenue between 49th and 50th Streets was a somewhat less distinguished eight-story brick structure with limestone detail. Like the adjacent powerhouse, it enjoyed direct access to the train platforms beneath.[39] The later Merchants Loft Building (1911), Mail Services Building (1914) and Railroad Y.M.C.A. (1914) on Park Avenue harmonized with the completed improvements. As part of Reed & Stem's scheme, Warren & Wetmore designed the Park Avenue viaduct in 1912, with engineer Olaf Hoff, to connect lower Park Avenue (then Fourth Avenue) at 40th Street to Reed & Stem's elevated driveways, which extended around the terminal building and rejoined Park Avenue at 45th Street. When completed in 1919, the roadway, supported by three broad spanning steel arches, would be instrumental in moving traffic through the area and in opening up the midtown stretch of Park Avenue for development.[40]

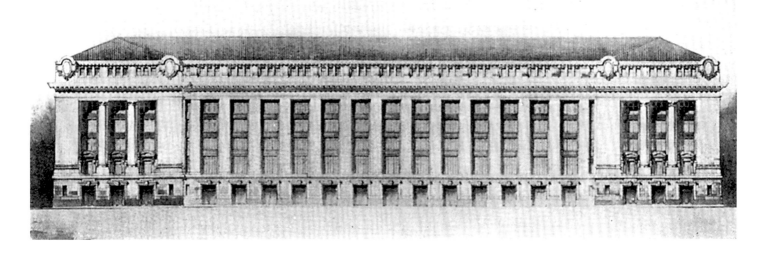

3.25. Post Office Building, New York Central Railroad. Proposed Lexington facade. The American Architect 90 (November 24, 1906).

3.26. Grand Central Palace, 480 Lexington Avenue, New York City. Architecture 24 (August 1911): pl. 84.

3.27 (opposite). Biltmore Hotel, 335 Madison Avenue, New York City. From the roof of Grand Central Terminal. Museum of the City of New York, Byron Collection, #93.1.1.5783.

3.28 (left). Biltmore Hotel. Upper floors. The American Architect 105 (February 11, 1914).

The twenty-six-story Biltmore Hotel, the most complex early design to rise out of Terminal City, also reflected a portion of Wilgus's original concept (fig. 3.27).[41] Located on the block bound by 43rd and 44th Streets, Madison and Vanderbilt Avenues, the hotel enclosed the upper part of Grand Central's Incoming Station and was situated directly over its tracks. Arriving passengers could pass directly from their trains up into the hotel without entering the street or the main concourse. Like all construction over the train yards, the Biltmore did not have a conventional foundation or basement, and the underlying tracks dictated the location of the building columns—which, to avoid vibration, had to be kept entirely separate from the tracks.

The Biltmore, with one thousand rooms and extensive entertaining space, represented the new wave of hotels built to support the influx of travelers moving in and out of the city. While the New York Central and New York, New Haven, and Hartford Railroads jointly owned the building, hotel entrepreneurs Gustave Baumann and John McE. Bowman operated the business. Bowman, a self-made man, would turn the Biltmore Corporation into one of the country's most successful hotel chains.[42]

Although Warren & Wetmore executed most of the Biltmore's design, the Associated Architects were responsible for the Incoming Station, a fundamental part of the overall scheme. Preliminary plans formed a portion of the work completed by the Associated Architects; however, Warren & Wetmore carried the Biltmore, its fourth New York City hotel, from the initial design phase to its completion in 1913.[43] Despite its overwhelming bulk, the Biltmore deferred to the stouter terminal building across the street. Warren & Wetmore created a strong visual divide between the five-story granite and limestone base, consistent in height with Grand Central, and the soaring brick structure of the hotel on top of the stone pedestal. To avoid overshadowing Grand Central Terminal, the architects created a sixth floor setback on Vanderbilt Avenue to open the airspace around the building. They distinguished the Biltmore's roofline with a distinctive triple-height Italian Renaissance colonnade with paired engaged Ionic columns, iron spandrel panels, and dentillated cornice (fig. 3.28).

The Biltmore was a world unto itself with guest rooms, apartments, restaurants, bars, ballrooms, and a guest hospital—what one critic would describe as "a living thing, a machine to do many things, to perform a hundred functions."[44] Because the hotel did not have a base-

ment, the kitchen and service quarters occupied floors in the base above the Incoming Station, grillroom, restaurant, reception, and palm court. The brick shaft, with its regular grid of windows, contained bedrooms with bathrooms en suite and a number of apartments available for long-term lease.[45] The top floors, expressed by the triple-height terra-cotta colonnade, housed the hotel's formal entertaining spaces: a grand Louis XIV–style ballroom, three stories in height, and a banquet hall whose 25-foot-high windows were removed during the summer months to create an "outdoor" restaurant. One critic noted that "the architect of a skyscraping hotel has advantages over the architect of a skyscraping office building." While designers of office buildings often used arbitrary architectural language to enliven their designs, hotel architects could create successful elevations simply by expressing the form of the myriad functions within the building on the facade.[46]

When the hotel opened on New Year's Eve, 1913, *The New York Times* declared that "in interior finishing the hotel [was] striking." Theodore Starrett, writing for *Architecture and Building*, remarked that the rooms were carried out "with the usual care which characterize[d] the work of Warren and Wetmore. Many of the rooms [were] treated with extreme richness of decoration, but without flamboyant display."[47] The Biltmore's interiors showcased the firm's approach of drawing from a variety of different styles and influences—a quality manifested in its house designs. Working with decorators W. & J. Sloane, Warren & Wetmore incorporated several Jacobean-inspired rooms, including the oak-paneled grillroom, and executed the bedrooms in a restrained Adam style. Many of the spaces were designed in variations of the French mode, such as the sumptuous yellow and blue ballroom and sixth-floor terrace with treillage, caryatids, urns, and Le Nôtre–style gardens; others interpreted the Italian Renaissance, including the opulent dining room with its pink-veined marble pilasters and the banquet room with Caen stone walls and ceiling reminiscent of the Davanzati Palace in Florence (figs. 3.29, 3.31, 3.32). The hotel's central lounge and its celebrated clock became a preferred New York rendezvous, captured in countless books and movies, including J. D. Salinger's *Catcher in the Rye*: "meet me under the clock at the Biltmore at two o'clock (fig. 3.30)."[48]

3.29 (opposite top). Biltmore Hotel. Ballroom. The American Architect 105 (February 11, 1914).

3.30 (opposite bottom). Biltmore Hotel. Palm court. Architectural Record 35 (March 1914): 232.

3.31 (above). Biltmore Hotel. Restaurant. The American Architect 105 (February 11, 1914).

3.32 (following pages). Biltmore Hotel. Ballroom foyer. The American Architect 105 (February 11, 1914).

3.33. Hartsdale Station, Hartsdale, New York. *The American Architect* 107 (June 23, 1915).

3.34. White Plains Station, White Plains, New York. *The American Architect* 107 (June 23, 1915).

BRANCH STATIONS AND TERMINALS

The New York Central and Hudson River Railroad's redevelopment plan also included new suburban stations along the newly electrified Hudson and Harlem lines. Designed by the Associated Architects, these stations were planned at the same time as the main terminal complex and constructed between 1910 and 1918. As at Grand Central, Reed & Stem was likely responsible for the planning and practical issues and Warren & Wetmore the architectural treatment. Improvements for both train speed and vehicular traffic included the elimination of crossings where the tracks intersected with local streets. Typically, the suburban streets were lowered, creating underpasses. For even the smallest stations, these changes in grade required the architects to use ramps, stairs, and (albeit on a small scale) the ingenuity that marked the planning devices for Grand Central Terminal.

Most of the fifteen stations were modest buildings with waiting rooms, baggage facilities, and ticket offices that incorporated a range of stylistic influences.[49] At the Hartsdale station (1915), the architects used an informal Tudor style, reminiscent of Warren & Wetmore's estate outbuilding designs, and added a fireplace inside (fig. 3.33). At the Bronxville (1916)

3.35. *Terminal for the Michigan Central Railroad, Detroit, Michigan.* Warren & Wetmore Collection, Avery Architectural and Fine Arts Library, Columbia University.

and Hyde Park (1914) stations, they designed one-story mission-style buildings with tiled roofs. For most of the stations, the architects used brick and incorporated French details. At White Plains (1915), a smaller station, they executed a rectangular building with diamond-patterned brickwork and three round-arched windows as the central motif (fig. 3.34). The architects distinguished the Yonkers station (1911), the largest on the Hudson line, with a central arched window and boldly ornamented facades. On entering, commuters passed through a Guastavino-tiled rotunda into a large waiting room that was accented with diamond-patterned walls, chandeliers, and terra-cotta details. The suburban stations formed a substantial share of the Associated Architects' work; however, there was little or no profit involved in their execution.[50] Although they were initially designed by the two firms, Warren & Wetmore received much of the credit, because most of the stations were built subsequent to Charles Reed's death in 1911.

During their partnership, Reed & Stem and Warren & Wetmore also designed a larger terminal building in Detroit (1912–13) for the Michigan Central Railroad, a subsidiary of New York Central (fig. 3.35).[51] Located two miles from downtown, the terminal marked the portal of a new two-and-a-half mile tunnel—an important international artery—under the Detroit River, which completed the railroad's connection between Detroit and Windsor,

Ontario. Part real estate development, the project also included an eighteen-story office block that stretched the width of the street-level train station. The architects clearly attempted to visually divorce the office building from the terminal by choosing distinct proportions, materials, and details for each section and setting the taller block behind the station. The elegant classical base, executed in granite and blue limestone, established a civic presence on the street while the light brick tower seemed to hover above. By assuming the architects had simply failed to mold the program into one coherent design, some critics misunderstood their design strategy. *Architectural Record* complained that "the exterior of the Detroit Station presents an extraordinary lack of continuity of conception . . . each part taken separately might be good. Joined together, they are architecturally incongruous."[52]

With automobile travel in its infancy, it was expected that most travelers would arrive at the terminal by streetcar, given its distance from downtown. Rather than entering through the principal northern facade, which was dominated by three colossal arched windows and Corinthian columns, passengers accessed the building from the east, where the streetcar platforms were located. Passengers moved down a central axis to the ticket area—a grand space defined by pairs of massive Doric columns, ornamental ceiling panels, and elegant chandeliers—that connected the waiting room and the concourse. As the station's showcase, the 76-foot-high waiting room had a barrel-vaulted ceiling with plaster ribs, lunettes with ornamental ironwork, and marble Doric columns. Bronze chandeliers, incorporating tiny light bulbs, extended from the intricately carved ribs. Although substantially less decorative, the concourse had textured brick walls and an immense copper skylight that stretched the length of the room. As they had done at Grand Central, the architects incorporated ramps that led to eleven tracks located in low-lying, top-lit sheds, under which large areas for baggage, express, and mail were situated. Because the terminal was designed to accommodate large numbers of people waiting to make connections, the Associated Architects incorporated reading rooms, smoking rooms, women's waiting rooms, and dining rooms into the plan. The opulent terminal and office, however, never realized its full potential. When built, it was assumed that the terminal would draw on the city's expanding business districts. But, during the depression, the streetcars connecting the terminal to Detroit's downtown were closed, limiting passenger access and leaving the building in isolation. With the dawn of the automobile age, public transportation in Detroit never took hold.[53]

Warren & Wetmore's involvement in Grand Central Terminal brought the firm individual railroad commissions in Winnipeg, Manitoba, and Houston.[54] In 1909 the firm designed a station building and the track layout for Fort Garry Terminal in Winnipeg (fig. 3.36). Replacing the Canadian Northern Railroad outdated depot, Warren & Wetmore's new building served as a transportation hub connecting several Canadian train lines, including the Grand Trunk Pacific Railway and Transcontinental Railway of Canada.[55] As at Grand Central, Warren & Wetmore used the triumphal arch to express the monumentality of the design. Four-story wings for the railroad's office space extended to the north and south, and a great dome capped the central portion. The building's warm buff-colored limestone facades were austere; the imposing power of the design was derived from the architects' use of proportion and simple volumes. Off the central ticket lobby—a circular space surmounted by a 93-foot dome and skylight—opened a waiting room in the north wing and offices to the south (fig. 3.37). Warren & Wetmore carried out the public interiors in imitation Caen stone with Red Durance marble wainscoting and terrazzo floors.

In Houston the firm designed a restrained brick and limestone terminal for the Houston Belt & Terminal Railway Company.[56] The building, which opened in 1911, enclosed a large rectangular room with barrel-vaulted side aisles and lunette windows (fig. 3.38). Because the building was smaller than the Winnipeg and Detroit terminals, Warren & Wetmore combined the waiting area and ticket booths in one room and cleverly divided the space by using arcades of fluted Ionic columns with marble bases that corresponded in height to the mahogany benches. The firm's use of rich materials and bronze multibulb chandeliers gave the space depth and texture.

3.36 (opposite top). Fort Garry Terminal for the Canadian Northern Railroad, Winnipeg, Canada. Warren & Wetmore Collection, Avery Architectural and Fine Arts Library, Columbia University.

3.37 (opposite bottom). Fort Garry Terminal. Entrance rotunda. Warren & Wetmore Collection, Avery Architectural and Fine Arts Library, Columbia University.

3.38 (following pages). Union Station, Houston Belt and Terminal Railroad, Houston, Texas. Warren & Wetmore Collection, Avery Architectural and Fine Arts Library, Columbia University.

3.39. *James Hazen Hyde's Ball, Dining room at Sherry's, January 31, 1905.* Museum of the City of New York, Byron Collection, #93.1.1.20209.

HOTELS AND APARTMENTS

> There are endless things in "Europe," to your vision, behind and beyond the hotel, a multitudinous complicated life; in the States, on the other hand, you see the hotel as itself that life, as constituting for vast numbers of people the richest form of existence. . . . I remember how often, in moving about, the observation that most remained with me appeared to be this note of the hotel . . . as the supreme social expression.
>
> — HENRY JAMES, *The American Scene*

As luxurious transatlantic ocean liners and expanding railroads prompted increasing numbers of Americans to travel, the modern hotel emerged as an important setting to the new social order. Since the 1830s, New York's hotels had stood at the forefront of design. Hotels such as the Astor House (Isaiah Rogers, 1836) on Broadway, between Barclay and Vesey Streets, and the Fifth Avenue Hotel (William Washburn, 1859) at Madison Square offered modern amenities and technological advances unavailable in the homes of even the wealthiest New Yorkers.[57] In the post–Civil War period, the city's grand hotels grew in size and architectural splendor as a reflection of the era's escalating wealth and their patrons' cultural expectations. In addition to offering conveniences such as telephones and electric lights, hotels such as Henry J. Hardenbergh's châteauesque Waldorf-Astoria at 34th Street and Fifth Avenue (1893 and 1897) included grand entertaining suites and dining rooms inspired by the Italian Renaissance or Louis XV period. Within such opulent settings, society's emerging passion for socializing, lounging, and dining in public flourished.

Americans who spent an increasing amount of time in Europe brought the French fascination with exotic fêtes and pageantry to New York. At the turn of the twentieth century, Sherry's—Stanford White's hotel at Fifth Avenue and 44th Street (1898)—played host to the period's most extravagant affairs, and its magnificent French ballroom was redecorated to suit the occasion. In 1905, the Equitable Life Assurance Society heir and ardent Francophile

3.40. Group photograph from James Hazen Hyde's Ball, January 31, 1905. William Baylies, Montgomery Hare, William Burden, Mrs. F. K. Pendleton, Cornelius Vanderbilt, James A. Burden, Mr. and Mrs. Charles Munn, Mr. and Mrs. August Belmont and Charles Wetmore (sixth from the right). Museum of the City of New York, Byron Collection, #93.1.1.9592.

3.41. Whitney Warren, menu for a dinner given by James Hazen Hyde, January 31, 1905. Etching, printed in red ink on tan laid paper, 8 9/16 x 6 ½ in. (218 x 165 mm). Cooper-Hewitt, National Design Museum, Smithsonian Institution. Gift of Mrs. William Greenhough, 1943-51-469. Photo: Matt Flynn.

James Hazen Hyde held his notorious ball at Sherry's for the exorbitant cost of $200,000 (fig. 3.39). Whitney Warren transformed the hotel's ballroom into a dazzling spectacle of eighteenth-century France, creating a set for the most famous party of the decade and the downfall of his client. Social New York, dressed in court costumes, mixed among formal grass parterres that evoked the fantastic extravagance of the *ancien régime* (fig. 3.40).[58] For Hyde, Warren created elaborate menus, programs, and decorations for the affair, which featured entertainment by celebrated French actress Gabrielle Réjane and a special commission by the Metropolitan Opera (fig. 3.41). However, the opulence of Warren's creation made Hyde's ball a public symbol of the era's excess. Shareholders, the press, and government committees all focused on the financing of the ball and the deal making behind the insurance giant. Hyde's career came to a crashing end, and he spent the rest of his life as an exile in Paris.[59]

Abroad, the pairing of César Ritz and chef Auguste Escoffier initiated significant changes within the hotel industry during the final decade of the nineteenth century. At his elegant hotels, Ritz established a reputation for comfort and service, and Escoffier revolutionized hotel dining with his haute cuisine. Seasonal trips to Europe had provided high society and its preferred architects with a familiarity with the venerable European institutions, such as Ritz's eponymous hotel on the Place Vendôme in Paris (1898), London's Savoy (1889) and Carlton Hotel (1899), and Rome's Grand Hotel (1894), which catered to a discerning clientele and set a superior standard of luxury and comfort. As the American economy recovered from the recession of the mid-1890s, an elegant and sophisticated hotel emerged that, like their European counterparts, emphasized service, comfort, and refinement.

By the time construction on Warren & Wetmore's Biltmore Hotel began in 1912, the firm had successfully carved a niche for itself as hotel architect with earlier designs for the Belmont, Ritz, and Vanderbilt hotels. All located within walking distance of Grand Central Terminal, these establishments ushered in an era of unparalleled elegance and comfort within the realm of American hotel design. Refining the scale and proportion of the grand hotels of the 1890s, Warren & Wetmore produced dignified designs that exuded exclusivity. While the firm's design for the Biltmore epitomized the essence of the large and impersonal railroad hotel, the Belmont, Ritz, and Vanderbilt hotels represented a new breed of hotel, part of which—if not all—was intended for permanent guests. Residential hotels offered the same services and conveniences but lacked the ornate ballrooms and opulent entertaining suites of the grand hotel tradition. As many prominent New Yorkers—as well as social aspirants from out-of-town—discovered their luxury and convenience, residential hotels grew in popularity. Essentially apartment houses with extensive services, they evoked an atmosphere of comfort and exclusive domesticity.

With its city hotels, Warren & Wetmore successfully demonstrated that a hotel's complex program could be shaped into a functional, efficient, and livable form capable of providing the scenographic variety demanded for society's stage. As a designer, Wetmore appears to have been interested in hotels and was largely responsible for the firm's Ritz-Carlton Hotel in Montreal (1910–12), the Condado-Vanderbilt in Puerto Rico (1918), and the Royal Hawaiian at Waikiki Beach (1926–27).[60] In discussing the development of the building type, Wetmore, in writing for *The Architectural Review*, emphasized the importance of the plan, economy of material, and texture in designing simple and dignified hotels that the "educated traveling public" could enjoy.[61] To enliven the interiors, the firm took a multidimensional approach toward finishes that went beyond iconic style. As expressed by firm associate Walter Hopkins, "if the entire building has been conceived in one of the orthodox 'styles,' and it is the intention to have the public rooms designed and furnished in the same 'period,' the imagination and individuality of the designer will be held rather strongly in check. . . . the great value of contrast should not be lost sight of, and especially in large hotels with many public rooms does the danger of monotony become imminent. . . . By varying the materials used and the shapes and proportions of the rooms, schemes of the decoration, hangings and furniture, a harmonious effect can be obtained for the ensemble and yet each of the rooms be given a distinct individuality."[62] The firm mastered the complex problem of

3.42. Hotel Belmont, Fourth Avenue between 41st and 42nd Streets, New York City. Warren & Wetmore Collection, Avery Architectural and Fine Arts Library, Columbia University.

arranging the public rooms, bedrooms, apartments, and service spaces in plan, often creating elaborate sequences for entertaining rooms, while placing the more private rooms in an adjacent atmosphere of domesticity.

The firm's first major hotel commission, the Belmont Hotel, came through wealthy banker August Belmont Jr. (1853–1924), financier of the new city subway (fig. 3.42). After hotel entrepreneur B. L. M. Bates convinced Belmont to finance a luxury hotel in midtown Manhattan, Belmont gave Bates carte blanche to realize the full magnitude of his vision. When the hotel opened in May 1906, it was the tallest building in the Grand Central region and hailed as a veritable palace of luxury. However, the exterior of the twenty-two-story, buff-brick building with cut limestone detail, on the west side of Park Avenue between 41st and 42nd Streets, received lukewarm reviews. Critics remarked that the enormous bracketed cornice, festooned with giant copper garlands, overpowered the building's facades and understated base.[63]

Inside, the force of Warren & Wetmore's spirited French style was unleashed. From the 42nd Street entrance, visitors and guests entered into a double-height lobby—a space described by firm associate Walter Hopkins as the "most difficult room in which to inject any degree of charm"—executed in imitation Caen stone and red marble with a gallery stretching around three sides (fig. 3.43).[64] The architects attempted to enhance the lobby, which contained the necessary office desk, news stand, public telephone, and telegraph offices, by incorporating Gertrude Vanderbilt Whitney's boldly unorthodox sculpted atlantes

3.43 (opposite). Hotel Belmont. Lobby. Museum of the City of New York, Wurts Collection, #111221.

3.44 (right). Hotel Belmont. Palm court. Architecture and Building 38 (May 1906): 331.

into the design of the gallery piers. However, H. W. Frohne, writing for *Architectural Record*, found them "ponderous" because "aesthetically one can find no excuse for them, nor do they give any particular character to the room."[65] Off the lobby extended a sequence of sumptuous architectural spaces, lavishly decorated by W. & J. Sloane with fine furniture and tapestries from Paris. The palm court, an artistic showcase of frescoes, lofty barrel vaults, red marble columns, and shimmering crystal chandeliers, opened onto a double-height galleried dining room frescoed in pale blue and green (fig. 3.44). Wealthy families and passing visitors in the building's seven-hundred-fifty guest rooms resided in opulent comfort. As a modern hotel, the Belmont offered amenities such as pneumatic tube systems to carry messages, telephones, advanced water filtration systems, and air conditioners. With five sublevels, the Belmont conveniently connected to the new subway and the terminal building.

Warren & Wetmore's next hotel, the sixteen-story Ritz-Carlton (1908–10), offered a quieter, subtler version of elegance (fig. 3.45). A group of wealthy New Yorkers, accustomed to staying at the Ritz hotels abroad, originated the idea of developing a hotel run along similar lines in New York. Robert W. Goelet, Warren's nephew, owned land on the west side of Madison Avenue between 46th and 47th Streets and encouraged William Harris, chairman of the Carlton and Ritz Hotels of London, to establish a branch in New York.[66] Although César Ritz initially hesitated to endorse an American hotel under his flagship, the Ritz was an immediate success upon its opening.

Warren & Wetmore accurately anticipated the shift in taste away from the grandiose French styles and turned to the Georgian architecture of London for its inspiration for the

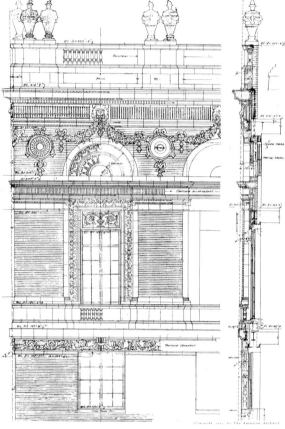

3.45 (above left). Ritz-Carlton, 370–384 Madison Avenue, New York City. Byron Co., New York. Prints and Photographs Division, Library of Congress, #6673.

3.46 (above right). Ritz-Carlton. Detail of corner at upper part of building. The American Architect 99 (February 1, 1911).

3.47 (opposite top). Ritz-Carlton. Dining room. Museum of the City of New York, Byron Collection, #93.1.1.6579.

3.48 (opposite bottom). Ritz-Carlton. Ground and typical floor plans. The American Architect 99 (February 1, 1911).

3.49 (following pages). Ritz-Carlton. Palm court. Museum of the City of New York, Byron Collection, #93.1.1.17401.

Ritz. Despite the hotel's height, the architects infused the reserved Adam-style facades with a comfortable and domestic spirit reminiscent of English terrace houses. The building's three-story limestone base, punctuated by entrances and windows interspersed between Ionic columns, rose into a brick shaft capped by refined limestone arches over the windows at the attic story. As a typically flamboyant Warren feature, the architects boldly articulated the roofline with giant terra-cotta urns—each of which measured 5 feet 7 inches tall and weighed three-quarters of a ton—to distinguish the hotel's block mass (fig. 3.46). *The American Architect* considered the motif—characteristic of so many eighteenth-century English buildings—"less pleasing" than its smaller-scaled prototype, but deemed it "preferable to the great projecting cornice so often resorted to; for to get such a cornice in scale with the rest of the structure, it ha[d] to overshadow several stories and, furthermore, to mar the silhouette."[67] Fanciful Japanese rooftop gardens with bridges, pagodas, and lanterns lent a contrasting and exotic note.

As opposed to the conspicuous gilding and frescoes used in the Belmont's interiors, the Ritz exuded an atmosphere of rich but refined domesticity through the use, principally, of an Adam-style decor that was widely emulated by other hotel designs and gave rise to the term "Adam-style Ritz." Small-scale details and fine proportions created an effect of quiet perfection (fig. 3.49). The gray-green elliptical dining room, decorated with an Adam ceiling and Wedgwood medallions, seated two hundred fifty guests and appeared more intimate than its size suggested (figs. 3.47, 3.48). With celebrated French chef Auguste Escoffier installed in the kitchens, dining at the Ritz became the height of fashion.

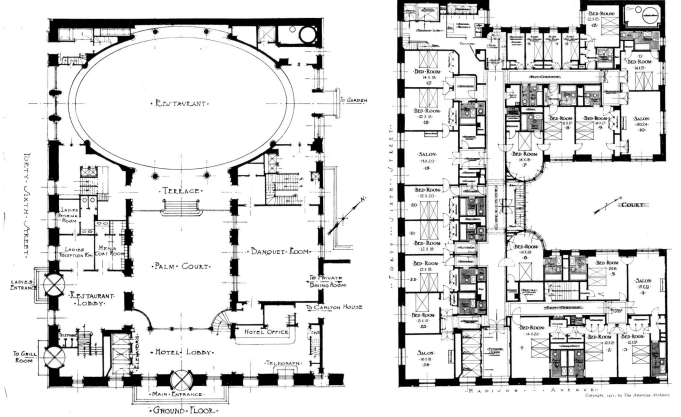

123

3.50. Hotel Vanderbilt, 4 Park
Avenue, New York City. Warren
& Wetmore Collection, Avery
Architectural and Fine Arts Library,
Columbia University.

3.51 (opposite). Hotel
Vanderbilt. Dining room. Warren
& Wetmore Collection, Avery
Architectural and Fine Arts Library,
Columbia University.

3.52 (following pages). Hotel
Vanderbilt. Lobby. Warren &
Wetmore Collection, Avery
Architectural and Fine Arts Library,
Columbia University.

In 1911 the firm designed an eighteen-story addition to the west with guest rooms and
ballroom. In admiring the hotel's elegant sequence of entertaining spaces, architect
Lawrence White remarked in 1956, "the entertainment suite of the Ritz oval ball-room and
the oval dining-room and the green ball-room with the staircase escalier d'honneur that went
up to it, was one of the handsomest settings for public entertainment that I've seen anywhere in the world. I've seen palaces, but I've never seen a public hotel that could touch
it."[68] After the addition was completed, Warren & Wetmore moved its offices to the northern portion of the Ritz at 16 East 47th Street, and Warren moved his family into Carlton
House, the residential section of the hotel, at 22 East 47th Street.

The firm's twenty-story Hotel Vanderbilt, on the west side of Park Avenue between 33rd
and 34th Streets, catered specifically to permanent residents (fig. 3.50).[69] On land once owned
by his great-grandfather Commodore Cornelius Vanderbilt, Alfred Gwynne Vanderbilt developed a six-hundred-room hotel where he and his second wife, Margaret Emerson McKim,
occupied a duplex penthouse accessed by a separate entry and private elevator. Relatively
inactive in the business world, Vanderbilt, a professional horseman and traveler who had
inherited the bulk of his father's estate in 1899, took "a personal interest in the construction
and furnishing of the hotel."[70] However, Vanderbilt's time in the hotel, which opened in
1913, was short-lived; in 1915 he died aboard the ill-fated Lusitania.[71]

Like the Ritz, Warren & Wetmore's design for the Vanderbilt also featured architectural
terra-cotta detail but displayed a wider interpretation of the Adam style. On the base of the

3.53. *Hotel Vanderbilt. Della Robbia Restaurant.* Warren & Wetmore Collection, Avery Architectural and Fine Arts Library, Columbia University.

building, the architects featured elegant brick pilasters, terra-cotta band courses, Adam medallions, and two massive Palladian windows delicately carved with fans of terra-cotta fluting. On the upper E-shaped bedroom floors they used a multihued blue-gray brick. Again, Warren & Wetmore abandoned the traditional projecting cornice for a flat decorative approach and an interesting parapet silhouette. Described by *The Brickbuilder* as "a pleasing example of the artistic and practical qualities of architectural terra cotta," the terra-cotta detailing, carved crests of the Vanderbilt "V," and rams' head pier capitals created the semblance of a colonnade at the attic story; caryatids supported the arched trusses that spanned the building's two courtyards.[72] The hotel's undulating parapet, adorned with figures of Hermes that were cast into outline by electric lights at night, transformed the top of the building into a sculptural event on the city skyline.

Inside, Warren & Wetmore collaborated with artists and artisans in designing the informal lounge space, palm court, and dining room on the hotel's main floor. Flowing seamlessly into one another, the main lobby and vaulted dining room featured Beatrice Astor Chanler's panels in plaster relief depicting cherubic children (figs. 3.51, 3.52). The hotel's cavernous Della Robbia Restaurant also displayed the possibilities of color and mural art in design (fig. 3.53). In the sublevel grillroom and bar, the architects created a stunning spectacle of blue-glazed Guastavino tiled vaults, cream-colored faience, and exotic murals of tropical birds and

3.54. Ritz-Carlton, Montreal, Quebec. Ballroom detail. Warren & Wetmore Collection, Avery Architectural and Fine Arts Library, Columbia University.

foliage, which *The American Architect* described as "an eloquent testimony to the wisdom of making the construction decorate the building."[73] Throughout the hotel, Warren & Wetmore's attention to detail was scrupulous down to even the most minor element: Paul Helleu's dry-point etchings graced the walls of the guest rooms, and Wedgwood knobs were used on all the doors.

The Belmont, Ritz, and Vanderbilt hotels firmly established Warren & Wetmore's reputation for hotel design and brought in commissions beyond the city. In 1910 a group of Canadian businessmen commissioned the firm to design a first-class residential hotel on Sherbrooke Street in Montreal.[74] The members of the syndicate were also familiar with the relaxed club-like surroundings of London's Carlton Hotel and aspired to create an establishment of similar stature and atmosphere. Soon after, they approached César Ritz to lend his name to their venture; by that time, the Ritz Hotel Development Company had developed hotels in Europe, South America, New York, and Philadelphia. Like the New York Ritz, the Montreal branch, which opened December 31, 1912, embraced the Adam revival. Warren & Wetmore's ten-story limestone building with restrained terra-cotta details included an elliptical dining room with carved plaster ceiling and a double-height cream-colored ballroom festooned with delicate Adam-style carvings and moldings (fig. 3.54).[75] The Philadelphia Ritz (1912), designed by Horace Trumbauer in association with Warren & Wetmore, was similarly tasteful and reserved.[76]

3.55. *903 Park Avenue,*
New York City. Museum of the
City of New York, Wurts Collection,
#1155569.

With established relationships with some of the country's expanding hotel corporations—the Ritz, Vanderbilt, and Biltmore—Warren & Wetmore went on to design hotels across the country during the 1910s and 1920s. In New York the firm successfully translated its expertise in hotel design into the developing field of apartment design. Apartment living—like hotel living—was then gaining popularity in society's upper echelons. Delano & Aldrich's 925 Park Avenue (1907–9), on the northeast corner of 80th Street, prompted Park Avenue's rapid transformation as upscale residential apartment buildings replaced the tenements and brownstones built during the period when railroad tracks ran in an open cut down the center of the avenue. Along with McKim, Mead & White's palatial 998 Fifth Avenue, Warren & Wetmore's 903 Park Avenue, designed in 1912 in association with Robert T. Lyons, was the epitome of luxurious apartment living (fig. 3.55). The seventeen-story building at the northeast corner of 79th Street, developed by Bing & Bing, presented buff-colored brick facades, broken by band courses and balconies and topped with a heavy bracketed copper cornice. The interiors were appropriately expansive: each floor contained one apartment with seventeen rooms, five baths, a circular entry hall, and six servants' rooms.[77]

3.56. *William K. Vanderbilt Sr.'s guesthouse, 49 East 52nd Street, New York City.* Museum of the City of New York, Wurts Collection, #800377.

Houses and Estates

Since its establishment, Warren & Wetmore had been the architect of choice for the William K. Vanderbilt family, succeeding Richard Morris Hunt who had died in 1895. Vanderbilt and his socially ambitious wife, Alva Erskine Smith, whom he divorced in 1896, had commissioned Hunt to design Idle Hour and a grand French Renaissance château at 660 Fifth Avenue (1883). In 1908 Vanderbilt called upon Warren & Wetmore to design a guesthouse at 49 East 52nd Street, one block away from his mansion on Fifth Avenue and 52nd Street (fig. 3.56).

Warren & Wetmore's restrained brick and limestone facades manifested the degree to which tastes had changed since the Vanderbilts had commissioned Hunt to design 600 Fifth Avenue. At 50 feet wide and seven stories tall, the guesthouse was a larger version of Warren & Wetmore's private houses, such as those for the Wilson and Burden families, carried out in the firm's modern French mode. The firm's extravagant rooms accommodated the Vanderbilt guests in grand style. The floors alternated living rooms and bedrooms; each floor

of bedrooms had a corresponding floor for entertaining. The first, third, and fifth floors contained salons, reception rooms, and elliptical dining rooms decorated with deep colors, marble fireplaces, and crystal chandeliers; a number of bedrooms and sitting rooms occupied the second, fourth, and sixth floors. Servants lived in rooms beneath the mansard roof, lit by bull's-eye windows. A ramp that extended down from the arched entrance on 52nd Street led to an underground garage.[78]

During the years the firm was working with Reed & Stem on Grand Central Terminal, the Vanderbilt guesthouse would be the most ambitious design for a private residence to come out of its offices. The streets of the Upper East Side were rapidly being improved with smaller, more manageable town houses executed in the restrained Georgian mode by such firms as Delano & Aldrich and Walker & Gillette. However, as this trend increased, Warren & Wetmore was moving away from the large private house commissions and was transferring the grand scale and style for which it was known into the developing field of apartment and hotel design. To a lesser degree, New York's rich continued to build large city homes; however, little land was available on the fashionable Upper East Side. Houses for Marion Brookman, the widow of shipping magnate H. D. Brookman, at 5 East 70th Street (1909), and S. Reading Bertron, a Houston executive, at 935 Fifth Avenue (1910) exhibited Warren & Wetmore's exuberant modern French style, but, in the spirit of the age, were smaller and less imposing than those designed a decade earlier.[79]

The number of country house commissions also dwindled. Notable designs included a series of picturesque, high-roofed outbuildings (1907) for capitalist Isaac Guggenheim at his estate Villa Carola on Sand's Point, Long Island, and a tennis court building for Harry Payne

3.58. *William K. Vanderbilt Jr. estate, Eagle's Nest, Centerport, New York, 1910.* Suffolk County Vanderbilt Museum.

3.59. *Eagle's Nest. Boathouse.* Suffolk County Vanderbilt Museum.

3.60. Chelsea Piers. Little West 12th Street to West 23rd Street, New York City. Warren & Wetmore Collection, Avery Architectural and Fine Arts Library, Columbia University.

Whitney (1912) at the Whitney compound in Old Westbury, Long Island (fig. 3.57). Also in 1912, Warren & Wetmore completed a six-room bachelor's retreat for the recently separated William K. Vanderbilt Jr. (1898–1944) at Eagle's Nest in Centerport, Long Island, on Northport Harbor. Like the Guggenheim outbuildings, the firm carried out Vanderbilt's English-style cottage and small boathouse in a picturesque vernacular, distinguishing the modest house with an overhanging bracketed roof and the dramatically perched boathouse with half-timber details (figs. 3.58, 3.59). In the 1920s the firm returned to Eagle's Nest and radically transformed Vanderbilt's retreat into a sprawling estate. Although the boathouse would remain untouched, the house and grounds were significantly expanded past the point of recognition (see pages 220–27).[80]

In 1906 Frederick and Louise Vanderbilt called upon Warren to redesign portions of their Hudson River manor house, Hyde Park; Charles McKim, who had designed the neoclassical mansion in 1895, was indisposed at the time. Sensitive to overstepping his bounds, Warren apprised the offices of McKim, Mead & White of the commission. In response, White wrote, "This of course is a surprise to us, and, in view of McKim's relations with Mr. Vanderbilt and the work, it will be a matter of great regret to him that its completion should pass out of his hands. We are certain, however, that, if Mr. Vanderbilt wishes you to do it, it is much better to leave you free to carry out his ideas in your own way, while appreciating and thanking you for your very kind letter."[81] Of Warren's renovations, his octagonal opening and heavy stone balustrade above the elliptical entrance hall were most notable. On the second floor, he transformed the central hall into a formal space with coved ceilings, skylight, and classical ornament.[82]

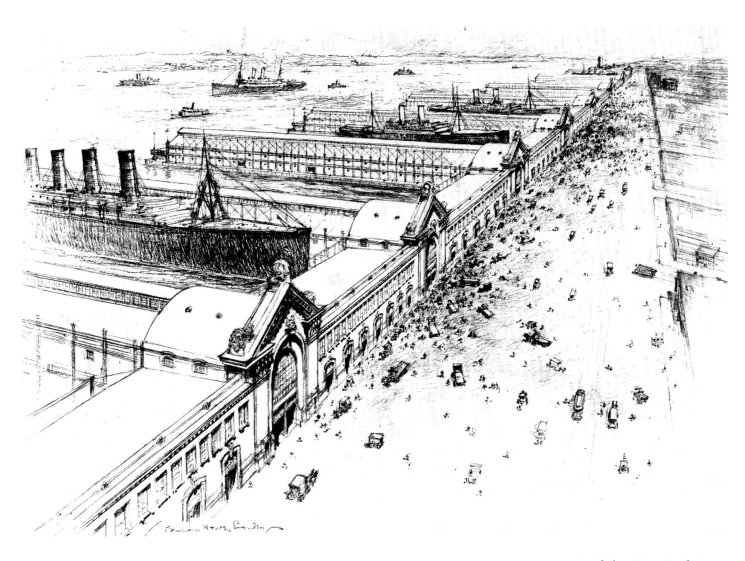

THE WATERFRONT

Throughout the 1900s and 1910s, Warren & Wetmore's practice grew larger and more diversified. Aside from Grand Central Terminal, the firm's most visible city improvement was the Chelsea Piers, completed in 1910 (fig. 3.60).[83] Like train terminals, piers and docks were considered major entry points into the city, though most were utilitarian, at best. Warren & Wetmore's design of the Chelsea Piers was a notable exception. Stretching from Little West 12th Street to West 23rd Street, they consisted of a continuous bulkhead behind which nine two-story sheds extended over the water to form slips that were big enough to accommodate the largest ocean liners and ships of the period.

The waterfront improvement, initiated by the city's Department for Docks and Ferries, had been in the making since the late 1880s. The department's engineers designed the piers, which were set on piles with stone fill, and innovative, long-span steel trusses to support the sheds. In 1907 Warren & Wetmore executed the elevations and ornamental aspects of the scheme, concentrating on the pier heads that faced the city. The firm had previously designed a recreational pier (Pier 30) on the East River for the city, and Warren, who had endorsed the principles of the New York City Improvement Commission's 1907 report, supported unified city design. The firm's elevations for the Chelsea improvement fused traditional architectural language with new technology and materials, confronting the city with a continuous concrete and pink-granite-trimmed facade articulated as a rhythm of arched entrances and pedimented cornices that rose above the two-story bulkhead (fig. 3.61).

3.62. Seamen's Church Institute, 25 South Street, New York City. Warren & Wetmore Collection, Avery Architectural and Fine Arts Library, Columbia University.

Allegorical details, described by one critic as "the most conspicuous ornamental concrete construction in [the] city," festooned the facades.[84] The architects distinguished the larger pier shed entrances from the bulkhead doors that accessed offices and stores with elaborately carved keystones modeled after Aphrodite and Mercury. At the cornice, Warren & Wetmore's copper finial globes and overscaled sculptural groups stood as symbols of transatlantic travel and shipping.

Warren & Wetmore's twelve-story brick clubhouse and hotel for the Seamen's Church Institute at Coenties Slip in lower Manhattan created a visible beacon on Manhattan's eastern waterfront (fig. 3.62). Backed by prominent lawyers, financiers, and clergymen, the

Seamen's Church Institute had been providing religious guidance and direction to sailors since 1844. Edmund L. Baylies, President of the institute and Wetmore's real estate investment partner, brought the commission to the firm in 1906; the building, an oversized interpretation of the Dutch warehouse type, was completed in 1912—the year of the *Titanic* tragedy. Unlike the New York Yacht Club, it established a home or clubhouse for "the ordinary man." In its design, Warren & Wetmore followed Ernest Flagg's plans for the Mills Hotels, which were boardinghouses with accommodations, restaurants, and lounges for working-class bachelors. At a moderate price, merchant seamen could find lodging in the institute's dormitory or hotel wing, dine in the restaurant, and use the building's library, game room, and auditorium. With its distinctive roofline, the building was visible to vessels coming into the historic harbor; the green light of the *Titanic* memorial lighthouse tower and time ball on the roof, dedicated in 1913, could be seen as far away as Sandy Hook.[85]

Retail Stores

> I have driven rapidly in a fast car, clinging to my hat and my hair against the New York wind, from one end of Fifth Avenue to the other, and what with the sunshine, and the flags wildly waving in the sunshine and the blue sky and cornices jutting into it, and roofs scraping it, and the large whiteness of the stores, and the invitation of the signs, and the display of the windows, and the swift sinuousness of the other cars, and the proud processions of American subjects . . . I have been positively intoxicated.
>
> — Arnold Bennett, *Those United States*

While the firm was working on Grand Central, Fifth Avenue from 34th Street to 57th Street was rapidly becoming the city's fashionable shopping district. In 1901 Charles Berg designed the fanciful Windsor Arcade on the east side of the avenue, between 46th and 47th Streets,

3.63. *J. Dreicer & Son, 560 Fifth Avenue, New York City.* Museum of the City of New York, Byron Collection, #93.1.1.18029.

3.64 *(following pages). J. Dreicer & Son. Showroom.* Museum of the City of New York, Byron Collection, #93.1.1.1932.

139

Byron N.Y.
25551.

3.65. Mrs. Osborn's dressmaking building, 24 East 46th Street, New York City. Warren & Wetmore Collection, Avery Architectural and Fine Arts Library, Columbia University.

on the site of the Windsor Hotel, which had been destroyed by fire. Berg's sculptural French building, which housed a number of upscale shops, lent a certain prestige to the area.[86] Warren & Wetmore's store buildings, clustered around 46th Street, were smaller than McKim, Mead & White's palazzi for Tiffany & Company (1906) and Gorham Company (1905) and the large department stores of the era. However, the firm's shops for two jewelers exploited the smaller scale of the establishments to create elegant and painstakingly detailed interiors. The firm's five-story French Renaissance–inspired building for J. Dreicer & Son, at 560 Fifth Avenue on the southwest corner of 46th Street, opened in 1907 (fig. 3.63).[87] Warren & Wetmore's black and gold marble base, gilded bronze Corinthian capitals, and broad expanses of plate glass at street level offered a contrasting note to the upper floors, which were executed in limestone with carved pilasters. Inside, the architects' use of scale and detail created the semblance of a private house. The interior decorators, P. W. French & Company, reinforced the atmosphere of reserved luxuriousness by using Louis XV commodes and tables (rather than conventional counters) and fixtures imported from Paris in the oak-paneled front room (fig. 3.64). One block north, Warren & Wetmore's shop for Theodore B. Starr (1911), at 576 Fifth Avenue, was located on the lower two floors of an office building.[88] In contrast to the Dreicer design, the firm used a reserved Adam style for the interiors, similar to that of the Ritz. Its nearby shop for Mrs. Osborn's dressmaking, a charming clubhouse-like Georgian design at 24 East 46th Street (1905), was described by the architect Francis S. Swales as "not in any sense typical of American shop-architecture as we should like it to be," but acquiesced that "it would hold its own Mayfair" (fig. 3.65).[89]

BANKS, COURTHOUSES, AND CHAPELS

With the exception of Grand Central's suburban stations and estate outbuildings, Warren & Wetmore designed few projects outside New York during the first two decades of the twentieth century. However, in 1909, the firm embarked on two projects in Hudson, New York: a bank and a courthouse.[90] These commissions probably came through Warren's family connections in the area; his grandmother, Mary Whitney Phoenix, owned Glenwood, an

3.66. Hudson City Savings Bank, Hudson, New York. Warren & Wetmore Collection, Avery Architectural and Fine Arts Library, Columbia University.

Italianate villa in Hudson where Warren had spent time as a child. The firm's Hudson City Savings Institution presented a monumental Greek Revival portico supported by bold Ionic columns (fig. 3.66). Warren & Wetmore enlivened the spare limestone facades with band courses, pilasters, and a boldly carved tympanum that complimented the design's compact, rectilinear quality. A large Palladian window generously lit the domed banking hall. The Columbia County Courthouse. the firm's only courthouse design, was appropriately stately with a large center dome and pedimented portico (fig. 3.67). Warren & Wetmore's burst of ornament above the arched second-story windows and in the tympanum, its use of delicately carved Corinthian capitals, and balustrades lent the design a sculptural depth that was highlighted by the building's straight lines and simple volumes.

In 1911, Warren & Wetmore also designed a mortuary chapel at Green-Wood Cemetery in Brooklyn that exhibited an uncharacteristic command of Gothic vocabulary: a style in which the firm rarely worked (fig. 3.68). The chapel was set within the rolling grounds of the 478-acre cemetery, which had been designed in the English landscape tradition by David B. Douglass in 1839. Over the years an impressive collection of mausolea and vaults marking the graves of some of New York's most prominent citizens—Ward McAllister, Dewitt Clinton, Horace Greeley, "Boss" Tweed—had grown within the gates of the cemetery. Warren & Wetmore's limestone chapel reflected the style of Richard M. Upjohn's brownstone gatehouse confection (1860) at the main entrance at Fifth Avenue and 25th Street. The firm adroitly combined taut facades and the rational plan of the Beaux-Arts tradition with ornament and a picturesque roofline characteristic of the Gothic style.[91]

CHAPTER FOUR

Inventors of the Modern Cityscape: 1914–1922

On August 5, 1914, just days after the eruption of World War One, Warren left for Europe aboard the steamer *Lorraine*. During the next five years, he had little interaction with his architectural offices, returning only briefly to the United States on two trips. In Paris Warren lived in rooms at the Grand Hotel at the Palais d'Orsay and worked tirelessly for the Allied cause. Although he had never been active in politics, Warren came to be regarded as a chief representative of American opinion abroad. He lectured and was interviewed frequently, and his views appeared regularly in leading publications on both sides of the Atlantic. Horrified by the Germans' senseless destruction of historic architecture, he traveled to devastated areas of France and Belgium and reported extensively on the damage, which he considered the "worst crimes by the Germans [because they were] against the helpless stones themselves" (fig. 4.1).[1] Warren was disappointed that his age prevented him from serving in the military even in a minor capacity, but he often visited the front to lend support as well as to visit his son, Whitney, who had received a commission in the French army.[2] Vehemently opposed to President Woodrow Wilson's policy of neutrality, Warren urged the United States' entry into the war. As the United States continued to postpone its entrance, Warren felt the weight of accountability for America's isolation and saw the mounting devastation in Europe as a direct consequence. His wife Charlotte, in New York, headed the Secours National, an organization that provided relief for French women and children as well as Belgian refugees, and sent her husband's articles to American newspapers and magazines to be published.

As Warren devoted himself wholeheartedly to France in what he considered "the chance of a lifetime," the offices of Warren & Wetmore continued to operate without his involvement.[3] Initially Warren felt guilty about his ongoing sabbatical from the firm. He tried to gauge his partner's sentiments about his absence and wondered if the firm had been able to do "good business." During the war years, Julian Holland, a Brooklyn-born architect, ran the office with Wetmore, and the firm continued to draw commissions from major clients such as the New York Central and Hudson River Railroad and the Biltmore Corporation. In Warren's absence, the designs followed the same themes and spirit as those before the war, and the dedicated drafting room looked to the firm's body of work for inspiration. Leonard Schultze, the talented designer who, in partnership with S. Fullerton Weaver, went on to produce the Sherry Netherland (1927), Pierre (1929), and Waldorf Astoria (1931) hotels, supervised many of the projects.[4] The firm's office buildings, prestigious apartment houses, and residential hotels for the unimproved blocks north of Grand Central Terminal, produced between the years 1914 and 1922, created a dense pocket of design that formed one of New York's most impressive and cohesive improvements—Terminal City. Just as the firm's apartments and hotels established an influential model for high-rise living and its office designs gave rise to the emerging cityscape, its resorts outside the city set a luxurious standard for America's leisure class.

Apartments and Hotels in New York City

A mansion on Fifth Avenue used to be the badge of plutocracy; but plutocracy has moved to Park Avenue and changed its style of abode to the apartment domicile.

— *Architecture and Building*

By 1914 much of the railroad's property on Lexington Avenue had been developed, but most of Park Avenue north of 45th Street remained unimproved. While there were streets and sidewalks on the avenue and traffic moved freely through the area, most of the blocks were simply large open spaces that exposed the railroad yards beneath (fig. 4.2). In the next years Park Avenue would be dramatically transformed. Apartment living proved a success as the rich began to abandon their private houses and pay high prices for large suites on Park Avenue.

Warren & Wetmore's early design for 903 Park Avenue for Bing & Bing, and McKim, Mead & White's design for 998 Fifth Avenue, both dated 1912, established the standard for upscale apartment living. In the years following their construction, Park Avenue changed from a second-rate address to what the press described as the "second Fifth Avenue"; high-class apartment buildings and a number of private homes were built in rapid succession. A second wave of residential construction did not fully affect the scale and disposition of Fifth Avenue until the 1920s, when many of the mansions and large town houses built at the turn of the twentieth century were replaced by apartment buildings.

Park Avenue below 57th Street experienced a sweeping transformation as New York Central's real estate subsidiary extended long-term land leases for portions of its property, which stretched north to 57th Street, to various builders and companies. Between the years 1914 and 1922, Warren & Wetmore designed a string of luxury apartment buildings that occupied almost all of the avenue's western fringe from 47th to 56th Street (fig. 4.3). The firm's Hotel Ambassador, later joined by McKim, Mead & White's courtyard apartment building at 277 Park Avenue (1925) and Schultze & Weaver's Park Lane Hotel (1924), created an impressive ensemble on the east side of the avenue. While each building had a distinguishing character, the line of classically proportioned brick and limestone facades with consistent cornice lines, dictated by the zoning law enacted in 1916, formed a unified frame to Grand Central Terminal at the base of the avenue. Warren & Wetmore's first apartment building north of the terminal was at 340–50 Park Avenue, between 51st and 52nd Streets (fig. 4.4). Completed in 1915, the grand building stretched the length of the block and contained four large apartments per floor, serviced by two separate lobbies, each with its own elevator bank.[5] Warren & Wetmore was most successful in going beyond the standard tripartite division of tall buildings that required a full projecting cornice. In its best designs, the firm conceived the facade as a flat plane and applied decoration. In some cases, the Adam Revival or an interest in Mannerist architecture informed the architectural language. At 340–50 Park Avenue, the ornament, which made the lack of a projecting cornice irrelevant, encapsulated both styles. The block-long thirteen-story apartment formed a distinctive pair with 320–30 Park Avenue one block to the south, completed one year later.

4.1. Whitney Warren, inspecting the ruins of Reims Cathedral, 1914. bMS Am 2113.5. By permission of the Houghton Library, Harvard University.

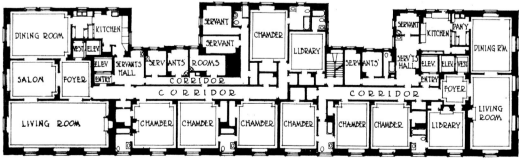

S. Fullerton Weaver (1879–1939) developed two buildings with Warren & Wetmore in 1914 and 1915. By that time, Weaver, a trained engineer, had acquired expertise in residential development, having worked with apartment specialist J. E. R. Carpenter on early luxury buildings at 635 Park Avenue (1909) and 960 Park Avenue (1910). In 1921 Weaver would form a practice with Leonard Schultze, Warren & Wetmore's chief executive in charge of all design and construction relating to the terminal—a title that included the Park Avenue apartment buildings and Hotel Ambassador. The press considered Warren & Wetmore and Weaver's first collaboration at 400 Park Avenue on the northwest corner of 54th Street a "pioneer among the high class apartment buildings . . . erected by the New York Central Railroad through its real estate operating subsidiary."[6] Like 903 Park Avenue, the twelve-story building contained one expansive apartment per floor, and its facades—defined by band courses, balustrades, and projecting cornice—formed a base, shaft, and capital in prototypical high-rise manner. For the block-long 420–30 Park Avenue building between 55th and 56th Streets, the firm designed a narrow brick edifice distinguished by limestone details and quoins (fig. 4.5).[7] Warren & Wetmore embellished the attic story of the

eighteen-story building with elaborately carved terra-cotta garlands, engaged columns, plaques, and medallions. A typical floor held two eighteen-room apartments that commanded outside views on all four sides (fig. 4.6). Two lobbies, each entered from one of the flanking side streets, contained fireplaces and a private elevator bank that opened onto one of the two apartments per floor. The building at 420–30 Park Avenue was rented out four months before construction was complete.

Work on the firm's most ambitious apartment design, at 270 Park Avenue, began in 1916 in collaboration with builder Dr. Charles Vincent Paterno.[8] Located opposite the Ritz, the immense courtyard building—known as "The Mansions"—covered the block between 47th and 48th Streets and Park and Madison Avenues and enclosed an Italian garden almost one block long (figs. 4.7, 4.8). At the time of its completion, *Architecture* noted that "in point of size and cost, this great structure exceed[ed] anything ever attempted of its kind, and it [was] likely to stand for many years as the maximum result of the apartment-builder's courage."[9] The twelve-story complex housed one hundred and eight suites in two distinct sections that the architects tied together with two three-story triumphal arches, through which Vanderbilt Avenue passed; a groin-vaulted Ionic arcade with herringbone brick floors and pendant fixtures set within the base of the building extended around the perimeter of the courtyard—through the triumphal arches—and joined the buildings (fig. 4.9). Like the Ritz, the brick structure presented restrained Adam-style facades accented with limestone details and decorative medallions. Behind the arcade, Warren & Wetmore incorporated a series of private lobbies appointed with upholstered furniture, rugs, and fixtures that reflected the

4.7 (opposite top). The Mansions, 270 Park Avenue, New York City. Museum of the City of New York, Wurts Collection, #117519.

4.8 (opposite bottom). The Mansions. Courtyard. Architecture 37 (May 1918): pl. 78.

4.9 (above). The Mansions. Arcade. Architecture 37 (May 1918).

refined elegance of the complex. All of the rooms in the apartments, which ranged in size from ten to seventeen rooms, commanded outside views. The Madison Avenue section housed mainly duplexes, whereas the smaller Park Avenue portion contained simplexes, a number of duplexes, and the Ritz-operated Avignon restaurant at street level. Publicized as "the utmost in housekeeping apartments," the building also provided servants from the nearby hotel upon request. Warren & Wetmore's courtyard building displayed an innovative response to urban design and inspired several offshoots, including McKim, Mead & White's impressive 277 Park Avenue, later built across the avenue.

The firm's twelve-story corner building at 927 Fifth Avenue, on the southeast corner of 74th Street, which replaced William Picard's 1889 brownstone mansion, followed the growing trend of razing mansions to free space for apartment construction (fig. 4.10). After the completion of the pioneering 998 Fifth Avenue, a number of architects and developers followed suit. J. E. R. Carpenter and Starrett & Van Vleck contributed luxurious apartments at 907 Fifth Avenue (1915) and 820 Fifth Avenue (1916), replacing the homes of James A. Burden and the Progress Club. Warren & Wetmore's limestone-clad building at 927 Fifth Avenue also exemplified the elegant, understated classicism of the early Fifth Avenue apartment house.[10] Completed in 1917, it housed twelve fifteen-room apartments and an intimate lobby appointed with a fireplace and arched ceiling painted with frescoes (fig. 4.11). Warren & Wetmore successfully balanced the building's composition with a three-story rusticated base and a band course carved with shells and fleur-de-lis above the tenth floor, and enlivened the limestone-sheathed facades with a head-scroll keystone above a two-story arched entrance and eleventh-floor medallions of eagles copied from Trajan's Forum.

*4.12. 280–90 Park Avenue, New
York City.* Warren & Wetmore
Collection, Avery Architectural and
Fine Arts Library, Columbia
University.

*4.13. 280–90 Park Avenue.
Typical floor plan.* Warren &
Wetmore Collection, Avery
Architectural and Fine Arts Library,
Columbia University.

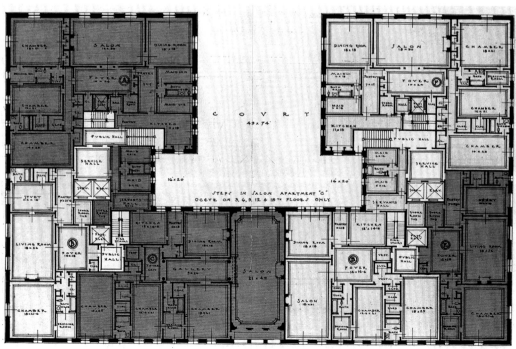

Although building activity diminished during the war years, it quickly revived in the early 1920s. Soon after Warren's return from France in 1919, the firm began construction on a pair of block-long U-shaped brick and limestone apartment houses at 280–90 Park Avenue and 300–10 Park Avenue, each with a light court opening to the west. Like 270 Park Avenue one block south, the buildings offered housekeeping service to "solve the servant problem." The seventeen-story 280–90 Park Avenue building between 48th and 49th Streets contained six apartments per floor and one full story dedicated to servants' quarters (fig. 4.12).[11] Whereas the larger apartments in the southern wing had kitchens, tenants of the smaller suites in the northern section relied on Pierre's ground-level restaurant for provisions and room service. Resident proprietors, who funded the $4-million-dollar project, owned sixty of the building's apartments, and the remaining thirty suites were rented out to cover expenses. As one of the proprietors, Warren and his wife gave up their apartment in Carlton House and moved into 280 Park Avenue upon its completion in 1922. The Warrens' apartment, the largest in the building, opened onto a long gallery defined by freestanding columns that led to a double-height salon (20 by 46 feet) with arched windows to the east and west (fig. 4.13). With the inclusion of double-height space—a feature articulated on the Park Avenue facade—Warren & Wetmore split the levels of the building so that every other apartment had a one-and-a-half-story drawing room. Tenants in the firm's sixteen-story building at 300–10

4.14. 300–10 Park Avenue, New York City. Warren & Wetmore Collection, Avery Architectural and Fine Arts Library, Columbia University.

4.15 (following pages). 300–10 Park Avenue, New York City. Sherry's Restaurant. Warren & Wetmore Collection, Avery Architectural and Fine Arts Library, Columbia University.

*4.16. Hotel Chatham, 23–29
East 48th Street, New York City.
Architecture* 36 (December 1917):
pl. 207.

Park Avenue, between 49th and 50th Streets, also relied on the ground-floor restaurant for sustenance (fig. 4.14). While a private lobby on 49th Street accessed the larger apartments with kitchens in the southern wing, the smaller suites without kitchens to the north shared an entrance with Sherry's, Louis Sherry's legendary establishment, which moved to the building from its 44th Street location (fig. 4.15). Sherry's lofty barrel-vaulted lounge and bright top-lit restaurant occupied the center of the building's first and second floors.[12] In the 1930s, after his wife's death, Wetmore moved into an apartment at 300 Park Avenue from his brownstone on West 53rd Street.

The relentless demand for center-city hotels and apartments around Grand Central Terminal resulted in Warren & Wetmore's fourteen-story Hotel Chatham, completed in 1917, which stretched between 48th and 49th Streets on Vanderbilt Avenue (fig. 4.16).[13] Its elegant brick facades reflected the reserved Adam Revival style of the Ritz; however, the top of the building was crowded with large limestone urns and shields, set between the triangular and arched pedimented attic story windows. Like the Ritz, design emphasis rested on creating a quiet and domestic environment for permanent and transient guests. Oak-paneled walls and elaborately patterned plastered ceilings raised the public spaces to the typical level of Warren & Wetmore's grand interiors. In the warmer months, guests enjoyed dining outside, where the restaurant took over a section on Vanderbilt Avenue known as Chatham Walk (fig. 4.17).

In 1919 Warren & Wetmore embarked on the larger Hotel Ambassador on the east side of Park Avenue between 51st and 52nd Streets (fig. 4.18).[14] Hotelier D. M. Linnard, who

4.17. Chatham Walk. View south from 49th Street and Vanderbilt Avenue with 280–90 Park Avenue (left), Hotel Chatham (right), and the arch of the 270 Park Avenue (center). Hewitt Smith Photograph Collection #77590d. The Collection of the New-York Historical Society.

operated a number of hotels in California and Atlantic City, and Chicago banker S. W. Straus collaborated on the development of the seventeen-story, block-long hotel. Although the limestone contrasted with the hotel's more subdued brick neighbors, Warren & Wetmore's classically proportioned facades and two-story arches framing the windows and doors at the base followed the compositions of the firm's apartment houses across the avenue. However, as opposed to their blocky, flat-roofed forms, the Ambassador's upper floors were expressed as a series of setbacks. Complying with the 1916 zoning regulations, the fourteenth and sixteenth floors set back to create roof terraces for the top rooms. When the hotel opened in April 1921, its proponents considered it an "an aristocrat of hotels." Of the building's five hundred rooms, the three hundred allocated for permanent guests were reserved well in advance of the building's completion (figs. 4.19). Inside, the architects nurtured the effect of luxurious domesticity by creating the impression of an exclusive apartment house with tasteful decor and residentially scaled public rooms. On the ground level, lounges and entertaining rooms in the French style were arranged *en suite* and connected to a trellised tea garden; individually decorated guest rooms and apartments were furnished with reproductions and antiques from the Belmaison Galleries of John Wanamaker (figs. 4.20–4.23).

Unlike the firm's residentially scaled hotels, Warren & Wetmore's twenty-eight-story Commodore Hotel (1917–19), named after New York Central Railroad's creator Commodore Cornelius Vanderbilt, was strictly a commercial establishment that connected directly to the terminal and the subway system and was designed to accommodate transient businessmen

4.18. Hotel Ambassador, 341–51 Park Avenue, New York City. Hewitt Smith Photograph Collection #77589d. The Collection of The New-York Historical Society.

4.19 (below). Hotel Ambassador. Ground floor and typical floor plans. The American Architect 119 (June 22, 1921).

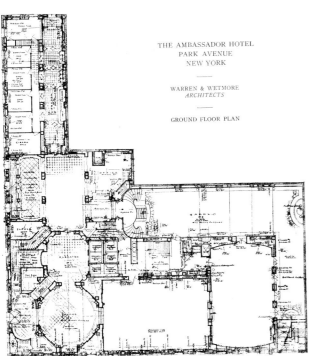

THE AMBASSADOR HOTEL
PARK AVENUE
NEW YORK

———

WARREN & WETMORE
ARCHITECTS

———

GROUND FLOOR PLAN

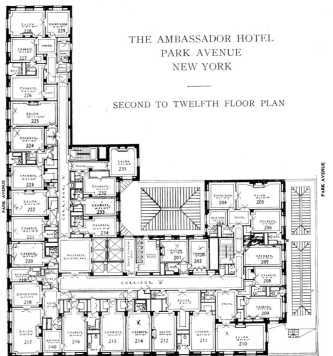

THE AMBASSADOR HOTEL
PARK AVENUE
NEW YORK

———

SECOND TO TWELFTH FLOOR PLAN

4.20 (left). Hotel Ambassador. Main lobby. The American Architect *119 (June 22, 1921): 644.*

4.21 (below left). Hotel Ambassador. Circular lounge on main floor. The American Architect *119 (June 22, 1921): 645.*

4.22 (above). Hotel Ambassador. Arcade. The American Architect *119 (June 22, 1921).*

4.23 (left). Hotel Ambassador. Tea garden. The American Architect *119 (June 22, 1921): 646.*

4.24. Hotel Commodore, 400–422 Lexington Avenue with Park Avenue Viaduct, New York City, 1919. Irving Underhill, Prints and Photographs Division, Library of Congress, #6673.

(fig. 4.24).[15] Marketed as "the world's largest and most complete hotel," the giant edifice on 42nd Street, between Lexington Avenue and Depew Place on the elevated Park Avenue viaduct, contained two thousand small guest rooms and myriad spaces for entertaining and gatherings.

Like the thriving Biltmore Hotel on Vanderbilt Avenue, which opened five years earlier, the Commodore was also financed by the railroad and operated by the Biltmore Corporation's entrepreneurial director, John McE. Bowman. The overwhelming size of the project impeded Warren & Wetmore's ability to compose a welcoming and distinctive exterior; however, as a bracket to Grand Central, the hotel's stark—almost astylar—buff-colored brick facades served as a neutral backdrop to the grandeur of the terminal building. In its design, the architects aligned the building with the drive around Grand Central and, in effect, continued its plinth as a five-story limestone base that supported the H-shaped mass of the hotel's twenty floors of bedrooms (fig. 4.25). Although large rectangular light courts gave the

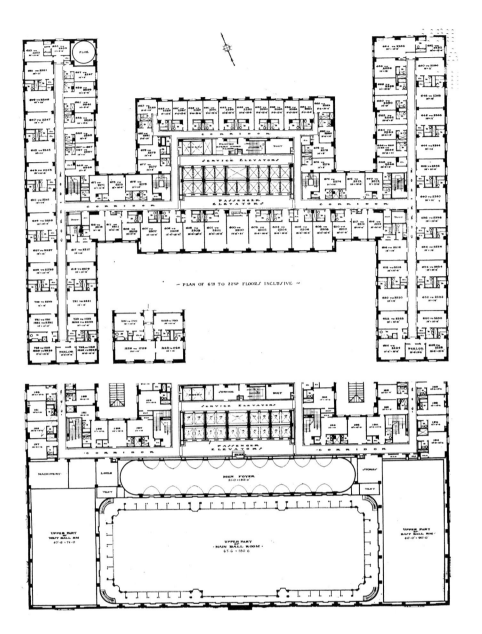

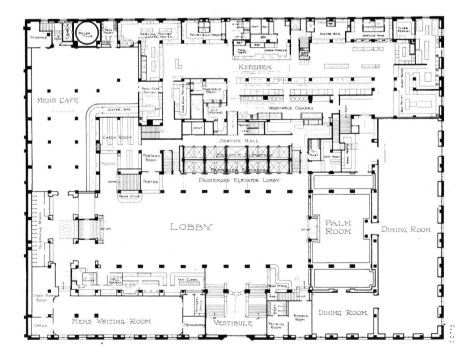

4.25. Hotel Commodore. Typical floor plan, ballroom level plan, and ground floor plan. *The American Architect* 115 (March 5, 1919): pl. 77.

4.26 (opposite). Hotel Commodore, 42nd Street entrance. Museum of the City of New York, Wurts Collection, #807874.

4.27 (above). Hotel Commodore. Entrance vestibule. Architecture 39 (April 1919): pl. 47.

design a blocky silhouette, Warren & Wetmore attempted to personalize the facades with ornament at the base and attic levels and groups of terra-cotta shells above the hotel's front entrance (fig. 4.26).

The Commodore's interiors epitomized the firm's attitude toward style. As Edith Wharton wrote, "the decorator is . . . not to explain illusions but to produce them."[16] From the architectural shell to the furnishings, the hotel's rooms were a sensory delight presenting a procession of styles and effects. A set of steps carved with aquatic forms led from the main entrance at 42nd Street to a double-height central lobby, designed to suggest an Italian courtyard (figs. 4.27, 4.28). Roofed in opaque white glass, the space was decorated with a profusion of palms, plants, vases, and statues of Roman basket carriers; flower boxes extending from an upper gallery, light stucco walls accented with Italian tiles, and dark woodwork evoked the out-of-doors. From an entrance on Depew Place, guests could enter the ballroom level directly. At 78 by 180 feet, the Commodore's great windowless ballroom was the largest in the United States. The grand double-height space, decorated in shades of purple, white, gold, and emerald green, contained an upper gallery divided into open boxes encircling the room and opened onto smaller ballrooms to the east and west (figs. 4.29, 4.30). Following its method of creating a variety of styles in its larger hotels, Warren & Wetmore executed the dining room, located off the main lobby, in a more restrained Adam style, while suggesting the Italian Renaissance Revival in the sublevel wood-paneled grillroom with large ceiling beams painted with heraldic decorations by the talented muralist John B. Smeraldi (fig. 4.31).[17] Confronted with the absence of natural light in the public spaces, Warren & Wetmore

4.28. Hotel Commodore. Lobby. The American Architect 115 (March 5, 1919): pl. 70.

4.29 (below). Hotel Commodore. Ballroom. Museum of the City of New York, Wurts Collection, #117491.

4.30 (opposite). Hotel Commodore. End of lobby to ballroom. Museum of the City of New York, Wurts Collection, #117490.

4.31. Hotel Commodore.
Grillroom. *The American Architect*
115 (March 5, 1919): pl. 72.

4.32. Plaza Hotel Addition, 55
West 58th Street, New York City.
Restaurant. *Architecture and
Building* 54 (February 1922): 16.

embraced the dramatic effects of electricity. In the lobby, fixtures concealed in vases and urns cast indirect light toward the ceiling, and fixtures behind the leaded windows in the basement grillroom gave the impression of sunlight. Seventeen multiblade fans, which were capable of moving 845,000 cubic feet of air per minute, ventilated the hotel's countless rooms.

Warren & Wetmore's expertise won the firm commissions for annexes to some of New York's most well-established hotels. In 1917 Warren & Wetmore expanded the Hotel McAlpin (1904) at Greeley Square, one of the first hotels in the vicinity of Pennsylvania Station (1901–11). Following the rather drab classical style set by the original builder, F. M. Andrews & Company, Warren & Wetmore's two hundred-room annex on 34th Street doubled the size of the hotel. In 1921 the firm completed a large extension to Henry Hardenbergh's châteauesque Plaza Hotel (1907) at 55 West 58th Street. In both designs, Warren & Wetmore worked in the architectural language of the existing building; as a result, it was difficult to distinguish the additions from the original. Inside, the firm created luxurious spaces on par with its own hotels. At the McAlpin, Warren & Wetmore's colonial ballroom, Turkish bathrooms, and extravagant entertaining spaces belied the understated exterior. At the Plaza, the firm designed a succession of Italian Renaissance foyers, Louis XVI restaurants, suites, and a grand ballroom (fig. 4.32).[18]

HOTELS OUTSIDE NEW YORK CITY

With its designs for the renowned, heavily traveled Terminal City establishments—from the Belmont to the Commodore—the firm had successfully carved out a niche as an expert in hotel design. Expanding companies such as the Ritz, Ambassador, Vanderbilt, and Biltmore, with whom the firm already had relationships, continued to hand commissions to Warren & Wetmore. Soon the firm was being called to the Caribbean, out west, and to the eastern seaboard to design hotels; at the same time, its national reputation attracted new clients. The Bowman–Biltmore Corporation continued as one of the firm's most important patrons. In addition to the Biltmore and Commodore hotels in New York, the company commissioned Warren & Wetmore to design a country club and hotel in suburban Westchester County, New York, a hotel in Providence, Rhode Island, and an addition to an existing hotel in Havana, Cuba.

Warren & Wetmore's Westchester-Biltmore Country Club and Hotel, one of John McE. Bowman's most ambitious projects, opened in May 1922.[19] Situated on a 650-acre property in Rye, New York, the club's grounds included two eighteen-hole golf courses, tennis courts, polo fields, and shooting traps as well as a diminutive Georgian casino at the beach on nearby Manursing Island. Working in an abstracted version of Italian Renaissance style, Warren & Wetmore produced an eight-story brick and stucco clubhouse and hotel, asymmetrical stucco sports building, and a three-story bachelors' wing around a center courtyard (figs. 4.33, 4.34). As the centerpiece of the composition, the clubhouse and hotel rose dramatically as a series of blocky setbacks that formed stepped terraces on the upper floors, which were decorated with stone vases, columns, and statues modeled after antique Italian models. At ground level, the architects connected the flanking sports and bachelors' buildings to the main section of the building with an arcade supported by carved columns in the shape of Roman basket carriers. However, although the Westchester-Biltmore was a successful venture for Bowman, Warren & Wetmore's combination of architectural elements missed the mark. Despite the firm's butterfly plan, the building's bulk made it seem bloated in the pastoral setting (fig. 4.35).

As was characteristic of Warren & Wetmore's hotel designs, the Westchester-Biltmore featured rich and stylistically varied interiors. In turning to Italian and Spanish Revival styles for inspiration, the firm incorporated more painted detail and less architectural sculp-

ture into the scheme. Along the front of the hotel, a lofty classical gallery with painted ceiling beams, 120 feet long, ran the width of the building and connected an intimate oak-paneled Tudor-style grillroom at one end and various shops and offices at the other. Behind the gallery, a paneled and vaulted lobby space with painted ribbing opened onto the rear terrace and golf courses beyond. In the wings extending off the lobby on either side, Warren & Wetmore located a large paneled lounge with a carved plaster ceiling and a ballroom decorated with columns of Cippelino marble and stone moldings. However, in one respect the design strayed from one fundamental Beaux-Arts tenet: The plan of firm's elegant ballroom had no relationship with the exterior of the building.

One month after Warren & Wetmore had completed the Westchester-Biltmore, in June 1922, the firm's Providence-Biltmore Hotel opened (fig. 4.36). Providence's first grand hotel became the focus of civic pride; at the time of its completion, the nineteen-story hotel, the tallest and most modern structure in the city, proudly announced that Providence, a flourishing manufacturing and commercial center, had finally arrived.[20] The Providence-Biltmore's Georgianesque building, deferring to regional preferences, presented dignified, gently bowed Harvard brick facades, ornamented with stonework at the base and attic sto-

4.33 (opposite). Westchester-Biltmore Country Club, Rye, New York. Rendering by Chester B. Price. Courtesy of the Westchester Country Club, Rye, New York.

4.34 (above). Westchester-Biltmore Country Club. Sports house. Courtesy of the Westchester Country Club, Rye, New York.

4.35 (following pages). Westchester-Biltmore Country Club. View from golf course. Courtesy of the Westchester Country Club, Rye, New York.

171

4.36. *Providence-Biltmore Hotel,*
Providence, Rhode Island.
Museum of the City of New York,
Byron Collection, #93.1.1.5785.

ries. Due to the trapezoidal shape of the lot, the hotel's three-story base was essentially tri-angular and supported an L-shaped mass containing bedroom levels. Like the New York Biltmore, a double-height ballroom occupied the hotel's top floors. Warren & Wetmore employed a reserved Adam style throughout the interior, with the exception of the Tudor-style grillroom.

In 1919, as Warren & Wetmore began work on the Westchester and Providence Biltmores, Bowman purchased the Hotel Sevilla in Havana, Cuba, and commissioned the firm to perform a $500,000 renovation in time for the upcoming tourist season.[21] The fact that Havana's hotels were more overcrowded than New York's inspired Bowman to venture onto foreign terrain, and even before the renovated hotel opened, he was already considering building a larger one there. When Leonard Schultze left to form his own practice with S. Fullerton Weaver in 1921, Bowman and the Biltmore Corporation followed. Schultze & Weaver went on to design hotels for the expanding company in Los Angeles (1923), Atlanta (1924), and Coral Gables (1926), as well as the Sevilla Biltmore in Cuba.

At the same time, Warren & Wetmore was expanding its reach to Colorado and Puerto Rico. In 1916, Spencer Penrose, a transplanted Philadelphian made rich through mining investments, and his associate, C. M. MacNeill, commissioned the firm to design a large lux-ury hotel in Colorado Springs, Colorado. Originally, Penrose had hired Frederick J. Sterner,

4.37. *Broadmoor Hotel,*
Colorado Springs, Colorado.
Entrance facade. Denver Public
Library, Western History
Collection, L. C. McClure,
MCC-3532.

architect of the renowned Greenbrier in West Virginia and the Antlers in Colorado Springs;
however, Penrose disliked the elaborate classical scheme Sterner produced and turned to
Warren & Wetmore.

Upon its opening in 1918, Penrose's venture—the Broadmoor—quickly became a
favorite among New York society (fig. 4.37).[22] Its picturesque Italianate Renaissance design
consisted of four low-lying wings connected by covered passages that stepped up to a nine-
story building capped with a bell tower. The composition, thoroughly informed by the site,
was far more successful than the Westchester-Biltmore, completed four years later. Its cascading quality harmonized beautifully with the contours of the mountainous backdrop, and
the warm colors of the pink stucco facades, sepia details in sgraffito, and green tile roof
blended with the natural surroundings. The grounds included an eighteen-hole golf course,
landscape design by the Olmsted Brothers, and a scenic man-made lake to the rear with a
Japanese garden accessed by footbridge (fig. 4.38).

Inside, frescoes and polychromy created a dazzling effect. On the eastern facade, a
vaulted entrance loggia, painted blue with a spray of stars, led into a polychrome lobby
inspired by the Davanzati Palace, with ceiling beams painted with Italian Renaissance
revival ornament (fig. 4.39). From the ground floor, a curving stair ascended to the *piano*
nobile. Because the Broadmoor was built on a slope, the rear of the main floor sat level with

4.38 (following pages).
Broadmoor Hotel. View from
lake. Denver Public Library,
Western History Collection,
L. C. McClure, MCC-3607.

the lake. The palm court, decorated with murals in the Pompeian manner, stretched along the front of the building, and the arched roof of the enclosed rear terrace simulated latticework; in the central lounge and airy hall, Warren & Wetmore incorporated trompe l'oeil plaster work in relief on the ceilings (fig. 4.40).

Like the Broadmoor, Warren & Wetmore's Condado-Vanderbilt in San Juan, Puerto Rico, completed in 1919, exhibited Italian and Mediterranean overtones.[23] The hotel, marketed as "the finest resort hotel in the West Indies," reflected "the wholesome atmosphere of luxury and refinement that characterize[d] the Vanderbilt in New York." Owned and operated by the New York flagship, the Condado-Vanderbilt included all of the features its discerning guests might expect of a modern American hotel. Grounds included a golf course, tennis courts, and bathing beach, and the resort's ninety-eight guest rooms enjoyed views of the ocean or Condado Bay. The hotel's primary vaulted spaces, made bright and breezy by French doors and windows, opened onto a loggia that encircled the building and looked onto the water. The stark simplicity of the stucco facades and red tile roof created an impression of quiet and easy luxury well suited to the tropical surroundings.

Working nearer to New York, Warren & Wetmore also embarked on several hotel projects in Atlantic City, New Jersey, then a popular health and pleasure resort. Large wood-framed seaside hotels had formed the backbone of the city's colorful social life since the 1870s. When the city lifted the 300-foot development ban along the shoreline after the turn of the twentieth century, a new generation of hotels and additions was spurred. In 1919, *The New York Times* announced a $20-million building venture along the boardwalk in the city's Chelsea District, which included a new 600-room Ritz-Carlton and 450-room addition to the Hotel Ambassador located directly south of it.[24] Following in the spirit of the New York and Philadelphia Ritz-Carltons, the firm produced a fourteen-story red brick block for the Atlantic City branch (fig. 4.41). But, in this commission, Warren & Wetmore's Adam-style terra-cotta detailing appeared anemic, almost vestigial. Guests enjoyed views of the ocean from the broad arched windows of the main dining room, the shaded terrace, or the trellised tearoom, whose ceiling was brightly painted by John B. Smeraldi to suggest a garden with darting birds and blue skies. For bathers, a private elevator descended from the guest quarters to a basement corridor leading out to the beach.[25]

Warren & Wetmore's addition to the Hotel Ambassador more than doubled the size of Clinton & Russell's 1919 building on the boardwalk.[26] The new twelve-story building stretched away from the beach and was connected to the original hotel only at the first level. As in the firm's additions to the McAlpin and Plaza Hotels, Warren & Wetmore avoided attempts to distract from the importance of the original structure. However, whereas Warren & Wetmore's buff-colored brick facades for the Ambassador were simple and unadorned, its interiors, which included a saltwater swimming pool, grillroom, convention hall, ballroom, and four hundred and fifty guest rooms, unfolded in dramatic fashion. In the sunken orange and black grillroom, the firm painted the walls and columns with winged sphinxes, seahorses, shells, and cupids in shades of blue, green, and red, and included a dancing floor, set

4.39 (opposite top). Broadmoor Hotel. Lobby. Denver Public Library, Western History Collection, L. C. McClure, MCC-3887.

4.40 (opposite bottom). Broadmoor Hotel. Lounge. Denver Public Library, Western History Collection, L. C. McClure, MCC-3886.

4.41 (above). Ritz-Carlton, rendering, Atlantic City, New Jersey. Warren & Wetmore Collection, Avery Architectural and Fine Arts Library, Columbia University.

5 feet below the main floor level, that could be converted into a ice rink during the winter months. Further north on the boardwalk, in 1922, Warren & Wetmore added a nine-story wing to the Shelburne Hotel that included a ballroom and seaside dining room, and, four years later, a twelve-story tower.[27] Around the same time, the firm completed a fourteen-story tower for the St. Charles Hotel.

OFFICE BUILDINGS AND BANKS

Office building design represented a growing portion of Warren & Wetmore's practice. Generally, the firm's early office buildings tended to be blocky volumes with ornamentation and detail at the base and roofline. The firm's thirteen-story headquarters for the oil corporation, Texas Company (now known as Texaco), in Houston, Texas, illustrated an innovative twist on this compositional approach (fig. 4.42). While the design presented straightforward massing and regular window patterns, an arcade supported by pairs of Doric columns circumscribed the base of the building and contained vaulted arches intricately laid with Guastavino tile.[28]

New York provided fertile ground for office commissions as tall buildings continued to go up downtown and in the growing midtown business district. At Fifth Avenue and 37th Street, the firm completed two buildings that exhibited variations on the office block. For Robert W. Goelet, the firm designed a building at 402 Fifth Avenue on the southwest corner of 37th Street in 1914 that displayed a thoroughly novel approach to terra-cotta facades (fig. 4.43).[29] Slender blue and white terra-cotta panels and large windows lent the upper floors a lofty quality, and the intricacy and color of the terra-cotta patterning, carved in the shape of wreathes, urns, and flowers, created a light and decorative effect. Specialty stores, Stewart & Company and Mark Cross, moved to the fashionable address, taking up residence in the building's dark stone base. Diagonally across the street, at 411 Fifth Avenue on the northeast corner of 37th Street, Warren & Wetmore's store and loft building for the Murray Hill Investing Company, designed in 1915, presented one of its signature design approaches (fig. 4.44). Although carried out in light stucco and terra-cotta rather than brick, the building also included the more flamboyant and sculptural design features—an undulating cornice encrusted with scrolling garlands and figures of heads—that also distinguished the rooflines of the Vanderbilt Hotel and 340–50 Park Avenue.[30] The building's three-story base—an isolated use of a glass curtain wall—counterbalanced the heavy treatment of the upper floors.

Warren & Wetmore's Vanderbilt Concourse Building at 52 Vanderbilt Avenue (1915) and offices for the Equitable Trust Company at 347 Madison Avenue (1918) and Marlin Rockwell Corporation

4.42 (opposite). Texas Company Building, Houston, Texas. Arcade. Warren & Wetmore Collection, Avery Architectural and Fine Arts Library, Columbia University.

4.43. Robert Goelet Building, 402 Fifth Avenue, New York City. Warren & Wetmore Collection, Avery Architectural and Fine Arts Library, Columbia University.

(1920) at 366 Madison Avenue harmonized with the Grand Central group and complemented the restrained facades of the neighboring Biltmore and Ritz Hotels. However, their designs were less daring and evocative than the Goelet Building at 37th Street.[31] With its stark facades, blocky massing, and open light court, the exterior of the Equitable Trust Company Building verged on the mundane (fig. 4.45). The interiors recaptured some of the vigor and color that its exterior lacked: Warren & Wetmore grandly appointed the main barrel-vaulted lobby with marble, chandeliers, and overscaled carved detail. On nearby land owned by the Phipps Estate, the firearm and machinery manufacturer Marlin Rockwell Corporation built a stately brick office and store that the firm distinguished with a heavy bracketed cornice and granite and limestone base.

Downtown, the firm was also busy with designs for the Kerr Steamship Company at 38–46 Beaver Street (1919) and the Barrett Building Company at 40 Rector Street (1920). In 1920 Warren & Wetmore completed the limestone-faced eight-story All America Cables Building at 89 Broad Street (fig. 4.46). Distinguished by a green tile roof and attic-story bull's-eye windows set within arches, the design also creatively incorporated cartouches and crests on the facades, carved with the arms of the cities and countries of Central and South America that the company's cable system served.[32]

Many companies, however, felt that the Wall Street area was inconvenient for clients. In 1920 leading mortgage bank S. W. Straus and Company initiated a move uptown from its offices at 150 Broadway to the developing financial district near Grand Central. Bank president Straus noted that the new location at the northeast corner of 46th Street and Fifth Avenue—on the site of the old Windsor Hotel and subsequent Windsor Arcade—"was carefully selected with a view to the greater convenience for those we serve. It is convenient of access, readily reached by rail or bus lines, subways, elevated or surface lines."[33] Like recent branches established in the area by the Guaranty Trust Company (Cross & Cross, 1920) and

4.46 (above left). All America
Cables Building, 89 Broad
Street, New York City. The
Architectural Review 11 (October
1920): 109.

4.47 (above right). S. W. Straus
and Company Building, rendering, 565 Fifth Avenue, New York
City. Warren & Wetmore
Collection, Avery Architectural
and Fine Arts Library, Columbia
University.

the Astor Trust Company (Montague Flagg, 1917), Warren & Wetmore's distinctive eleven-
story building for S. W. Straus and Company glorified the banking establishment (fig. 4.47).
On the limestone exterior, the firm achieved the aura of monumentality through ample scale
rather than ornate decorative treatment. Four colossal Corinthian columns at the banking
entrance and a great arched window above the door dominated the Fifth Avenue facade. Bas-
relief panels by Italian sculptor Leo Lentelli (1879–1962) representing the banking and building trades accentuated the proportions of the bays on the base of the building.[34] From a broad
set of stairs, clients entered a lofty banking hall 14 feet above the street level. Inspired by the
basilica of S. Spirito in Ravenna, Italy, it was a typically sculpted space with an arched cof-
fered ceiling and vaulted side aisles (figs. 4.48, 4.49).[35]

In 1920 Warren & Wetmore also embarked on a project at the southwest corner of 57th
Street and Fifth Avenue with a syndicate that included property owner August Heckscher,
builder George Backer, and Charles D. Wetmore. Heckscher (1848–1941), a German immi-
grant, built a fortune around Lehigh Zinc & Iron Company and later became a leading New
York real estate investor. By 1923 Heckscher's Anahma Corporation owned and controlled a
large portion of realty in the Grand Central zone, including the Vanderbilt Concourse
Building, where Heckscher kept offices and a penthouse apartment, the adjoining Equitable
Trust Company Building, the Marlin Rockwell Building, the Grand Central Palace, and
Warren & Wetmore's newly completed Park-Lexington Building at 245 Park Avenue.
Heckscher was also responsible for developing 277 Park Avenue, McKim, Mead & White's
luxurious courtyard apartment house. At 57th Street, the Heckscher Building was located
well above the midtown district.[36] As the northernmost office building at the time, its pres-

ence in the middle of the prestigious residential neighborhood—home to the Vanderbilts and Whitneys—served as an anchor for the expanding Fifth Avenue business section.[37]

One of the first important office and retail buildings constructed under the new 1916 zoning regulations, Heckscher's pioneering multiple-use structure also represented an emerging type (fig. 4.51). By 1920 the lull in building activity experienced during the war had subsided and the economy had recovered. Only when construction resumed were the height and setback controls, established to protect light and air, manifested in built form. The composition of the Heckscher Building, consisting of a series of blocky setbacks capped by an elaborate picturesque tower, followed the prescribed parameters. Originally, the design encompassed a thirty-two-story building that connected to an eight-story wing opening onto 56th Street, which contained a theater and concert hall. However, as the design evolved, the program was reduced. The theater program was abandoned, and the heights of the two buildings were lowered to twenty-five and six floors, respectively. The final scheme exhibited Warren's mastery of the setback tower: a ten-story base, constructed to the limit of 125 feet, set back to a twenty-story tower. Additional setbacks above the tenth, fourteenth, and twenty-second floors culminated in a richly decorated octagonal tower with a steep pyramidal roof, bull's-eye dormers, and a 10-foot rooster weathervane.[38] On the ground floor, the building contained a string of shops with bronze-framed windows set along a black and gold marble arcade running from 56th to 57th Street. Large showrooms occupied the nine-story limestone-clad base, and the tower stories, faced in buff-colored brick and terra cotta, contained office space.

Warren & Wetmore's French Renaissance detailing defined the facades. Verde copper spandrel panels, embossed in relief, created strong vertical lines that balanced the flat setbacks, which were accentuated by textured terra cotta banding unevenly realized on the

4.48 (below left). S. W. Straus and Company. Side aisle. Architecture 44 (August 1921): pl. 118.

4.49 (below right). S. W. Straus and Company. Banking hall. Architecture 44 (August 1921): pl. 118.

building's windowless backside (fig. 4.50). A diaper-patterned terra-cotta chimney rose against the southwest corner of the building. As seen in his early sketches from his grand tour, Warren was drawn to towers as monuments of beauty. The Heckscher Building clearly reflected that fascination.

When the building opened in 1921, its spaces quickly filled with upscale jewelers and art dealers; in 1929 the newly founded Museum of Modern Art began renting space for loan exhibitions on the twelfth floor. The critics also approved of the building. *Architecture and Building* enthusiastically noted that "the architectural results of the New York Zoning Regulations are magnificent" and went on to describe the Heckscher Building as a "glorified chateau."[39] However, George Harold Edgell, dean of Harvard's School of Architecture, observed that the horizontality of the building was overemphasized, and the distinct masses of the design were not successfully bound.[40] For Warren & Wetmore, the zoning regulations created a new set of challenges in the solution to the skyscraper, which only reinforced the firm's penchant for architecturally distinct rooflines. As Warren & Wetmore's reputation as hotel and apartment architects crystallized, its proficiency in the sphere of office and commercial design developed significantly. The Heckscher Building was the first of many spectacular solutions following the setback controls to come out of the firm.

CHAPTER FIVE

Late Projects: 1922–1931

The final decade of Warren and Wetmore's practice produced a number of distinct and memorable projects. In 1919 Warren returned from his wartime stint in Paris, but he continued to move between New York and Paris for the better part of the decade. What he described as his most important commission—the reconstruction of the university library in Louvain, Belgium—occupied much of his time and focus.

At home, the firm continued to design luxurious apartment houses, city hotels, and resorts throughout the country. Increasingly, however, Warren & Wetmore's practice was dedicated to office buildings and towers. As the firm developed its understanding of this building type, its style evolved and produced, in its later years, a number of buildings that contributed a distinct sense of beauty and monumentality to New York's expanding skyline. The firm's final design—the heroic New York Central Building at 230 Park Avenue—represented the pinnacle of its achievement as office designers as well as the culmination of Warren & Wetmore's long association with the New York Central Railroad. The firm's final country estate project, commissioned by William K. Vanderbilt Jr., the railroad company's president, in Centerport, Long Island, epitomized the firm's fanciful and scenographic approach in its mature form.

OFFICE BUILDINGS AND STORES

Building on its pioneering design of the Heckscher Building, Warren & Wetmore went on to create some of its most compelling schemes for setback office buildings and towers. Its next significant effort, the Tower Building—a twenty-five-story combination office and apartment house at 200 Madison Avenue—took shape as a boxy pedestal and tower (fig. 5.1).[1] Stretching 194 feet along the west side of Madison Avenue, the building extended back 196 feet on 35th Street and 220 feet on 36th Street to form an essentially square footprint. Its nine-story base contained shops and a Marshall Field showroom at street level and apartments on the upper floors that faced onto the avenue and extended 40 feet back into the depth of the building. As primarily an office building, Warren & Wetmore dedicated the remaining floor area in the western portion of the base and the tower to office space. Above the ninth floor, the building mass abruptly set back to a blocky office tower that was crowned with an illuminated lantern. Again, Warren & Wetmore countered the strong horizontal character of the design by emphasizing its verticality with black glazed terra-cotta spandrel panels under the windows. Nonetheless, the modern French red brick and limestone facades lacked the energy and detail that distinguished the Heckscher Building.

5.1. Tower Building, 200
Madison Avenue, New York
City. Rendering by N. Vasselieff.
Museum of the City of New York,
Wurts Collection, #809156.

5.2. Tower Building. Lobby.
Architecture and Building 58
(July 1926): pl. 139.

Upon its completion in 1926, *Architecture and Building* proclaimed the Tower Building the sixth largest office structure in the country. Located across from the Morgan family compound, its construction embodied the sort of commercial infringement the Morgan family had tried so intensely to deter for decades. When the 200 Madison Corporation purchased the site from William Waldorf Astor's estate for the high-rise's construction, the well-known feud between the two established Manhattan families concluded and the quiet character of the exclusive Murray Hill residential district was upended by the tide of commercial development. In keeping with the area's zoning, Warren & Wetmore situated the Tower Building's residential section on Madison Avenue, with a separate lobby, and located the office entrances on the flanking side streets. What the exterior lacked in exuberance was recovered in the broad corridor and lobby that ran through the building. A multicolored terrazzo marble floor, walls in shades of yellow and red marble, and richly ornamented ceiling with gold detail, coffers, and medallions in relief created a rich and stunning prelude to the office section (fig. 5.2).

As at the Tower Building, the architects incorporated spandrel panels into its design of the nearby Madison-Belmont Building at the southeast corner of Madison Avenue and 34th Street. Robert M. Catts, of the Merchants and Manufacturers Exchange, erected the seventeen-story office and loft building in 1925 after commissioning the firm to design the Grand Central Palace (1911) and the connecting Park-Lexington Building, (1923) where he kept a penthouse apartment.[2] Aside from the spandrels, the upper floors of the L-shaped structure, extending to 33rd Street, were conventional. However, the bottom levels of the building, which contained Cheney Silk Company's showrooms, featured one of New York's earliest examples of art deco—stylized French metalwork by established French *ferronnier* Edgar Brandt.[3]

By the mid-1920s, Warren & Wetmore's tower designs were becoming increasingly sophisticated. In 1924 W. L. Hopkins, of the firm, planned the exteriors and interiors of Steinway Hall for esteemed piano makers Steinway & Sons at 109–113 West 57th Street (fig. 5.3). Founded by Heinrich Engelhard Steinweg in 1853, the historic company had resided near the Academy of Music on East 14th Street since 1864. However, with the opening of Carnegie Hall in 1891, 57th Street was reborn as a cultural center that attracted related musical enterprises. The headquarters of the American Piano Company moved to Cross & Cross's Chickering Hall at 29 West 57th Street in 1924, and elegant shops, art dealers such as Joseph Duveen and M. Knoedler, and the American Fine Arts Society Building drew the cultured elite into the area. By 1923 Steinway & Sons, then operated by second- and third-generation Steinways, assembled eight lots on 57th and 58th Streets for new showrooms and speculative offices.[4]

Warren & Wetmore's through-block building, completed in 1925, was a thin L-shaped structure with 63 feet fronting 57th Street and 100 feet on 58th Street. Although the austere design verged on the severe, its classical proportions, exquisitely carved stonework, picturesque roofline, and highly decorative interiors showed the best of Warren & Wetmore's artistic approach toward architecture. The architects broke the primary limestone-clad facade on 57th Street into a three-story base demarcated by a frieze of laurel festoons with portrait medallions of the great composers and a nine-story office block with regular window patterns. At street level, they balanced the composition with entrances on either side of

5.3 (opposite). Steinway Hall, 109–113 West 57th Street, New York City. Warren & Wetmore Collection, Avery Architectural and Fine Arts Library, Columbia University.

5.4. Steinway Hall. Detail of base. Architectural Record 58 (September 1925): 208.

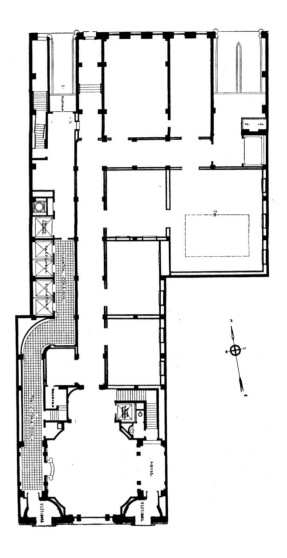

5.5 (above left). Steinway Hall. Detail of upper floors. Warren & Wetmore Collection, Avery Architectural and Fine Arts Library, Columbia University.

5.6 (above right). Steinway Hall. Entrance floor plan. *Architectural Record* 58 (September 1925): 208.

the smooth limestone expanse and placed at center a large display window embellished by Ionic columns (fig. 5.4). Set within a lunette over the window was Leo Lentelli's sculpture of Apollo receiving the crown of musical triumph from the Muse. At the twelfth floor, a balustrade and pairs of giant urns articulated the setback to a copper-roofed four-story pavilion, and a pyramidal roof and lantern capped the square one-story tower that cleverly disguised tanks and mechanical systems (fig. 5.5).

Inside the building, Warren & Wetmore designed some of its most sumptuous and important public spaces. A separate street entrance to the east led to Steinway & Son's showrooms and 250-seat concert hall on the first three levels. A double-height octagonal reception room at the front of the building formed the entry point to a sequence of showrooms extending back toward 58th Street (fig. 5.6). Brescia Verde Ionic columns supported a soaring dome painted in soft colors with panels by Paul Arndt in the manner of Pergolzi and Angelica Kaufmann and murals by Cooper & Gentiluomo (fig. 5.7). Tinos Green marble pilasters and trim, crystal chandeliers, ironwork in the shape of lyres, replicas of furniture from the British Museum, and oil portraits of composers Mendelssohn, Berlioz, and Schubert created an atmosphere of rich and intimate luxury. From the reception room, described by *Architecture and Building* as "an architectural and decorative inspiration," the architects aligned a broad barrel-vaulted corridor on axis with the reception room's singular display window.[5] Extending the length of the building, it opened onto a number of wood-paneled and sky-lit showrooms that were furnished with antiques and Steinway pianos (fig. 5.8). An interior elevator ascended to additional showrooms on the mezzanine level, a windowless concert hall decorated to evoke a private living room on the second story, and the company's executive

5.7. *Steinway Hall. Reception room. Architectural Record* 58 (September 1925): 208.

5.8. *Steinway Hall. Showroom.* Warren & Wetmore Collection, Avery Architectural and Fine Arts Library, Columbia University.

5.9. *Aeolian Building, 689 Fifth Avenue, New York City.* Museum of the City of New York, Wurts Collection, #807557.

offices on the third floor. On 57th Street, an entrance to the west led to a glass-walled lobby that looked onto Steinway's extravagant hall, with elevators to the offices and musical studios on the upper floors.

As work on Steinway Hall drew to a close, construction of the firm's Aeolian Building on the northeast corner of Fifth Avenue and 54th Street began (fig. 5.9).[6] The Aeolian Company, founded by William B. Tremaine in 1887, was the era's leading manufacturer of roll-operated instruments. At the turn of the twentieth century, self-playing organs and pianos became enormously popular among the wealthy. The company grew substantially during this period and in 1912 commissioned Warren & Wetmore to design its fourth headquarters at 33 West 42nd Street on a site overlooking Bryant Park. Set on the periphery of the Grand Central zone, the sixteen-story through-block structure presented austere French Renaissance–inspired facades enlivened by Gertrude Vanderbilt Whitney and Sylvain Salières's bronze busts. The building's large concert hall, where Paul Whiteman conducted the world premiere of George Gershwin's *Rhapsody in Blue* on February 12, 1924, stood for many years as a major musical venue, hosting performances by Igor Stravinsky, Ferruccio Busoni, and Sergei Rachmaninoff.[7] However, by 1925, the cultural center at 57th Street had eclipsed the 42nd Street area, prompting the Aeolian Company to move north.

In early 1925 the Gould Realty Corporation purchased the site of William G. Rockefeller's brownstone mansion at 689 Fifth Avenue, on the northeast corner of 54th Street, and one month later the Aeolian Company signed a lease to occupy the projected building. Commodore Charles Albert Gould (1849–1926), director of Gould Realty, was a prominent New York real estate investor who had built a fortune from steel and iron manufacturing. He commissioned Warren & Wetmore, Aeolian's former architects, to design a luxurious fourteen-story limestone-clad building for the site with showrooms, offices, and small recital hall. Warren's graceful design presented the architect's most fluid and sophisticated interpretation of the zoning regulations. In carrying out the building, Warren & Wetmore avoided the use of hard edges and lines to create an original and artistic commercial structure. A pink granite base inset with Italian marble panels and detailed with gilded garlands created a strong horizontal balance to the sculptural discourse of the upper floors, and the firm's distinctive rounded windows on the first through ninth floors softened the corner of the building (fig. 5.10). Above the ninth floor, Warren articulated the setbacks as a cascade of sculptural, almost baroque, curves and forms. Large terra-cotta urns marking the corners of the building, concave walls, chamfered corners, windows set within arches, and carved garlands gave rise to a supple and distinct roofline. As at the Steinway Building, a two-story penthouse tower, with its distinct copper pyramidal roof and lantern, housed the mechanical systems. Six floors of showrooms were executed in a medley of architectural styles, ranging from Spanish to French to early American. From the street-level showroom with its marble floors, Jaspe Oriental marble pilasters, and a mural interpretation of Beethoven's Ninth Symphony, elevators led to a small wood-paneled recital hall on the second floor and recording studios and offices above.[8]

For Warren, the building represented an oasis in the city's skyscraping culture. During the building's dedication in February 1927, he announced that Warren & Wetmore's inspiration for the design "lay everywhere, difficult to fix." Regarding his design goals, Warren stated: "Ancient traditions of pure melody clash along the avenue with the modern dissonance of jazz: the towering aggressive structures of industry and commerce are like the clarion calls of architecture, all about us. . . . Man is not always strident, the soul is not always

5.10. Aeolian Building.
Base. The Architect 8
(June 1927): 337.

5.11. Consolidated Gas
Company Tower, 14th Street
and Irving Place, New York City.
Museum of the City of New York,
Wurts Collection, #809295.

5.12 (opposite). Consolidated
Gas Company Tower. Museum of
the City of New York, Wurts
Collection, #809296.

in haste, the eye does not always seek the restless gesture of the skyscraper never attaining its sky—a little rest, a little peace, a simplicity complete, a dream realized. . . . I hope that the Aeolian Building conveys something of this. . . . "[9] Michael Friedsam, the president of the Fifth Avenue Association, awarded Gould Realty its gold medal for Warren & Wetmore's architectural contribution, declaring that "this splendid building is a Fifth Avenue-New York message to the country. Such beautiful structures as this insure to our common country the commercial leadership of the world."[10]

In 1926 Warren & Wetmore began work on a twenty-six-story office tower for the Consolidated Gas Company in collaboration with engineer and designer Thomas E. Murray.[11] By this time, the gas company had established its headquarters near Union Square and was operating out of two buildings on the east side of Irving Place.[12] Warren & Wetmore's plans for the northeast corner of Irving Place and 14th Street more than doubled the size of the company's holdings. The extent to which the downtown music sector had fallen out of favor was compounded by the fact that the new tower replaced the venerable Academy of Music.

With the completion of Consolidated Gas's limestone tower in 1928, yet another distinct beacon marked New York's expanding skyline (fig. 5.11). As with its Heckscher, Steinway, and Aeolian designs, Warren & Wetmore applied bold and dramatic strategies to exploring the tall building. Consolidated Gas's monumental rooftop features encompassed much of the design but did not contain any rentable space. The square tower stepped seamlessly into a heavy limestone pedestal, with large clocks on each of the four faces and colos-

sal urns at the corners (fig. 5.12). Crowning the pedestal was a pavilion embellished with Ionic colonnades, a pyramidal roof, and a 38-foot-tall solid bronze lantern at its pinnacle. Creative lighting became an important design feature: At the top of the lantern, a strong searchlight beamed light upward, and horizontal beams marked the points of the compass. *The New Yorker*'s "T-Square" remarked that the edifice "set back ingeniously to the splendid lantern," and *The Architect* emphatically declared the tower a "building of unusual merit and distinction. . . . It is in fact a memorial, a Tower of Light."[13] Noteworthy interiors included the main corridor, which was wainscoted in rare Old Convent Siena marble. According to *The Architect*, "[its] vaulted ceiling [was] decorated with a flame motive which Whitney Warren [had] noted in his sketch book in his earliest student days during his wanderings in the old churches of Italy" (fig. 5.13).[14]

As architects and builders developed ways to exploit the economic viability of their sites under the new zoning, a new interpretation of the office tower emerged. Soaring rectangular slabs with sharp, shallow setbacks, such as Sloan & Robertson's Chanin Building (1926–29) and H. Douglas Ives and John Sloan's Fred F. French Building (1927), added to the striking verticality of New York's skyline. However, as modernist sensibilities took hold, architects reduced the depth of the elements on these new towers and buildings and eschewed ornament and sculpture. Warren & Wetmore's thirty-three-story Empire Trust and Knabe Building (1928) at the northwest corner of 47th Street and Fifth Avenue reflected this

5.13. Consolidated Gas Company Tower. Street front. Museum of the City of New York, Wurts Collection, #809293.

5.14. New York Central Building, 230 Park Avenue, New York City. View south from 49th Street, c. 1930. Museum of the City of New York, Wurts Collection #808981.

new approach. Collaborating with developer Max J. Kramer, the firm produced a narrow tower of light brick with gradually receding, boxy setbacks and little relief. Although the sharp, stylized details and gargoyles reinforced the design's crisp, sharp rise, they seemed uninspired compared to the sculptural ornament that had defined previous projects. Warren & Wetmore's tower connected through the lobby to the neighboring Brentano's Building (Cross & Cross, 1925) and housed a Tudor banking hall for the Empire Trust Company on the second and third floors of the building, elaborate classical showrooms for the Knabe Piano Company on Fifth Avenue, and ample office space on the upper floors.[15]

The magnificent New York Central Building at 230 Park Avenue (now known as the Helmsley Building) culminated Warren & Wetmore's involvement in the design of Terminal City and was the firm's last major project in New York (fig. 5.14).[16] In fact, it would be one of the final great commissions enjoyed by any architectural firm in New York before the depression's onset. In September 1927 Warren & Wetmore completed plans for the dramatic Beaux-Arts edifice at the base of Park Avenue directly north of the terminal. A product of

5.15. *Photostat of an architectural rendering showing traffic flow at the intersection of Park Avenue and East 46th Street, around the northern end of Grand Central Station, from proposal album prepared by Warren & Wetmore, after 1926. 9 ¹³/₁₆ x 13 ¹/₈ in. (241 x 332 mm).* Cooper-Hewitt, National Design Museum, Smithsonian Institution. Gift of Cooper Union Museum Picture Library, 1959-39-1 (5). Photo: Matt Flynn.

5.16. *Photostat of a rendering by Chesley Bonestell of the northern facade of the New York Central Railroad Office Building from proposal album prepared by Warren & Wetmore, after 1926. 12 ¹⁵/₁₆ x 9 ¹¹/₁₆ in. (329 x 246 mm).* Cooper-Hewitt, National Design Museum, Smithsonian Institution. Gift of Cooper Union Museum Picture Library, 1959-39-1 (2). Photo: Matt Flynn.

5.17. New York Central Building. Edward McCartan's clock ensemble, 2005. Photo: Jonathan Wallen.

negotiation and collaboration between the city and the railroad, the building had been in development since 1919, when the Park Avenue viaduct had opened.[17] As tunnels allowed for north–south vehicular traffic to pass continuously through its base, the thirty-five-story campanile-like structure formed a critical link between the upper and lower sections of Park Avenue. When completed in 1929, the existing raised roadways on Depew Place and on the western side of the terminal streamed together at the rear of the building and passed on viaducts over 45th Street (fig. 5.15). They then funneled through the base of the New York Central Building and emptied on Park Avenue, the road beds of which were widened at that time to accommodate the increased flow of traffic.[18]

Like the hotels and offices surrounding the terminal, the immense building supported by steel columns over Grand Central's complicated double track system was a remarkable engineering achievement. The fifteen-story base stretched from Depew Place to Vanderbilt Avenue and from 45th to 46th Street and presented a central tower with gently curved wings to upper Park Avenue. The soaring tower ascended above the three-story base an additional nineteen floors and set back to an elaborate copper pyramidal roof and spire. Detailed with antique green and gold finish, the roof was punctuated with three levels of progressively smaller bull's-eye dormers and was capped by a giant lantern originally fitted with a 6,000-watt bulb (fig. 5.16). Framed by the line of buildings on either side of the Park Avenue, it stood as the crowning achievement of the railroad's development plan and as a glorified symbol of the company's empire.

Sculptural ornament was integral to Warren & Wetmore's architectural scheme. Above the two arched tunnels, the three-story limestone and pink granite base supported Edward McCartan's heroic clock ensemble featuring symbolic figures of Transportation and Industry (fig. 5.17). Critic Royal Cortissoz marveled at McCartan's contribution, calling it "one of the most conspicuous sculptural decorations ever erected in the city."[19] Warren judiciously applied terra-cotta detail to balance the strong lines created by the windows and spandrels. At the fifteenth-floor setback, seventy-eight terra-cotta bison heads—alluding to the railroad's western expansion—festooned the cornice and details symbolic of research, discovery, and engineering hung between the upper window bays.[20] Like the profile of Ernest Flagg's bold design for the Singer Building (1908), the upper floors of the building bowed outward. A three-story Ionic colonnade deepened the sculptural quality of the facades and reinforced the building's presence from afar.

5.18. New York Central Building. Lobby. Through the Ages 8 (May 1930) 23.

The New York Central's lobby reflected Warren & Wetmore's propensity for rich color and material (fig. 5.18). Located between the two vehicular ramps, the narrow lobby stretched through the block between 45th and 46th Streets and was flanked by the viaducts and through-block arcades that created continuous sidewalks. Inside, tall travertine walls, accented with Rouge Jaspe Oriental marble wainscoting and Elmer Garnsey's chandeliers, created a bold and elegant setting.[21] Barrel-vaulted alcoves that extended off the central passage led to elevators with vermilion doors set beneath stylized cast-iron New York Central logos. Even the elevator cabs were given a full decorative program of red walls, gilded wood moldings, and domed ceilings painted with impressionistic clouds. *The New Yorker's* "T-Square" defended the relative grandeur of the hall: "True, it is lavish and opulent, but it is done with the grand air of Louis XIV, the deity of Warren & Wetmore. It is bold, colorful, and masculine." However, he was less enthusiastic about the marble trimmings: "the sanguinary marble trim of this *salle de parade* is not pretty. It is the red meat of a vigorous period when kings were kings and architects were princes."[22] As the offices of the kings of empire, the company's executive space was also carried out in a range of rich marbles: Tinos, travertine, Porta Santa, and Verde Campan Melange.

In a period when the modern movement and its Beaux-Arts counterpart—stripped classicism—were gaining ground, to some critics, the New York Central Building represented a step backward. Lewis Mumford wrote, "between 1924 and 1928, it seemed that American architecture had at last emerged from its feeble romantic, pseudo-historic posturing. . . . The past year, alas! has been marked by a series of retreats, or one had better say atavisms: most of the new buildings that have been put up around Grand Central Station have followed the lamentable example of the New York Central Building; they belong to the period of design dated by the Singer Building and the Woolworth Tower and are distinguished only by their essential mediocrity. . . . "[23] Architect Harry T. Cunningham, writing for *The American Yearbook*, agreed, describing the project—while designed "in the best 'Pompier' manner of some twenty years ago"—as "one of the greatest steps in the present backwards tendency shown in American Architecture."[24]

However, as the linchpin of the city's greatest urban scheme to date, Warren & Wetmore's final addition gave a monumental and awe-inspiring quality to the Park Avenue corridor (fig. 5.19). One New Yorker noted: "This afternoon I crossed Park Avenue at Fiftieth Street and, looking down toward the colossal building now going up at the Grand Central, I was suddenly arrested by the realization that its effect has been to turn Park Avenue into the nave of a mighty cathedral. . . . Here, then, is another of the many instances of sudden beauty in this amazing city. One would hardly expect to have one's thoughts stimulated in the direction of the Cologne Cathedral while crossing Park Avenue. But such was my experience. New York grows and grows: and she grows in startling and unexpected beauty."[25]

5.19. New York Central Building. View from 50th Street and Park Avenue. William Wilgus Papers, Manuscripts and Archives Division, The New York Public Library, Astor, Lenox and Tilden Foundations.

5.20. *Stewart and Company,*
721 Fifth Avenue, New York
City. Museum of the City of New
York, Wurts Collection, #809310.

5.21 (opposite). *Stewart and*
Company. Entrance detail.
Museum of the City of New York,
Wurts Collection, #809311.

In contrast to the New York Central Building, the firm's design for the Stewart and Company Building at 721 Fifth Avenue, also completed in 1929, presented stark, unadorned limestone facades (fig. 5.20).[26] While stripped classicism more accurately reflected the prevailing taste of the late 1920s and 1930s, Warren & Wetmore's adoption of the modern style, bereft of their signature sculpture and overscaled architectural details, was both progressive and uncharacteristic of the firm. In the late 1920s, the repercussions of the 1925 Exposition des Arts Décoratif et Industriels Modernes, held in Paris, were only beginning to be felt in this country; however, an architecture defined by minimalist vocabulary, albeit classically proportioned, was the antithesis of what Warren strove for in his art. Nonetheless, the building was a success. *Architecture and Building* proclaimed it "a splendid example of modern architecture in design," while *The New Yorker's* "T-Square" called the building "a notable achievement."[27]

The fashionable women's specialty store, Stewart and Company, had established shops in the base of Warren & Wetmore's Goelet Building at Fifth Avenue and 37th Street in 1914. However, like most of its competitors, the company felt the pull of the uptown shopping district. In 1928 Stewart and Company purchased property at the northeast corner of 56th Street and Fifth Avenue, occupied by a row of French Renaissance–style mansions designed by Clinton & Russell originally commissioned by William Waldorf Astor in 1895 to generate income. Julian Holland, Warren & Wetmore's supervising architect, produced a design of crisp massing, taut, undecorated surfaces, and stout proportions that gave rise to what critic R. W. Sexton described as "a particularly successful example of store architecture."[28] The entrance—the focal point of the twelve-story building—burst forth in a dash of color. Norwegian sculptor Trygve Hammer's golden yellow faience panels above the Pompeian green doors and elaborate cast-aluminum ornament of female figures—backlit at night—attracted patrons at the street level, and René Chambellan's elegant bas-relief panels of draped women between the eighth and ninth floors suggested elements of a classical frieze (fig. 5.21).[29]

Stewart and Company's move was ill timed: Thirteen days after the store's opening on October 16, 1929, the stock market crashed. Just months later, the more established and financially stable Bonwit Teller department store leased the building and Ely Jacques Kahn was commissioned to renovate Warren & Wetmore's design, which months earlier had been acclaimed "the finest achievement in industrial art in the world."[30] Warren & Wetmore's interiors had been divided into individually decorated shops. Rare woods, ornamental glass, and stylized nickel-silver grilles and details by artisans Eugene Schoen, Jacques Carlu, and J. Franklin Whitman Jr. created a dynamic backdrop to the *vendeuse* system of selling employed within the store.[31] However, Kahn and his associate James B. Newman felt that "the merchandise was necessarily relegated to the background, leaving the patroness the center of attraction in a dramatic setting," and opted for simpler interiors deemed more "proper in the modern department store."[32] Warren & Wetmore's colorful faience entry, metalwork, and grilles were replaced by a restrained facade design by Kahn.

APARTMENTS

Fifth Avenue is pre-eminently the historic residential thoroughfare of America. Its palatial mansions have set architectural fashions in fine homes. As the cooperative apartment takes the place of the townhouse in large cities, upper Fifth Avenue will continue to be a favored spot for this type of housing. The increased height permitted under the new law, and the terraces resulting from set-backs, open the way for distinctive expressions of the architectural art such as were represented in another field by the fine Fifth Avenue mansions now so rapidly being replaced.

— ANTHONY PATERNO, *The New York Times*

In the mid-1920s, Fifth Avenue experienced a transforming second wave of construction when the 150-foot height limit, set by the 1916 zoning regulations, and recovering economy facilitated a sweeping redevelopment of the Fifth Avenue corridor.[33] As speculative builders began to control the cooperative construction market, mansions built during the 1890s and 1900s were taken down and replaced by stately apartment buildings. While Warren & Wetmore designed one apartment building individually on Fifth Avenue under the new zoning, it worked in association with the emergent apartment specialist Rosario Candela in creating some of the grandest and more prestigious buildings on the avenue.

In 1925 Michael Paterno commissioned Warren & Wetmore to design an elegant and exclusive cooperative at 1020 Fifth Avenue, at the northeast corner of 83rd Street (fig. 5.22). While Paterno's apartment house presented sedate limestone facades distinguished by a three-story rusticated base and cornice balustrade, in section it had a sophisticated floor configuration. Apartments and maisonettes on the lower floors had common ceiling heights, but the fourteen-room suites on the fifth, eighth, and eleventh floors contained giant salons with eighteen-foot ceilings and double-height windows (fig. 5.23). Because the soaring height of the salons reduced the size of the intermediary apartments, the seventh- and tenth-floor apartments contained step-down living rooms with thirteen-foot ceilings, and the apartments on the sixth, ninth, and twelfth stories had ten-foot ceilings throughout, less the floor area of the salon space. Warren & Wetmore had explored interlocking spaces and volumes in its design of 280–90 Park Avenue, where Warren kept his apartment, and the concept was expanded at 1020 Fifth Avenue. All apartments enjoyed a "distinct individuality," "big, open fireplaces, large sunshiny sleeping chambers and plenty of servants' rooms."[34]

Beginning in 1926, Warren & Wetmore embarked on several projects in association with Rosario Candela. Candela (1890–1953), son of a plasterer, had emigrated from Palermo, Sicily, in 1909 and attended Columbia's School of Architecture. After stints working for Gaetano Ajello, an architect specializing in apartment houses, and Frederick Sterner (architect of the Greenbrier in White Sulphur Springs, West Virginia, and the Antlers in Colorado

5.22. *1020 Fifth Avenue,
New York City.* Museum of the
City of New York, Wurts Collection,
#807237.

5.23. *1020 Fifth Avenue. Plan.*
*Pease & Elliman's Catalogue of East
Side New York Apartment Plans.*

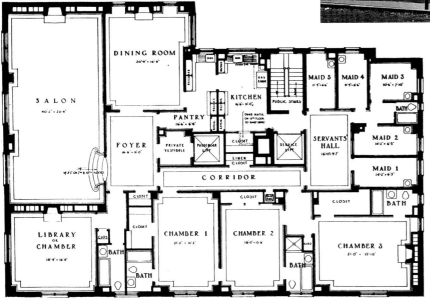

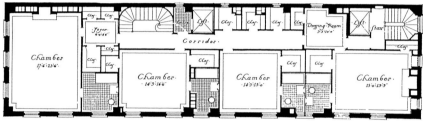

5.24 (above left). 990 Fifth
Avenue, New York City. Museum
of the City of New York, Wurts
Collection, #808316.

5.25 (above right). 990 Fifth
Avenue. Plan. Pease & Elliman's
Catalogue of East Side New York
Apartment Plans.

Springs, Colorado), Candela struck out on his own in 1920. During his early years of prac-
tice, he designed a number of middle-class apartment houses on West End Avenue and
Riverside Drive, many of which were developed by fellow Italians—mainly the Paterno and
Campagna families. With designs for the upscale One Sutton Place South (1925) and 775 Park
Avenue (1926), Candela made his foray into the east side of Manhattan.

In 1926 Warren & Wetmore and Candela began work on 990 Fifth Avenue, a refined thirteen-story limestone palazzo on the northeast corner of 80th Street (fig. 5.24). Built on land
previously occupied by C. P. H. Gilbert's 1901 house for Frank W. Woolworth, 990 Fifth
Avenue contained only six apartments: five duplexes of thirteen rooms and a penthouse
triplex. Living rooms with 11-foot ceilings and master bedrooms stacked above spanned the
27-foot width of the slender building (fig. 5.25).[35] Construction on Michael Paterno's 856
Fifth Avenue on the southeast corner of 67th Street began in 1927 (fig. 5.26).[36] By 1926, land
on Fifth Avenue had become too valuable for private homes. Judge Elbert H. Gary, chairman
of the U. S. Steel Corporation, reluctantly leased the site of his Italian Renaissance mansion
(1910), also by C. P. H. Gilbert, and the adjacent site to the south, to Paterno for the construction of another luxurious apartment house. Paterno brought Shreve & Lamb to the project as supervising architects.[37] Warren & Wetmore and Candela's limestone-clad building,
completed in 1928, contained nine fourteen-room apartments, two duplex maisonettes with
private street entrances, and a grand duplex penthouse with a terrace and solarium. Like 990
Fifth Avenue, the design—within and without—was the epitome of restraint and elegance.

The collaboration of Warren & Wetmore and Candela culminated in the design of 960 Fifth Avenue at the northeast corner of 77th Street (fig. 5.27).[38] The building—one of the city's grandest apartment houses—stood on the site of one of the Gilded Age's most expensive and ostentatious private homes. In 1907 Senator William Clark of Montana, a copper magnate, built an immense and exceedingly ornate baroque mansion, designed by Lord, Hewlett & Hull and Henri Deglane. After Clark's death in 1925, the property stood vacant for several years; despite its desirable location, potential builders were intimidated by the tremendous prospect of dismantling the structure. Eventually, developer Anthony Campagna purchased the property and enlisted Warren & Wetmore and Candela, with Cross & Cross as supervising architects, to design a "worthy successor to the townhouse."[39]

The team produced a large and stately limestone building broken into two distinct sections: 960 Fifth Avenue and 3 East 77th Street. The front portion of the building contained fourteen spacious, cooperative apartments, and the 77th Street side housed fifty-two smaller rental suites with stepped terraces, in accordance with zoning. At 960 Fifth Avenue, the architects further developed the concept of interlocking volumes and alternating ceiling heights that Warren & Wetmore had explored earlier at 1020 Fifth Avenue. With the exception of three apartments, none of the layouts followed the same plan. Ceiling heights alternated throughout and duplex apartments commingled with simplexes in a complex spatial arrangement that changed from floor to floor (fig. 5.28). Behind the three central arched windows on the tenth floor was Dr. Preston Pope Satterwhite's unusually large double-height

5.27. 960 Fifth Avenue, New York City. Museum of the City of New York, Gottscho-Schleisner Collection, #88.1.1.644.

5.28. 960 Fifth Avenue. Plan of one of the building's simplex apartments. Pease & Elliman's Catalogue of East Side New York Apartment Plans.

salon—just one room in his sprawling duplex located on the tenth and a portion of the eleventh floors. Financier James Cox Brady purchased part of the twelfth floor and the entire penthouse, which was configured as a twenty-four-room duplex. Interior designer Dorothy Draper decorated all of the public halls and lounges in the Georgian style, including the restaurant and large dining suite off the lobby. As was its strategy in other tall buildings, such as 340–50 Park Avenue and the Hotel Chatham, Warren & Wetmore applied architectural orders and ornament to the top floors without following the canonical rules of classicism. At the cornice of 960 Fifth Avenue, distinctive caryatids and carved garlands boldly distinguished the roofline, balancing the complex pattern of double- and single-height windows that hinted at the sophisticated apartment layout within the building.

Just before the Depression, Candela designed several remarkable apartment buildings, including 1040 Fifth Avenue at the northeast corner of 85th Street in 1929 for Anthony Paterno. In 1926, Warren, who owned his late brother Lloyd's brownstone at 1041 Fifth Avenue, had earlier attempted to place an apartment house on the same site without the inclusion of the corner lot. Warren & Wetmore's plans detailed a twelve-story building with an arrangement of duplex and simplex apartments with high ceilings. Unlike most of the speculative builders, Warren had intended to retain full ownership of the property and to lease the apartments.[40]

HOTELS AND RESORTS

Despite the loss of one of its most profitable clients, the Biltmore Corporation, the firm continued to design hotels and resorts to produce over thirty major hotels and additions by 1931.[41] The Mayflower Hotel in Washington, D.C., designed in association with Robert F. Beresford, reflected the scale and sophistication of Warren & Wetmore's New York City establishments (fig. 5.29).[42] Prominent businessman and developer Allen E. Walker enlisted

5.29. Mayflower Hotel, Washington, D.C. Warren & Wetmore Collection, Avery Architectural and Fine Arts Library, Columbia University.

5.30. Royal Hawaiian, Waikiki
Beach, Honolulu, Hawaii. Aerial
view. Prints and Photographs
Division, Library of Congress, #6673.

the firm to design a large hotel for transient guests and long-term residents on Connecticut Avenue, four blocks from the White House. When completed in 1925, the portion of the building fronting Connecticut Avenue contained 650 guest rooms, and three smaller sections divided by deep light courts, extending along DeSales Street to 17th Street, housed 112 apartments.[43] A limestone pedestal, punctuated by arched entries and bull's-eye windows, encircled the base of the building and tied the various masses of the composition together, and the gentle bow of the Connecticut Avenue facade differentiated the hotel entrance from the rear apartment section. Like the firm's seminal design for the New York Ritz, the Mayflower's brick facades were characteristically reserved, and its distinctive roofline displayed the bold silhouette of colossal urns. On the base of the building were profuse terracotta details: Carved fleur de lis, garlands, urns, and flowers accented the smooth stone. The interiors of the Mayflower expressed the same urbane grandeur that marked the firm's New York hotels. A 475-foot gallery ran through the length of the building and opened onto the public rooms and entertaining spaces. Notable were the glass-roofed palm court, appointed with lattice and screen work of Spanish design; the grand ballroom, decorated in gold, ivory, and blue, with balcony boxes and a small stage; and murals by Edward Laning.

Newly established steamship lines expanded the reach of the hotel industry substantially in the postwar period, and the tourist industry flourished in remote regions. Following the completion of the Mayflower Hotel, the firm designed several upscale resort hotels in tropical locations. In 1919 Bermuda's Trade Development Board formed an agreement with the British steamship company Furness, Withy and Company. In exchange for regular departures for Bermuda from New York, the board would provide Furness Withy with a subsidy for transporting tourists. To boost tourist appeal, the island heavily promoted golf. Furness, Withy capitalized on this arrangement and, in 1922, commissioned Warren & Wetmore to design the elegant but undercooked Mediterranean-style Bermuda Golf Club in

Tucker's Town.[44] The firm's six-story stucco Italian Renaissance–style Hotel Bermudiana, a later phase of the board's development plan, was completed in 1925. Among the island's three largest hotels, the Bermudiana created an additional 247 guest rooms in Hamilton for tourists.[45] In 1928 the firm embarked on a resort six miles outside of Kingston, Jamaica. When the island's historic Constant Spring Hotel was destroyed by fire in 1927, the Canadian National Railway and the United Hotel Company purchased the site and commissioned Warren & Wetmore to design a modern hotel of the same name with a colony of separate cottages, swimming pools, and a golf course. The resort reopened in 1931 in conjunction with the inauguration of the railroad's new steamship line, departing from Canadian ports for Jamaica.[46] In the tradition of the invention of appropriate styles in new colonies, the architects looked to the heritage of Europe and simplified the language of the architecture to achieve a rudimentary classicism appropriate to the islands.

Of Warren & Wetmore's resorts, the Royal Hawaiian at Waikiki Beach was the most distinctive (figs. 5.30, 5.32). In 1927 the Matson Navigation Company launched its luxury steamship *Malolo* to provide service between San Francisco and Hawaii. The Royal Hawaiian, the conception of William Roth, manager of the Matson Company, and Edward Tenney, president of Honolulu's stalwart financial company Castle & Cook, created comfortable and elegant accommodations for the wealthy passengers and tourists once they arrived in Hawaii. Warren & Wetmore's plans were completed in 1925, and despite several construction setbacks, the hotel opened two years later, on January 31, 1927, to immediate success.[47] The distinctive pink stucco building created a picturesque and colorful vision on Waikiki Beach. The open arcades, bluish-green tile floor, bell towers, and crisp lines of the design displayed Moorish and Spanish overtones, and deep blue jardinieres set into the building's undulating roofline accented the pink walls (fig. 5.31). The smooth, clean stucco surfaces created a neutral backdrop for Warren & Wetmore's scrolling baroque relief.

Many of the hotel's four hundred rooms, located in three L-shaped wings extending off the building's central block, opened onto lanais, or private balconies, and enjoyed views of the ocean, banyan, or coconut groves. Landscape architect R. T. Stevens transformed the grounds of the hotel, which were enclosed by a hedge of hibiscus, into a playground of tennis courts, archery, and croquet lawns. Warren & Wetmore imported materials from Spain, Persia, Italy, and Holland; the richness of the interiors—the long arcaded gallery extending along the beachfront and large ballroom—reflected these exotic reaches. The Persian dining room, decorated with Persian and Dutch tiles, travertine columns, and gilded ornament, offered a more formal option than the seaside terrace with its trellised walls and tiled roof. Throughout, porches and generous open arches took advantage of light and air to create a luxurious and relaxed atmosphere (fig. 5.33).

In 1929 Warren & Wetmore completed a ten-story tower addition to the historic and prestigious Homestead Hotel in Hot Springs, Virginia. Reputably the oldest resort in the country, the Homestead was located high in the Allegheny Mountains and, with its restorative mineral springs, had been drawing visitors since the 1700s. Although hotels had existed on the site since 1766, it was not until J. Pierpont Morgan and a group of wealthy investors capitalized on the resort's potential in 1888 that the Homestead—a hotel building and spa designed by Yarnall & Goforth, and a golf course—were constructed. In 1903 and 1913 the Cincinnati firm Elzner & Anderson completed two large wings in the Georgian style, and the Olmsted Brothers landscaped the grounds in the 1920s.[48]

By the time that Warren & Wetmore was commissioned to design yet another addition, the resort was an established stop on society's seasonal tour (fig. 5.34). The fashionable spa attracted New York's elite, and Wetmore, a frequent guest, spent the June season in Hot Springs with his family in the company of Chauncey Depew and William K.

5.33. Royal Hawaiian. Lanai.
Hawaii State Archives.

5.34. The Homestead, Hot Springs, Virginia. Tower addition, 1946. Gottscho-Schleisner Collection, Prints and Photographs Division, Library of Congress, #8504.

Vanderbilt. The firm's tower addition, with one hundred additional rooms and baths, was intentionally understated to blend with the existing buildings. Its red brick walls stepped up from a wide five-story base to a square tower accented by white pilasters, loggias, lintels, and urns. The design's pyramidal copper roof, embellished with lunettes and bull's-eye windows, a clock tower, and soaring spire, created an impressive silhouette against the Allegheny Mountains.

THEATERS

Despite Warren & Wetmore's affinity for drama and scenography, the firm realized only one major theater project in New York: the Erlanger Theater at 246–51 West 44th Street in 1927.[49] Earlier, in 1906, the firm came close to winning a large commission for the New Theater, one of the city's most costly playhouses. A group of prominent New Yorkers—composed of many who had been clients of the firm—planned the theater to stimulate art and recreate an environment akin to Paris's Opéra Comique, to be sustained through charitable donation.[50] Although the competition guidelines called for a "very severe and simple exterior," Warren & Wetmore produced an ambitious design reminiscent of Charles Garnier's Opera House, replete with sculpture, niches, overscaled ornament, and trellised roof garden (fig. 5.35). Warren & Wetmore and Carrère & Hastings's entries were the top contenders of

5.35. *New Theater, Central Park West, New York City. Competition entry, 1908.* Warren & Wetmore Collection, Avery Architectural and Fine Arts Library, Columbia University.

the nine plans submitted; Carrère & Hastings's chaste design won. However, due to its inconvenient location on Central Park West and 63rd Street, far from its affluent audience across the park, the theater quickly failed.[51]

Compared to its scheme for the New Theater, Warren & Wetmore's architectural language for the Erlanger Theater, designed twenty years later, was restrained (fig. 5.36).[52] Abraham Erlanger (1860–1930) and his partner Marc Klaw had commissioned theater specialists Herts & Tallant to design the popular New Amsterdam (1902–3), an art nouveau playhouse, and the Beaux-Arts-inspired Liberty Theater (1904). But after the partners split, Erlanger chose Warren & Wetmore to execute his first solo venture in New York; at the same time, the firm also designed a three-story brick and limestone Renaissance Revival theater (1926–27) for the Statler Hotel in Erlanger's hometown of Buffalo, New York, which Erlanger leased and gave his name.[53] As the postwar economy revived, the Times Square theater district thrived; the Erlanger was one of over thirty new playhouses. Its broad stucco facade embodied Warren & Wetmore's classical language stripped to its essence. Ornamented with quoins, a thin cornice of molded masks, and a central enclosed balcony, the building's flat exterior served mainly as a backdrop for electric lights and signage. Although more elaborate than the exterior, the Georgian interiors were similarly restrained. Walls and ceilings were given over to trompe l'oeil paintings of coffering, swags, and musical instruments but did not include the ornate plasterwork or gilding typical of many of the other Times Square theaters.

Warren & Wetmore also designed the Paramount Theater and Convention Hall, completed in 1930, in Asbury Park, New Jersey, as part of the city's plan to develop the seaside resort founded by James A. Bradley in 1871 into a booming beachfront community (fig. 5.37). Bradley's property was sold to the city of Asbury Park in 1903; in 1923 the city embarked on a sweeping campaign to revitalize it. Warren & Wetmore was called upon to design a movie theater, convention hall, and casino in association with Arthur Cottrell, Ernest Arend, and

5.36. *Erlanger Theater, 246–51 West 44th Street, New York City.* Architecture and Building 59 (September 1927): pl. 189.

5.37. *Paramount Theater and Convention Hall, Asbury Park, New Jersey.* Architecture and Building 62 (August 1930): pl. 138.

Kenneth Towner; at the same time, the Berkeley-Carteret Company commissioned the firm to design an adjacent four-hundred-room hotel.[54] The formal Italian Renaissance Revival building for the Paramount Theater and Convention Hall complex created an imposing presence on the waterfront. Spanning the boardwalk, the large brick structure extended on piles over the water.[55] Warren & Wetmore returned to a whimsical and patently decorative mode of design. Polychrome terra-cotta ornament, tiled panels in shades of purple, and gilded details of ships at the cornice adorned the facades, and lanterns festively outlined the building's silhouette against the night sky. In contrast to the Erlanger, the movie theater contained a simple and undecorated auditorium with seating for two thousand spectators. It connected through the boardwalk arcade to the sky-lit convention hall on the pier, which enclosed a more decorative auditorium with gilded ornament and marine mural panels. The brick casino building featured a large copper screen, embellished with mythological sea creatures, that spanned the boardwalk.[56]

HOUSES AND ESTATES

In the 1920s Warren & Wetmore resumed work on William K. Vanderbilt Jr.'s estate, Eagle's Nest, in Centerport, Long Island, to produce one of its most original and distinctive designs.[57] When Vanderbilt and his first wife Virginia Graham Fair separated in 1910, Vanderbilt sold Deepdale, his large Georgian estate designed by Carrère & Hastings, in Lake Success, Long Island, and moved to Centerport, where the firm had designed a six-room retreat for the bachelor. When the couple divorced in 1927, Vanderbilt married Rosamond Lancaster Warburton, whom he had met aboard his yacht *Ara* on a four-month cruise through the Caribbean. Intensely interested in auto racing and aviation, the energetic Vanderbilt was also dedicated to yachting and deep-sea fishing and spent much of his time collecting marine specimens during his sailing expeditions. His marriage to Warburton coincided with an ambitious building campaign at Eagle's Nest during which Warren & Wetmore transformed its modest cottage for Vanderbilt into a sprawling hacienda. The property, which grew to include a marine museum, swimming pool, private golf course, a Spanish-style chauffeur's apartment, and an airplane hangar, not only exhibited Vanderbilt's range of interests but also showed Warren & Wetmore's exuberant architecture in full flower (fig. 5.38).

Warren & Wetmore's stucco house and bell tower, built around three sides of a courtyard paved in Belgian block, bore no resemblance to the English-style cottage formerly on the site. According to Augusta Owen Patterson of *Town & Country*, Vanderbilt sent Ronald Pearce, the supervising architect on the project, to Spain to study the country's architecture; Pearce's observations took shape at Eagle's Nest as an exotic amalgam of northern and southern European styles.[58] Well incorporated into the sloping site, the upper floors of the house perched dramatically on the edge of a cliff overlooking Northport Harbor, and the lower levels spilled down toward the water in a series of stepped walls and terraces. The crisp white stucco facades stood in contrast to the natural surroundings and were complemented by colorful bursts of Spanish baroque ornament at the door and window openings. Carried out in a range of colors from buff to deep rose, the robust details harmonized with the red tile of the multilevel roofs. A polychromed bell tower containing an antique Russian bell rose from the low-lying building mass surrounding the courtyard. Its heavy wooden doors, portcullis, floridly carved urns, and scrolling Vanderbilt coat-of-arms created an impressive approach to the house (fig. 5.39).

The house's entrance arcade on the southern periphery of the courtyard connected two sections of the house and looked out onto a charming boxwood garden with baroque gates, fountains, and a colorful mural and sundial painted on one of the sidewalls. The main portion of the house was entered from the east, where a door, embellished with richly carved stone, opened into a double-height travertine entrance hall that led to a study, game room, several

5.38. *William K. Vanderbilt Jr. estate, Eagle's Nest, Centerport, New York. View to the north.* Suffolk County Vanderbilt Museum.

5.39. *Eagle's Nest. Bell tower.* Suffolk County Vanderbilt Museum.

5.40 (opposite). Eagle's Nest. William K. Vanderbilt Jr.'s bedroom, 2005. Photo: Jonathan Wallen.

5.41 (left). Eagle's Nest. Vanderbilt's bathroom, 2005. Photo: Jonathan Wallen.

bedrooms, and an intimate dining room with a hand-carved cypress ceiling, stucco walls, and Portuguese tiled floor (fig. 5.42). Upstairs, the wood-paneled organ room contained a massive fireplace and 2,000-pipe Aeolian organ. Vanderbilt's French Empire master bedroom, located in the slender eastern wing, offered both water and courtyard views and was decorated with furniture from the Napoleonic era; the bathroom *en suite* was luxuriously trimmed with marble and appointed with mural panels by Henri Courtais (figs. 5.40, 5.41). Mrs. Vanderbilt's Louis XVI–style bedroom, dressing rooms, and octagonal bathroom connected through a long sunlit hall. Kitchens and servants' quarters were located on lower levels, and a large library and additional bedrooms occupied the western wing off the entrance arcade. All exterior and interior ironwork was executed by renowned metalworker Samuel Yellin of Philadelphia.

Previously unassuming, Eagle's Nest was an enclave of Vanderbilt's personal taste. A pair of cast-iron eagles from the original Grand Central Terminal, transported to the Centerport property when Warren & Wetmore's original house was constructed, perched on the entrance gates to the estate. Just beyond stood six Corinthian columns from the ruins of Carthage, salvaged by Vanderbilt and moved from the Deepdale estate, which marked the curve in the drive as it turned north and descended over an arching bridge and through the opening in the bell tower. A lower road, running beneath the bridge, led to the harbor and boathouse. A one-story brick museum (1922), known as the Hall of Fishes, sat at the northwestern edge of the property and was embellished by an elaborate entry with spiraling columns and a baroque pediment (fig. 5.43). Inside, Vanderbilt's collections of marine specimens were displayed in cases. Also in 1922, Warren & Wetmore designed a circular swimming pool and two stucco bathhouses, decorated with large imitation travertine stone vases, statuary, and ironwork by Yellin (fig. 5.44).

Although Ronald Pearce oversaw much of the design and construction of Eagle's Nest, Warren remained involved. When working on the museum building, Pearce urged Vanderbilt to "incorporate as many yellow flowering shrubs and flowers . . . to carry a more or less yellow base line along the building to further carry out the light stone color at the main entrance" and reiterated that "Mr. Warren also feels very strongly on this same subject."[59] Later, in 1930, Warren stepped in when Vanderbilt expressed discontent with Pearce for employing artists

5.42 (following pages). Eagle's Nest. Dining room. Suffolk County Vanderbilt Museum.

223

5.43. Eagle's Nest. Museum.
Suffolk County Vanderbilt Museum.

5.44. Eagle's Nest. Swimming pool. Suffolk County Vanderbilt Museum.

without his knowledge or approval. Warren emphatically wrote, "You are our one star client and I can assure you everything is done to please you and expedite your work."[60]

Ronald Pearce continued to work on Eagle's Nest after Warren's retirement from the firm. As Vanderbilt's collections continued to grow, Pearce added a second floor to the Hall of Fishes (1930–31) and refaced the building in stucco (its flat roof was used as the first tee for Vanderbilt's golf course). In 1936 he completed a wing on the northern edge of the courtyard in memory of Vanderbilt's son, who had tragically died in an automobile accident in 1933. The addition, also executed in white stucco with Spanish detail, harmonized with the house and provided additional museum space for Vanderbilt's expanding anthropological and ornithological collections. Pearce had also acted as supervising architect for Vanderbilt's exclusive Deepdale Golf and Country Club (1925) in Lake Success, near the avid sportsman's former estate. Warren & Wetmore's small Spanish-style stucco clubhouse was "more like a private country house in which members would feel at ease to do as they wished."[61] With Warren, Pearce also renovated Vanderbilt's triplex maisonette at 651 Park Avenue (1930), in Mott Schmidt's Georgian apartment house between 67th and 68th Streets, into a sumptuous spectacle of French taste (fig. 5.45).

Apart from the Vanderbilt commissions, Warren & Wetmore's postwar residential projects included tennis court buildings, pool houses, and town houses. In 1923 the firm designed a Georgian tennis court building for Mrs. Marshall Field at Caumsett in Lloyd Neck, Long Island (fig. 5.46). The restrained red brick building blended with John Russell Pope's mansion and outbuildings, built at the same time.[62] Also in 1923, the firm completed an imposing Georgian-style tennis court and pool building for Florence A. V. Twombly, a granddaughter of

5.46. *Mrs. Marshall Field estate,
Caumsett, Lloyd's Neck, New
York. Tennis court building.*
Warren & Wetmore Collection, Avery
Architectural and Fine Arts Library,
Columbia University.

Commodore Cornelius Vanderbilt, and her daughter Ruth at Florham, the family's estate in Convent, New Jersey, designed by McKim, Mead & White (1899). A reflection of the grand brick mansion, Warren & Wetmore's brick sports building was luxuriously equipped with a Grecian-style swimming pool, wall and ceiling murals by Robert Winthrop Chanler, and a championship clay tennis court.[63] Mrs. Twombly was also responsible for commissioning Warren & Wetmore's last city mansion. In 1927, the firm executed a restrained Italian Renaissance palazzo at 900 Fifth Avenue, on the northwest corner of 71st Street.

University Library, Louvain

> "Furore Teutonica Diruta, Dono Americano Restituta"—Destroyed by Teutonic Fury, Restored by American Generosity
>
> — Cardinal Mercier

Of the firm's innumerable projects, the reconstruction of the library in the ancient university town of Louvain, outside Brussels, held the greatest significance for Warren (fig. 5.47). At the onset of World War One, in August 1914, the Germans had pillaged the historic city and burned over eighteen hundred buildings, including the university's fifteenth-century library. As previously mentioned, while living in France, Warren had invested his energy in the war effort and had been deeply affected by the Germans' destruction of France's and Belgium's architectural monuments, particularly the destruction of the venerable library, regarded as one of Europe's preeminent repositories. The library, established in 1636, had occupied the historic building, originally used as a cloth market by Louvain's merchants, since the mid-1700s. As early as 1915, the Institut de France, of which Warren was a member, began discussions regarding the reconstruction of the fallen monument.

In 1918 the International Committee for the Reconstruction of the Library at Louvain, headed by Imbart de la Tour, president of the Institut de France, was established, and its American counterpart, the National Committee of the United States for the Reconstruction of the University of Louvain, directed by Columbia University's president, Dr. Nicholas Murray Butler, began collecting subscriptions to fund the reconstruction. Subsequently, the American committee requested full responsibility for the project. At the same time, Warren and Wetmore began considering the possibility of rebuilding war-torn areas in France and Belgium. To his wife Charlotte, Warren wrote enthusiastically: "I don't know whether Charlie has spoken to you about a scheme of rebuilding the devastated regions of Belgium and of France with the aid of American construction campaign, American Capital and ourselves W. & W at the head of the whole shooting match. It would be by all odds the greatest undertaking of the age. . . . "[64] However, it was not until 1920 that Warren was formally invited by Imbart de la Tour to take on the project of rebuilding the library at Louvain's Catholic University. Warren poured emotion and enthusiasm into its design, calling it a "labor of love"; its rebuilding was both a personal and moral achievement.[65]

Warren chose the library's prominent new site on the city's highest square—Place du Peuple—and collaborated with the aging head of the university, Cardinal Mercier, on the building's design.[66] Both men desired to acknowledge America's contribution to the war and

5.47. Rendering of the Library at Louvain, Belgium, 1922. Warren & Wetmore Collection, Avery Architectural and Fine Arts Library, Columbia University.

DESIGN FOR THE LIBRARY
AT LOUVAIN
DESTROYED BY THE GERMANS ·1914
RESTORED BY AMERICA ·1922
WARREN AND WETMORE ARCHITECTS

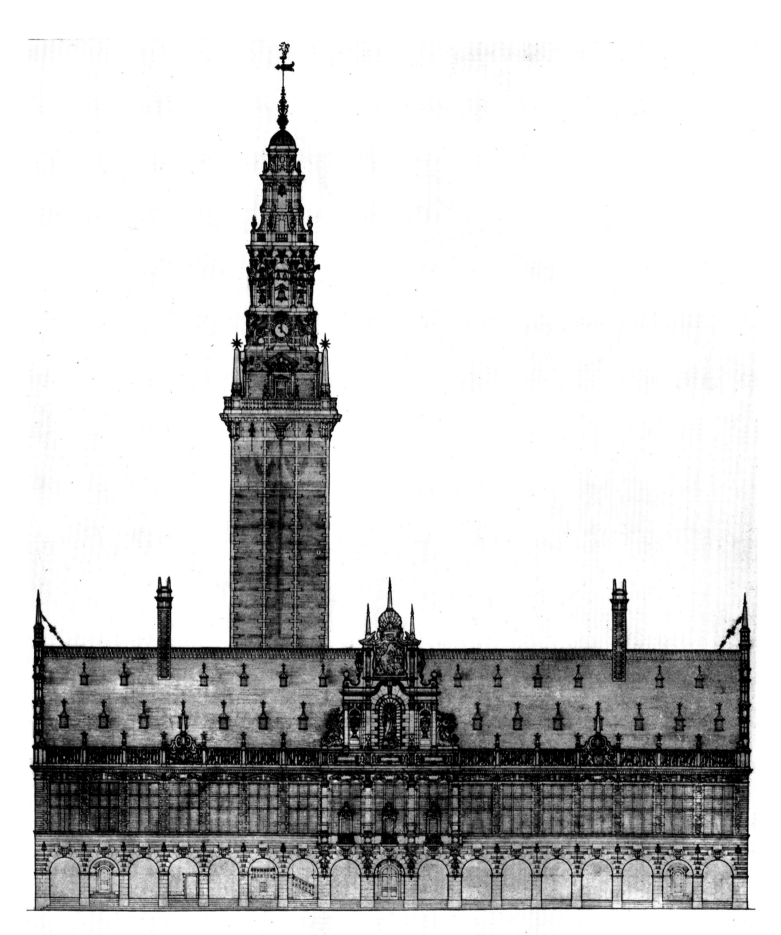

· LA NOUVELLE BIBLIOTHEQUE DE L'UNIVERSITE DE LOUVAIN ·
· LOUVAIN · BELGIQUE ·
· WARREN · ET · WETMORE · ARCHITECTES · NEW · YORK · E·U·A·

to create a permanent record of the library's history. Under Warren's careful guidance, a group of young architects spent months in Belgium sketching the masterpieces of Brabançonne art before preparing drawings for Warren's ambitious and contextual Flemish Renaissance design. On July 28, 1921, Dr. Butler laid the cornerstone of the building. By then, the American committee, composed of educators and prominent businessmen such as J. P. Morgan and Thomas Lamont, had raised $160,000 to fund the clearing of the site and the foundation.[67] Because work on the library progressed as money was raised, construction proceeded sporadically. Warren appealed to American colleges, urging them to collect subscriptions and donate books. By 1924 the rear section of the library, for stacks, was complete, providing much needed storage space for incoming books from the Allied countries and the Germans, who were ordered by the Treaty of Versailles to send ten thousand volumes a month in reparation. Herbert Hoover, then director of the American Commission for Relief in Belgium, raised an additional $650,000 for the building. In 1926, construction resumed.[68]

Lessing Williams, Warren's representative architect at Louvain, was devoted to the mission of achieving a truly Flemish building. In his work he used materials and resurrected crafts that were being swiftly abandoned as modernism swept through the profession. In his words, it included "inspecting stone in quarry, stone yard, and carver's shop, even carving and setting some with my own hand; arranging for brick to be specially made by hand, and inspecting them at the kiln for color and texture; figuring out how the old brick vaulting was built, and laying the brick to show the workmen how; modelling the ornament myself, because the professional modelers were trained in the French taste, thinner and colder than the native tradition."[69] In addition to Williams, Carroll Greenough, the brother of Warren's son-in-law William Greenough, was called upon to superintend the project. As the crowning element of the design, Warren incorporated an inscription that Cardinal Mercier had specified. In a decorative scrolling pattern, Warren wove Mercier's words—*Furore Teutonica Diruta, Dono Americano Restituta* (Destroyed by Teutonic fury, restored by American generosity)—into the balustrade extending the full length of the top of the facade (fig. 5.48). Mercier approved Warren's scheme before his death in January 1926; Brussels sculptor Pierre de Soete was commissioned to carve the lettering.

The new library drew a great deal of interest in the United States and in Europe. A model of Warren's design was displayed at the New York Public Library; the building featured prominently in the press and garnered much praise. Cass Gilbert, who visited the site, proclaimed that "the plan appear[ed]...to be admirably adapted to its purpose, the exterior design a graceful and charming adaptation of Flemish architecture." He admired the building's "excellent workmanship" and wished he "could get such good brick work done in America."[70] In France, a critic noted in *The Revue Critique des Idées et des Livres* that "like most Americans who have Beaux Arts diplomas, [Warren] has great regard for our balance, our taste, our great classic tradition. . . . It is not at all astonishing that his respect for our traditions is even greater than that of our young artists. . . . for he shows more repugnance than they do for that which seems foreign to the French genius and tradition."[71]

Critic Rexford Newcomb, writing for *The Western Architect*, noted that "while it had not been thought desirable or necessary to duplicate the architecture of the old library, a very beautiful and appropriate design, entirely in keeping with the high dignity and historic importance of the University, has been evolved by the architects."[72] Despite the local desire for a modern building, Warren's neo-Flemish red brick edifice was an important vehicle in reviving the historic style for rebuilding war-torn Louvain. In Lessing Williams's view, the design was

a concrete study of the modification of architecture, in mass and color and profile, to climatic conditions . . . and the adaptation of American ideas to the needs of a European university town. . . . the Belgians have attributed the revival of their traditional style, since then become widespread, to the influence of the Louvain Library, which they had begged us to make "modern." The play of light and shade in the old Brabançon buildings was better

5.48 (opposite). Louvain Library. Entrance elevation showing inscription in balustrade. Warren & Wetmore Collection, Avery Architectural and Fine Arts Library, Columbia University.

231

adapted to the peculiar climate, being an outgrowth of it, than modernistic white cement could be and we felt that this heritage should be preserved by grafting it on to modern planning and scale and methods of living. As archeology, it is deliberately distorted, but by knowing archeology well enough to use it not be hampered by it.[73]

Although Flemish in design, Warren's plan was clearly more American in inspiration. Carrère & Hastings's New York Public Library, completed in 1912, exemplified the grand scale of civic improvement during the first decades of the twentieth century. Warren's plan similarly incorporated a vast reading room, a separate wing to the rear for stacks, and two interior courtyards. Due to the size and program of the building, Louvain's exterior was over-scaled, compared to the Flemish models from which Warren drew inspiration.

The library, stretching majestically across the southeastern edge of the Place du Peuple (later renamed Mgr. Ladeuzeplein), consisted of a covered arcade that stretched the 220-foot width of the building and opened onto the square. A great stone stair extended up from the open arcade to the main entrance on the second floor and its brightly lit reading room, equal in height to four floors of stacks, which was articulated on the facade by giant windows made up of small panes of stained glass (fig. 5.49).[74] From the massive slate roof, punctuated with dormer windows and chimneys, rose the soaring memorial tower, crowned by a sculptural cupola, clock, and carillon paid for by funds raised by American engineers in memory of their colleagues who died during the war (fig. 5.50). The names of over seven hundred contributing institutions were carved in a variety of fonts into the limestone ashlar of the facade and arcade (figs. 5.51, 5.52).

As a memorial, the library was heavily detailed with images and symbols expressing the library's history and the Allied victory. The central motif, executed by French sculptor Jean

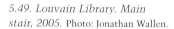

5.49. Louvain Library. Main stair, 2005. Photo: Jonathan Wallen.

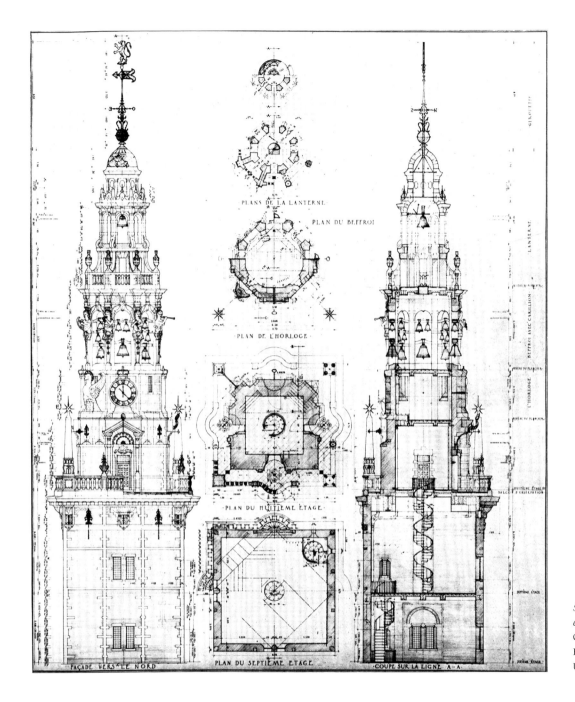

5.50. Louvain Library. Tower elevation. Warren & Wetmore Collection, Avery Architectural and Fine Arts Library, Columbia University.

Dampt, portrayed Notre Dame des Victoires flanked by figures of Saint George and Saint Michael crushing evil spirits; a bas relief above, set within a gilded baroque pediment, depicted the burning of the old library (fig. 5.53).[75] Busts of the king, queen, and crown prince of Belgium at the central windows and the coat of arms of the United States and Belgium in the high balustrade celebrated American–Belgian relations, and heraldic animals of the Allied countries glorified the triumph on the stepped gables on either end of the building.[76]

Cardinal Mercier's inscription for the balustrade proved controversial. As construction on the building resumed in 1926, Belgium was divided in passionate debate. Hoping to bury the atrocities of the war and to improve relations with the Germans, the president of the University, Monsignor Paulin Ladeuze, and a small but powerful group of faculty and Flemish students vehemently opposed the inscription. Warren, on the other hand, felt morally obliged to carry out the Cardinal's instructions and considered the inscription appropriate, if not necessary, for the Belgians to come to terms with the Germans' aggressions. Supported by the people of Louvain, French-speaking students, and the press, Warren became the hero for the cause. Each intent on achieving what he deemed appropriate, neither Warren nor Ladeuze was able to compromise on the issue.

The situation exploded in the months leading up to the library's completion and inauguration on July 4, 1928. Warren continued with his balustrade, despite the university's disapproval, while Ladeuze secretly commissioned a plain balustrade and attempted to install it without Warren's knowledge in June 1928. In response, Warren arranged to install his own balustrade in the early hours of the morning on June 22, 1928; however, the police intervened and work came to a standstill until lawyers could be consulted. As recalled by Ian MacCallum, who was working on the other inscriptions throughout the building, "as stones began to move, I looked across the square and saw Whitney Warren, cape flying and stick waving, streaming across the space with three lawyers in his wake carrying the legal injunction papers."[77] Because the parties were unable to resolve the situation for building's inauguration, Herbert Hoover, the primary fundraiser, intervened and authorized the plain balustrade.[78] Hordes of protesters gathered on the square outside the library, and riots erupted. Ladeuze's balustrade was smashed twice, once by enraged students breaking through police lines in June, then by Warren's Belgian foreman, Edmond Morren, in July, who became a national hero for his act. In November 1928 Warren was awarded the Grand Cordon of the Order of the Crown of Belgium.

As Ladeuze's third balustrade was installed, Warren brought suit against the university in Louvain's civil court for violating his contract and his rights as an artist. Because the university had accepted his design, Warren argued that he, as an artist, was empowered by law to complete his vision. Represented by three lawyers, he won the suit in 1929, and the court authorized the removal of Ladeuze's balustrade. However, the university won reversal of the

5.51 (below left). Louvain Library. Detail of arcade, 2005. Photo: Jonathan Wallen.

5.52 (below right). Louvain Library. Detail of first floor vaulting, 2005. Photo: Jonathan Wallen.

decision in the Brussels' Court of Appeals in 1930.[79] Although Hoover, by now president, emphatically disapproved of the "offensive" inscription, Warren refused to concede. He appealed the verdict in the highest Belgian court but, in 1932, lost again. In defeat, he said, "I look to the Belgian people to carry out the wishes of their beloved Cardinal Mercier. As far as I am concerned, I'm through, but whether or not the Belgian people are is another question."[80] One year later, Warren's foreman, Morren, smashed the balustrade yet again.[81]

When war swept through Europe for a second time, Warren, at the age of seventy-four was powerless to help. He was shattered by the loss of a cultural world that he revered and that had inspired him throughout his life. On May 16, 1940, Germans shelled the city of Louvain, set the library ablaze, and burned over 700,000 volumes. Foreign correspondent William Shirer was the first American on site. Writing in his diary, Shirer observed that "the great library is completely gutted. The ruins still smolder. Some of the girders that hold the roof remain. The Tudor-like facade, blackened by smoke, holds out proudly."[82] When asked by a reporter in 1940 whether Mercier's inscription should have been installed, Warren emphatically retorted, "More than ever! And how!"[83]

Throughout the Louvain controversy, Warren remained staunch in his opinions and refused to bend, despite strong opposition from both the university and the United States government. In much the same way, he clung to traditional language and architectural styles that made sense to him, undeterred by the rising tide of modernism that, in 1928, was sweeping Europe and gaining momentum in the United States. The crowning achievements of the architect's career—the library at Louvain and the New York Central Building—were singularly successful in their interpretation of historical styles, bold sculptural details, and creative artistry.

But by 1937, having known the heights of architectural and social fame, Warren conceded that the world had irrevocably changed. The architect had chaired the Beaux-Arts Ball since 1913 to benefit the educational programs of the Beaux-Arts Institute of Design; with his retirement from the organization, he announced that the popular themed galas would no longer be held. This was no small gesture for a man who forged his career around the tenets of the Beaux-Arts and fought his entire life to find a place for the past in architecture. Unwilling to accept the modern movement—the antithesis of his art—he may have recognized that his profession would soon find his work and its inspiration irrelevant. However, in the first three decades of the twentieth century, the influence of the Beaux-Arts education within the architectural world was fundamental, and Warren & Wetmore stood at center stage, dramatically shaping New York City around its ideals of beauty, urbanity, modernity, and monumentality. The firm's work is both an indelible imprint of the era leading up to the Great Depression and a remarkable testament to the sophisticated taste and European flair of its senior partner, Whitney Warren.

5.53. Louvain Library. Detail of entrance facade with Jean Dampt's Notre Dame des Victoires, 2005. Photo: Jonathan Wallen.

CATALOGUE RAISONNÉ

In 1952 Patrick Corry presented Avery Library a list of the works by Warren & Wetmore which has formed the basis of this catalogue raisonné, along with partial project lists from the Warren & Wetmore Collection in Avery's Drawings and Archives, input from books, historical societies, the architectural press, and the firm's drawings.

While the firm's project list includes over two thousand projects, many of them were either never realized or small renovations. Warren retired from the firm in 1931 and, although the firm continued to operate under Patrick Corry and Julian Holland until the early 1950s, later projects consited of renovations to existing buildings designed by the firm.

1893
Charles D. Wetmore, First Church of Christ Scientist, Prendergast Avenue, Jamestown, New York; extant.

1894
Whitney Warren, Newport Country Club, Harrison Avenue, Newport, Rhode Island, 1894–95; extant.

1898
New York Yacht Club, 37 West 44th Street, New York City; 1898–1901; (job # 1); extant.

1899
Court tennis court building, Tuxedo Tennis and Racquet Club, West Lake Road, Tuxedo Park, New York; (job # 4); extant.

1900
Honorable Francis K. Pendleton house, 7 East 86th Street, New York City; 1900–1; demolished: 1960.

Marshall Orme Wilson house, 3 East 64th Street, New York City; 1900–3; extant: Consulate General of India.

Amos Tuck French estate, Tucks Eden, Cliff Road, Tuxedo Park, New York; c. 1900; demolished: 1940s.

Henry Whitney Munroe estate, Crow's Nest, Crow's Nest Road, Tuxedo Park, New York; c. 1900; (job # 8); extant.

Moses Taylor V estate, Annandale Farm, Taylor Road, Mount Kisco, New York; house demolished in 1950; outbuildings extant (Mount Kisco Country Club).

William Starr Miller estate, High Tide, Ocean Avenue, Newport, Rhode Island; extant.

Jerry Crary estate, Warren, Pennsylvania. Warren & Wetmore Collection, Avery Architectural and Fine Arts Library, Columbia University.

Jerry Crary estate, Market Street, Warren, Pennsylvania; house demolished in 1937; carriage house extant.

Recreation Pier #30, East River, New York City. Warren & Wetmore Collection, Avery Architectural and Fine Arts Library, Columbia University.

Recreational Pier #30, East River, New York City; c. 1900; (job #121); demolished.

William Harrison Allen house, Conewango Avenue, Warren, Pennsylvania; c. 1900; demolished: 1971.

1901
Speculative houses, 832 and 834 Fifth Avenue, New York City; demolished: 1930.

Speculative houses, 9 and 11 East 84th Street, New York City; extant: no. 9 is private; no. 11 is the Republic of Bulgaria's Permanent Mission to the United Nations.

Frederick E. Edey house, 10 West 56th Street, New York City; extant: store.

Mrs. Sidney Dillon Ripley house, 16 East 79th Street, New York City; 1901–3; extant.

Windsor Trust Banking Rooms, Fifth Avenue, New York City; c. 1901; demolished: c. 1920.

John Hartness Brown Building, Euclid Avenue, Cleveland, Ohio; refaced and altered.

1902
James A. Burden Jr. house, 7 East 91st Street, New York City; 1902–5; extant: Convent of the Sacred Heart.

Theodore Frelinghuysen house, alteration, 15 West 47th Street, New York City; demolished: 1925.

Augustus van Horne Stuyvesant stable, 33 West 44th Street, New York City; demolished.

George Henry Warren house, 924 Fifth Avenue, New York City; 1902–3; demolished: 1950.

Clarence MacKay estate, Harbor Hill, carriage house, kennels, and dairyman's cottage, Harbor Hill Road, Roslyn, New York; extant: cottage; estate demolished: 1949.

William K. Vanderbilt Sr. estate, Idle Hour, guest wing and tennis court building, Idle Hour Boulevard, Oakdale, New York; 1902–4; extant (interiors demolished).

Winthrop Rutherfurd estate, Rutherfurd House, Route 517, Allamuchy, New Jersey; 1902–4; extant: Villa Madonna.

Court tennis court building, Myopia Hunt Club, Bay Avenue, South Hamilton, Massachusetts; extant.

Court tennis court building for William C. Whitney, Newbury Street, Aiken, South Carolina; extant.

Kean, Van Courtland Company Building, 28–30 Pine Street, New York City; 1902–3; (job # 82); demolished: 1956.

Imperial Hotel, addition to McKim, Mead & White's original building, Broadway between 31st and 32nd Streets, New York City; c. 1902; demolished: 1969.

Westmorly Court, Mt. Auburn Street, Cambridge, Massachusetts; extant: Adams House, Harvard University.

1903
Gov. R. Livingston Beeckman house, 854 Fifth Avenue, New York City; 1903–5; extant: Permanent Mission of Serbia and Montenegro to the United Nations.

Herbert L. Griggs house, alteration, 1 East 86th Street, New York City; demolished: 1958.

1904
James Henry Smith stable, 133–35 West 55th Street, New York City; demolished: 1922.

Ralph J. Preston estate, Ivy Hall, Kirby's Lane, Jericho, New York; c. 1904; demolished: c. 1950.

Joseph Sampson Stevens estate, Kirby Hill, Kirby's Lane, Jericho, New York, c. 1904; extant.

William Starr Miller estate, Rock Ledge, Ackert Hook Road, Rhinebeck, New York; 1904–6; with Francis L. V. Hoppin; extant.

William C. Whitney estate, Joye Cottage, squash court building, Newberry Street, Aiken, South Carolina; 1904–6; extant: private house.

Moses Taylor Hospital, Ridge Road, Lackawanna, New York; extant: Friendship House (Buffalo-Niagara Presbytery).

Stable for Street Cleaning Department, Flushing Avenue, Brooklyn, New York; 1904–5; extant.

Grand Central Terminal, New York City; 1904–1913; with Reed & Stem; (job # 702); extant.

1905
Lloyd Warren house, alteration, 1041 Fifth Avenue, New York City; demolished: 1930.

George F. Baker stable, Tuxedo Park, New York. Warren & Wetmore Collection, Avery Architectural and Fine Arts Library, Columbia University.

George F. Baker stable, East Lake Road, Tuxedo Park, New York; c. 1905; extant: private house.

John T. Magee estate, Wampus Farm, Wampus Pond Road, Mount Kisco, New York; c. 1905; demolished.

John Magee Ellsworth, alteration and addition, Bernardsville, New Jersey; demolished.

Hamilton Fountain, Riverside Park and 76th Street, New York City; extant.

Miss Osborn's Dressmaking building, 24 East 46th Street, New York City; (job #233); demolished: 1919.

Hotel Belmont, 120 Park Avenue, New York City; 1905–6; demolished: 1939.

1906

Frederick Vanderbilt estate, Hyde Park, alterations, Hyde Park, New York; extant: museum.

Clarence MacKay estate, Harbor Hill, court tennis court building, Harbor Hill Road, Roslyn, New York; 1906–7; (job #222); demolished.

Dreicer & Company, 560 Fifth Avenue, New York City; 1906–7; extant.

Grand Central Post Office Annex, 450 Lexington Avenue, New York City; with Reed & Stem; 1906–9; (job #703); extant.

1907

Isaac Guggenheim estate, Villa Carola, gatehouse, garage, barn, farmhouse, and conservatory, Middle Neck Road, Sands Point, New York; (job # 278); extant: Village Club at Sands Point.

Sir Donald D. Mann estate, Fallingbrook, Kingston Road, Scarborough, Canada; extant: gatehouse; house destroyed by fire in 1930.

Ritz Carlton and Carlton House, 370–84 Madison Avenue, New York City; 1907–10; (job # 275); demolished: 1951.

Seamen's Church Institute, 25 South Street, New York City; 1907–12; (job #265); demolished: 1967.

Chelsea Piers, Little West 12th Street to West 23rd Street, New York City; 1907–10; demolished.

1908

William K. Vanderbilt Sr. guesthouse, 49 East 52nd Street, New York City; (job # 348); altered and refaced.

1909

Mrs. Marion Brookman house, 5 East 70th Street, New York City; (job # 390); demolished: 1973.

John Magee Ellsworth estate, alteration and addition, Lake Road, Far Hills, New Jersey; c. 1909; extant.

Columbia County Courthouse, Hudson, New York. Warren & Wetmore Collection, Avery Architectural and Fine Arts Library, Columbia University.

Columbia County Courthouse, Union Street, Hudson, New York; extant.

Hudson City Savings Bank, Warren Street, Hudson, New York; extant.

Union Station, Houston Belt and Terminal Railroad, Crawford Street, Houston, Texas; 1909–11; extant: adaptively reused as the entrance to Minute Maid Park.

Union Station, Canadian Northern Railroad, Main Street, Winnipeg, Manitoba; 1909–11; (job #313); extant.

Prince Arthur Hotel, N. Cumberland Street, Port Arthur, Ontario; (job # 385); extant.

1910

S. Reading Betron house, 935 Fifth Avenue, New York City; demolished: 1953.

Lillian Nordica house, alteration, 6–8 West 9th Street, New York City.

William K. Vanderbilt Jr. estate, Eagle's Nest, cottage and boathouse, Little Neck Road, Centerport, New York; c. 1910; extant: boathouse, Suffolk County Vanderbilt Museum.

Vanderbilt Hotel, 4 Park Avenue, New York City; 1910–13; (job # 343); extant: converted into apartments in 1965.

Ritz-Carlton Hotel, Montreal, Canada. Architecture 27 [March 1913]: 46

Ritz Carlton, Sherbrooke Street, Montreal, Quebec; (job # 386); 1910–12; extant.

Biltmore Hotel, 335 Madison Avenue, New York City; 1910–13; (job # 728); refaced and rebuilt: 1981.

Downtown Association, addition, 60 Pine Street, New York City; 1910–11; extant.

1911

Theodore B. Starr store, 576 Fifth Avenue, New York City; (job # 482); altered.

Aeolian Hall, 33 West 42nd Street, New York City. Architectural Record 32 [October 1912]: 530.

Aeolian Building, 33 West 42nd Street, New York City; 1911–12; extant: SUNY State College of Optometry (remodeled in 1970 by Carl J. Petrilli).

Eagle Building, 257 Park Avenue South, New York City; 1911–13; (job # 497); extant: Gramercy Park Building.

Ritz Hotel addition, 370-84 Madison Avenue, New York City; 1911–12; (job # 334); demolished: 1951.

Green-Wood Cemetery Mortuary Chapel and 20th Street Gatehouse, Brooklyn, New York; (job # 657); extant.

Merchant's Loft Building, New York City; (job #705); with Reed & Stem.

Adams Express Company Building, 538–56 Lexington Avenue, New York City; with Reed & Stem; (job # 741); demolished: 1929 and replaced by the Waldorf Astoria.

Grand Central Palace, 480 Lexington Avenue, New York City; with Reed & Stem; demolished: 1963.

New York Central Power House, 100 East 50th Street, New York City; with Reed & Stem; demolished: 1929 and replaced by the Waldorf Astoria.

Hastings-on-Hudson Station, Southside Road, Hastings-on-Hudson, New York; with Reed & Stem; (job #714); extant.

Yonkers Station, Buena Vista Avenue, Yonkers, New York; with Reed & Stem; (job # 715); extant.

Newburgh Station, Water Street, Newburgh, New York; c. 1911; with Reed & Stem; (job # 717); extant: museum and restaurant.

Watertown Station, Watertown, New York; with Reed & Stem; (job #720); demolished: 1970s.

Mount Vernon Station, Mount Vernon, New York; with Reed & Stem; (job #728); demolished.

Ludlow Station, Ludlow Road, Ludlow, New York; with Reed & Stem; (job #735); demolished.

Glenwood Station, Glenwood Avenue, Glenwood, New York; with Reed & Stem; (job #736); extant.

Ossining Station, Main Street, Ossining, New York; with Reed & Stem; (job #737); extant.

Fordham Station, E. Fordham Road, Bronx, New York; with Reed & Stem; (job #745); extant.

Catskill Station, Catskill, New York; with Reed & Stem.

1912

Harry Payne Whitney estate, tennis court building, Roslyn, New York; extant.

Apartment House, 903 Park Avenue, New York City; with Robert T. Lyons; extant.

Goelet Office Building, 8–14 East 47th Street, New York City; demolished: 1960s.

Crypt for John Paul Jones, U. S. Navy Academy Chapel, Annapolis, Maryland. Warren & Wetmore Collection, Avery Architectural and Fine Arts Library, Columbia University.

Crypt for John Paul Jones, U. S. Navy Academy Chapel, Annapolis, Maryland; (job # 494); extant.

Ritz-Carlton Hotel, Walnut and Broad Streets, Philadelphia, Pennsylvania; with Horace Trumbauer; extant.

Park Avenue Viaduct, New York City; with Reed & Stem; (job #751); 1912–19; extant.

Grand Central Terminal Yard, outhouses, substations, sub interlocking stations, New York City.

Detroit Terminal, Michigan Central Railroad, West Vernor Highway, Detroit, Michigan; with Reed & Stem; 1912–13; (job # 727); extant: vacant.

1913

Apartment House, 340–50 Park Avenue, New York City; 1913–15; demolished: 1958.

Pantlind Hotel, Monroe Avenue, Grand Rapids, Michigan; (job # 760); extant: Amway Grand Plaza.

Old National Bank, in connection with the Pantilind Hotel, Grand Rapids, Michigan; (job #765).

1914

Apartment House, 400 Park Avenue, New York City; (job # 775); demolished: 1955.

35–39 West 35th Street, New York City; extant.

Goelet Building, 402 Fifth Avenue, New York City; extant: offices.

Vanderbilt Concourse Building, 52–58 Vanderbilt Avenue, New York City; 1914–15; (job # 764); extant.

Mail Services Building, 460–78 Lexington Avenue, New York City; 1914–15; (job # 832); rebuilt as the Park Avenue Atrium in 1984.

Railroad YMCA, 309 Park Avenue, New York City; (job # 726); demolished: 1929 and replaced by the Waldorf Astoria.

Texas Company Building, Rusk Avenue, Houston, Texas; 1914–15; (job # 768); extant.

Hyde Park Station, River Road, Hyde Park, New York; with Reed & Stem; (job # 763); extant: Hudson Valley Railroad Society.

Poughkeepsie Station, Main Street, Poughkeepsie, New York; with Reed & Stem; 1914–18; (job # 764); extant.

Mausoleum for William B. Hornblower, Woodlawn Cemetery, New York.

1915

Thomas A. Donoghue house, 17 Courtlandt Place, Houston, Texas; 1915–16; extant.

Apartment House, 320–30 Park Avenue, New York City; (job # 716); demolished: 1959.

Apartment House, 420–30 Park Avenue, New York City; 1915–16; stripped and rebuilt: 1953.

Stores and lofts for the Murray Hill Investing Company, 411 Fifth Avenue, New York City; extant.

American Drug Syndicate Factory Building, Borden and van Alst Avenues, Long Island City, New York.

Hill Top Inn, addition to a Richard Morris Hunt house, Bellevue Avenue, Newport, Rhode Island; demolished: 1926.

Warren Library, Market Street, Warren, Pennsylvania; 1915–16; extant.

White Plains Station, White Plains, New York; (job # 739); with Reed & Stem; demolished: 1992.

Hartsdale Station, East Hartsdale Avenue, Hartsdale, New York; with Reed & Stem; (job # 742); extant.

1916

W. D. Packard house, Packard Manor, Chautauqua, New York. Warren & Wetmore Collection, Avery Architectural and Fine Arts Library, Columbia University.

William Doud Packard estate, Packard Manor, North Lake Drive, Chautauqua, New York; extant.

Apartment House, 927 Fifth Avenue, New York City; 1916–17; extant.

The Mansions, 270 Park Avenue, New York City; 1916–18; demolished: 1960.

Commodore Hotel, 400–22 Lexington Avenue, New York City; 1916–19; (job # 758); rebuilt: 1980.

Consolidated Gas Company Branch Building, 212–18 West 57th Street, New York City. Architectural Forum 28 [March 1918]: pl. 36.

Consolidated Gas Company, 212–218 West 57th Street, New York City; demolished: 1931.

Gates Memorial Library, Proctor Street, Port Arthur, Texas; 1916–17; extant: Lamar University.

Bronxville Station, Parkway Road, Bronxville, New York; with Reed & Stem; (job # 740); extant.

Exposition Building, West Second Street, Jamestown, New York; 1916–17; extant: offices.

1917

Hotel Chatham, 23–29 East 48th Street, New York City; (job # 801); demolished: 1965.

McAlpin Hotel, addition, 34th Street and Herald Square, New York City; (job # 767); extant: apartments and offices.

Equitable Trust Company Building, 347 Madison Avenue, New York City; 1917–18; extant: offices.

Consulting or associate architects for the Chateau Laurier, Ottawa, Canada; designed by Ross & McFarlane; extant.

1918

Broadmoor Hotel, Lake Avenue, Colorado Springs, Colorado; (job # 891); extant.

Condado-Vanderbilt Hotel, San Juan, Puerto Rico. Architecture and Building 52 [July 1920]: pl. 80.

Condado-Vanderbilt Hotel, San Juan, Puerto Rico; (job # 883); extant.

Iroquois Club, Harvard University, Cambridge, Massachusetts. Architectural Forum 26 [March 1917]: pl. 40.

Iroquois Club, Mt. Auburn Street, Cambridge, Massachusetts; extant: Harvard offices.

All America Cables Building, 89 Broad Street, New York City; 1918–20; demolished: 1970.

Commodore-Biltmore Garage, 323–33 East 44th Street, New York City; 1918–19; demolished.

Cathedral of St. Paul, Baldaquino, Selby Avenue, St. Paul, Minnesota; (job #949); extant.

Mausoleum for William H. Newman, Woodlawn Cemetery, New York.

1919

Ambassador Hotel, 341–51 Park Avenue, New York City; 1919–21; demolished: 1967.

Westchester-Biltmore Hotel, country club, sports building and caddy house, Biltmore Avenue, Rye, New York; 1919–22; extant: Westchester Country Club.

Biltmore Beach Club, Manursing Island, Rye, New York; 1919–22; extant: Westchester Country Club.

Sevilla Hotel, addition, Trocadero, Old Havana, Cuba; extant.

Kerr Steamship Company Building, 44 Beaver Street, New York City; 1919–20; extant.

Warren Theater (Struthers Library Theater), addition and alteration, West Third Avenue, Warren, Pennsylvania; extant.

1920

Apartment House, 280–90 Park Avenue, New York City; 1920–22; demolished: 1960.

Columbia Trust Company Branch, 290 Park Avenue, New York City; demolished: 1960.

Apartment House, 300 Park Avenue and Sherry's Restaurant, New York City; 1920–22; (job # 1062); demolished: 1951.

Plaza Hotel, addition, 55 West 58th Street, New York City; 1920–21; extant.

Ambassador Hotel, addition, Belmont Avenue, Atlantic City, New Jersey; demolished.

St. Charles Hotel, addition, St. Charles Avenue, Atlantic City, New Jersey; demolished.

Mail Services Building, addition, 460–78 Lexington Avenue, New York City; 1920–21; rebuilt.

Heckscher Building, 730 Fifth Avenue, New York City; 1920–24; extant: Crown Building.

Barrett Building, 40 Rector Street, New York City; extant.

Marlin Rockwell Building, 366 Madison Avenue, New York City; extant.

S. W. Straus & Company Building, 565 Fifth Avenue, New York City; 1920–21; demolished: 1988.

Consulting or associate architects for the Chamberlain-Vanderbilt Hotel, Old Point Comfort, Virginia; designed by Marcellus Wright; c. 1920.

1921
Apartment House, 171 West 57th Street, New York City; with H. B. Mulliken; extant.

Providence-Biltmore Hotel, Dorrance Street, Providence, Rhode Island; 1921–22; (job # 1081); extant.

Ritz Carlton, Illinois Avenue, Atlantic City, New Jersey; (job # 1101); extant: condominiums.

1922
Mrs. Florence A. V. Twombly estate, Florham, tennis court building and pool house, Convent, New Jersey; (job # 1234); demolished: 1997.

William K. Vanderbilt Jr. estate, Eagle's Next, museum building and swimming pool, Little Neck Road, Centerport, New York; 1922–23; extant: Suffolk County Vanderbilt Museum.

Bermuda Golf Club, Tucker's Town, Bermuda.
Courtesy of the Mid Ocean Club.

Bermuda Golf Club, Tucker's Town, Bermuda; 1922–24; (job # 1292); demolished: 1972.

Mallow Sterling Hotel, tower addition, Wilkes-Barre, Pennsylvania; extant: vacant.

Shelburne Hotel, Atlantic City, New Jersey.
Architecture and Building 54 [November 1922]: pl. 184.

Shelburne Hotel, addition, Michigan Avenue, Atlantic City, New Jersey; demolished.

Seamen's Church Institute, Improvements to Jeanette Park, Coenties Slip, New York City.

Harper & Bros. Building, 49 East 33rd Street, New York City; 1922–23; (job # 1285); extant.

Park-Lexington Building, 245 Park Avenue, New York City; 1922–23; (job # 1194); demolished: 1967.

Home Club, addition and alterations, 11–15 East 45th Street, New York City; (job # 1203); demolished.

Memorial Gate for George v. L. Meyer, Hamilton, Massachusetts; (job # 1243); extant.

University Library, Mgr. Ladeuzeplein, Louvain, Belgium; 1922–28; (job # 1207); extant.

1923
The Mayflower Hotel, Connecticut Avenue N.W., Washington, D.C.; 1923–25; (job # 1291); extant.

Tower Building, 200 Madison Avenue, New York City; 1923–26; extant.

Steinway Hall, 109–13 West 57th Street, New York City; 1923–25; extant.

National Theater alteration and addition, 1321 Pennsylvania Avenue NW, Washington, D.C.; (job # 1275); extant.

B. P. O. Elks, No. 21, Camp and Broad Streets, Newark, New Jersey; extant: offices.

Sixteenth Street Bridge over Allegheny River, Pittsburgh, Pennsylvania; with sculpture by Leo Lentelli; extant.

Furniture and furnishings for the Bon Air Vanderbilt Hotel, Atlanta, Georgia.

Supervising architects for the Penn Athletic Club, Rittenhouse Square, Philadelphia, Pennsylvania; 1923–25; designed by Zantzinger, Borie, and Medary; extant.

1924
Mrs. Marshall Field estate, Caumsett, tennis court building, West Neck Road, Lloyd Harbor, New York; extant.

Hotel Bermudiana, Hamilton, Bermuda.
Architecture and Building 57 [April 1925]: pl. 79.

Hotel Bermudiana, Richmond Road, Hamilton, Bermuda; destroyed in fire: 1958.

Apartment House, 1020 Fifth Avenue, New York City; 1924–25; extant.

Madison-Belmont Building, 181 Madison Avenue, New York City; 1924–25; extant.

Consolidated Gas Company, 166th Street and Audubon Avenue, New York City.

Royal Italian Embassy, Fuller Street N.W., Washington, D.C.; extant: vacant.

Consulting or associate architects for Chateau Frontenac, tower addition, Quebec City, Quebec; extant.

1925
The Berkshire, 500 Madison Avenue, New York City; 1925–26; extant.

Berkeley-Carteret Hotel, Ocean Avenue, Asbury Park, New Jersey; extant.

Deepdale Golf and Country Club, Deepdale, New York. Architectural Record 60 [December 1926]: 519.

Deepdale Country Club, Lakeville Road, Deepdale, New York; 1925–26; extant: Lake Success town offices and golf course.

Aeolian Building, 689 Fifth Avenue, New York City; 1925–27; extant: offices and stores.

Cranleigh Hospital, 159–63 East 90th Street, New York City; extant: apartment building.

Butterfield Bank, Front and Burnaby Streets, Hamilton, Bermuda; extant.

Supervisiong architect for apartment house, 112 West 59th Street, New York City; designed by J. E. R. Carpenter; extant.

1926
Mrs. Florence A. V. Twombly, 900 Fifth Avenue, New York City; 1926–27; (job # 1744); demolished: 1958.

Apartment House, 990 Fifth Avenue, with Rosario Candela, New York City; extant.

Royal Hawaiian Hotel, Waikiki Beach, Honolulu, Hawaii; 1926–27; extant.

Shelburne Hotel, tower addition, Michigan Avenue, Atlantic City, New Jersey; demolished.

Consolidated Gas Company, tower addition, 4 Irving Place, New York City; with Thomas Murray; 1926–28; extant.

Seaman's Church Institute, addition, South Street, New York City; (job # 1064); demolished: 1967.

Erlanger Theater, 246–51 West 44th Street, New York City; 1926–27; extant: St. James Theater.

Theater for Hotel Statler, Delaware Avenue, Buffalo, New York; 1926–27; extant.

Supervising architects for the Michigan Theater and Office Building, Bagley Street, Detroit, Michigan; designed by C. W. and George L. Rapp; partially demolished and converted to parking garage.

Supervising architects for the Paramount Theater and Office Building, 1501 Broadway, New York City: 1926–27; designed by C. W. and George L. Rapp; extant.

1927

Apartment House, 856 Fifth Avenue, New York City; with Rosario Candela, extant.

Apartment House, 960 Fifth Avenue, New York City; with Rosario Candela, extant.

Constant Spring Hotel, Constant Spring Road, Kingston, Jamaica; 1927–31; extant: Immaculate Conception School.

New York Central Building, 230 Park Avenue, New York City; 1927–29; extant: Helmsley Building.

Medical Arts Building, 57 West 57th Street, New York City; 1927–29; extant: offices.

1928

William K. Vanderbilt Jr. estate, alterations and additions to house, Eagle's Next, Little Neck Road, Centerport, New York; c. 1928, extant: Suffolk Country Vanderbilt Museum.

Homestead Hotel, tower addition, Hot Springs, Virginia; 1928–29; extant.

Stewart and Company, 721 Fifth Avenue, New York City; 1928–29; (job # 1931); demolished: 1980.

Empire Trust Building, 580–86 Fifth Avenue, New York City. Architecture and Building 60 [May 1928]: 150.

Empire Trust and Knabe Tower Building, 580–86 Fifth Avenue, New York City; 1928–29; extant: offices.

Newport Trust Company, Newport, Rhode Island. Newport Historical Society

Newport Trust Company, Thames Street, Newport, Rhode Island; demolished.

Supervising architects for the Lincoln Building, 60 East 42nd Street, New York City; 1928–30; designed by J. E. R. Carpenter; extant.

Consulting or associate architects for the Vancouver Hotel, Vancouver, British Columbia; extant.

1929
Consulting or associate architects for the Dayton-Biltmore Hotel, North Main Street, Dayton, Ohio; designed by Frederick J. Hughes; extant: Biltmore Towers.

1930
William K. Vanderbilt Jr. estate, additional story to museum building and addition to main house, Eagle's Next, Little Neck Road, Centerport, New York; (job # 2017 and 2006); extant: Suffolk Country Vanderbilt Museum.

William K. Vanderbilt Jr. apartment, alterations, 651 Park Avenue, New York City; (job # 2013); extant.

Kirby Hall of Civil Rights, Lafayette College, Easton, Pennsylvania. Architecture and Building 62 [September 1930]: 261.

Kirby Hall of Rights, Lafayette College, Easton, Pennsylvania; c. 1930; with sculpture by Edward McCartan; extant.

Railroad YMCA, 220–30 East 47th Street, New York City; 1930–31; extant.

Silver Building, 32 Pearl Street, New York City; (job # 2045); extant.

Convention Hall, Pier, Paramount Theater, Casino, and Pier, Asbury Park, New Jersey; with Arthur Cottrell, Ernest Arend, and Kenneth Towner; extant.

Seacoast Trust Company, alterations and additions, Asbury Park, New Jersey.

UNDATED PROJECTS
Residential

Alexander, Charles B., alteration, New York City.

Green, Mary Amory estate, Mount Airy Road, Croton-on-Hudson, New York; extant.

Havemeyer, T. A. estate, addition and alterations, Brookville, New York.

Iselin, C. Oliver estate, addition and alterations, Wolver Hollow, Chicken Valley Road, Brookville; extant.

Kaufman, Louis G. estate, alteration, Short Hills, New Jersey.

Phoenix, Lloyd, alteration, 21 East 33rd Street, New York City; (job #621); demolished.

Preston, Veryl estate, addition and alterations, Glen Oaks, Hohokus, New Jersey.

Smith, Mrs. Sidney, alteration, New York City.

Winthrop, Egerton and Bronson, alteration, 23 East 33rd Street, New York City; (job #624); demolished.

Other

American Express Building, Tenth Avenue and 33rd Street, New York City.

Jamaica Water Supply Building, Jamaica, Queens.

Terminal Realty Building, Port Arthur, Texas.

United Cigar Stores Company Building, New York City; (job # 735).

George T. Slade Memorial, Mount Pleasant, New York.

Supervising Architects

Fulton-Flatbush Building, Brooklyn, New York
Chemical National Bank

UNBUILT PROJECTS

Unbuilt projects. Warren & Wetmore Collection, Avery
Architectural and Fine Arts Library, Columbia University.

*Whitney Warren's proposal for Hudson
River Bridge, 1909.* Margaret Brentano and
Nicholson Baker, *The World on Sunday*
(New York: Bulfinch Press, 2005): 115.

1. Grand Central Terminal, High Building
2. Madison Square Loft Building
3. Municipal Building
4. Peace Palace
5. University of California
6. Sing Sing Prison
7. Riker's Island Penitentiary
8. Bar Harbor Hotel
9. Grand Rapids Loft Building
10. Professional Building
11. McConkey Hotel
12. Mexico Hotel
13. Bankers Trust
14. New York Cotton Exchange
15. Ritz Hotel, Chicago
16. George Washington Memorial
17. Racquet and Tennis Club
18. Denver Terminal
19. Theater, 44th Street
20. Meadowbrook Tennis Court
21. D.S.C. Stable, New York City
22. Clinton Market D.S.C. Stable
23. Perry Belmont Residence
24. Dr. Pierce Stores and Offices
25. New Orleans Terminal
26. Baltimore Courthouse
27. Ritz Hotel, Rio de Janeiro
28. Winnipeg Hotel
29. New Theater
30. Cuban Palace
31. Dallas Terminal
32. Grant Memorial
33. Chemists Club
34. New York Public Library
35. Goelet Garage
36. Birmingham Terminal
37. Astor Tennis Court
38. Garbage Dock
39. Seton Hall
40. Conewango Club
41. Redmond Bank
42. Jamestown Hospital
43. Orange Post Office
44. Morgan Library
45. Union Club
46. Department of Justice
47. Denver Post Office
48. Consolidated Petroleum Exchange
49. Chemical Bank
50. Union Trust, San Francisco
51. Colgate Residence
52. Rathbone Residence
53. Astor Lodge
54. Munroe Residence
55. Leeds Residence
56. Robert Goelet Residence
57. Morganthau Residence
58. Whitney Swimming Pool
59. Hennings Residence

R. Allen
F. W. Bancroft
Sylvan Bien
M. G. Bitterbaum
Ralph Calder
R. C. Campi
E. F. Clapp
F. G. Colton
E. Conti
James E. Cooper
Henry Raymond Copeland
Patrick M. Corry
H. J. Cullen
R. J. Cummings
E. I. Daugherty
L. J. Eaton
F. K. English
Leon N. Gillette
E. Frey
F. Good
Carroll Greenough
Arthur W. Griffin
Clinton Gardner Harris
Charles Hartman
H. H. Heybeck
K. B. Hill
H. Hofmeister
Julian Holland
Walter Hopkins
John Edward Howe
William Iselin
C. M. Jaeger
R. A. Kluge
Morris Lapidus
Frederick Larkin
J. R. Lautenbach
Benjamin W. Levitan
E. S. Lyman
R. C. Lynch
Ian C. MacCallum
M. M. Mann
Bissell S. Mansfield
J. C. Marsh

Emmanuel Louis
    Masqueray
Eugene V. Meroni
Mortimer D. Metcalfe
S. M. Minoli
Lloyd Henry Morgan
C. G. Munsell
J. L. Newman
Ronald Pearce
A. Pieron
Henry Brooks Price
Harry M. Prince
John R. Rainbow
Frederick Garfield Robb
D. G. Rosenfeld
Leonard Schultze
Matthews M. Simpson
P. A. Singer
George C. Smith
L. H. Smith
William Sunderland
J. B. Surhoff
R. T. Swezey
H. D. Symonds
P. B. Tallman
Kristen Tangen
C. D. Thompson
H. Desmond Upton
N. T. Valentine
N. Vasselieff
T. E. Videto
Robert von Ezdorf
Alexander Stewart Walker
Richard A. Walker
G. Walling
Lloyd Warren
Richard Watmough
N. R. Webber
Lessing Whitford Williams
A. P. Wolf
L. M. Wolff
Eric Fisher Wood
A. Zaborowski

EPIGRAPHS

Whitney Warren, "Apologia," *Scientific American* 62 (December 7, 1912): 484.

Henry James, *The American Scene* (New York: Harper & Bros., 1907; New York: Charles Scribner's Sons, 1946): 406.

Arnold Bennett, *Those United States* (London: Martin Secker, 1912): 35.

"Apartment House, 300 Park Avenue, New York," *Architecture and Building* 54 (April 1922): 38.

"New Fifth Av. House on Clews Home Site," *The New York Times* (October 26, 1930): 11, 10.

INTRODUCTION

1. Patricia Beard, *After the Ball* (New York: Harper Collins Publishers, 2003): 8.
2. Republic's scale and pose referred to another colossal figure, the Statue of Liberty. Unlike Liberty, Republic was modeled strictly in the tradition of Greco-Roman heroic statuary—a classical goddess transformed into an icon of democratic virtue.
3. While the Ecole offered three *ateliers officiels* that were housed in the school's buildings, most ateliers were privately run—*ateliers libres*—and located in studios throughout Paris.
4. Herbert Dudley Hale (1866–1909), Joseph H. Freedlander (1870–1943), and John Vredenbergh Van Pelt (1874–1963) were the first three Americans to graduate from the Ecole des Beaux-Arts in 1895.
5. "Is There an American Architecture?," *The New York Times* (April 18, 1909): 4, 1.
6. Howard Greenley, "In Memorium, Whitney Warren, 1864–1943," from the archives of the American Institute of Architecture, Washington, D.C.
7. "Current Periodicals," *The Architectural Review* 8 (1901): 72.

CHAPTER ONE
BACKGROUND AND BEGINNINGS

1. "Whitney Warren Dies; Designed Grand Central," *New York Herald Tribune* (January 25, 1943): 8.
2. A traceable ancestor of the Warren family was William de Warrenne, who went to England with William the Conqueror (and was related to him by marriage and descent). The first Warren arrived in America during the 1660s. In 1798, the following generations of Warrens moved from Norwalk, Connecticut, to the thriving Hudson River town of Troy. There, Warren's grandfather, Nathan Warren (1779–1834), married his first cousin, Mary Bouton (1789–1859), and made a considerable fortune in banking, steamboats, and railroads. During their early years of marriage, George Henry and Mary Caroline Warren also lived at Mount Ida. In New York, they lived at 145 Madison Avenue and, later, at 520 Fifth Avenue; in 1890, George Henry Warren commissioned McKim, Mead & White to design the seven-story Warren Building at 903–7 Broadway. When he died in 1892, G.H. Warren's estate was valued at $7–8 million.
3. Warren's grandmother, Mary Bouton Warren, founded the Church of the Holy Cross and the Mary Warren Free Institute. Richard Upjohn enlarged the church in 1848, and Henry Dudley,

architect of the family vault, added a tower and antechapel in 1859. The adjoining school, the Mary Warren Free Institute of the City of Troy, was built in 1863.
4. An earlier child, also named Whitney, had died at age three. Warren's twin sister Anna also died shortly after birth.
5. Warren was called "Little Whitney" to differentiate him from his uncle Stephen Whitney Phoenix, also called Whitney. Letters of Mary Whitney Phoenix to her daughter Mary Caroline Phoenix Warren, 1875–76, Newport Historical Society, Newport, Rhode Island.
6. George Henry Warren was director of the Newport Casino.
7. Next to William K. Vanderbilt, George Henry Warren was said to be the largest subscriber in the formation of the Metropolitan Opera house.
8. "Whitney Warren, Architect, 78, Dies," *The New York Times* (January 25, 1943): 13.
9. Most aspiring architects, after arriving in Paris, typically spent at least one year studying for the notoriously grueling entrance examinations leading to admission to the Ecole des Beaux-Arts. Honoré Daumet was best known for his work on the restoration of the Château de Chantilly and the Palais de Justice in Paris. Charles Louis Girault, known for his designs for the Petit Palais on the Champs Élysées for the 1900 International Exhibition, joined Daumet in 1885 in heading the atelier.
10. Pierre Esquié succeeded Girault as *patron* in 1888; he was best known for his designs for the Ecole des Beaux-Arts and the Salle des Fetes et Capitole in Toulouse. Between the years of 1860 and 1907, the Daumet–Girault–Esquié atelier also placed second in the competition six times.
11. Warren, an *ancient éleve*—the recognition for students who spent at least five years at the Ecole—did not receive his diploma until March 7, 1919, when he was living in France. At that time, he wrote to his wife, "I received three days ago my Diploma as Architecte Diplôme par le Government! What I would have given to have it 25 years ago, and how hard I tried to get it! Well, I feel it has been earned!! At 55 years of age!!!" Whitney Warren to Charlotte A. Tooker Warren, Paris, May 28, 1919, Whitney Warren Papers, bMS Am 2113 (517). By permission of the Houghton Library, Harvard University.
12. Howard Greenley, "In Memorium, Whitney Warren, 1864–1943," from the archives of the A.I.A., Washington, D.C.; Whitney Warren [draft] to (?), Paris, January 13, 1915, Whitney Warren Papers, bMS Am 2113 (54). By permission of the Houghton Library, Harvard University.
13. A corresponding member, Warren replaced François Auguste Gevaert (1828–1908), the Belgian musician and composer.
14. Whitney Warren to Charlotte A. Tooker Warren, Paris, January 20, 1919, Whitney Warren Papers, bMS Am 2113 (477). By permission of the Houghton Library, Harvard University.
15. Warren's sketches and watercolors in the collections of the Cooper-Hewitt, National Design Museum, Smithsonian Institution, mostly cover the period from 1894 to 1898.
16. *Reminiscences of Lawrence Grant White*, 1956, pages 109–10 in the Columbia University Oral History Research Office Collection (hereafter CUOHROC).
17. According to *The New York Times*, architect L. Griffiths of Boston came in second in the club competition. "Newport Country Club's New Home," *The New York Times* (September 9, 1884): 8; Alan T. Schumacher, "The Newport Country Club: Its Curious History," *Newport History: Bulletin of the Newport Historical Society* 59 (Spring 1986): 47–106. In 1954 Warren's piazza was destroyed by a hurricane.
18. *The New York Times* (1895), as quoted in Schumacher, "The Newport Country Club: Its Curious History," *Newport History: Bulletin of the Newport Historical Society*, 67.

19. *Baltimore Courthouse*: "Baltimore Courthouse Competition," *The Inland Architect and News Record* 24 (August 1894); *New York Public Library*: Warren's entry is in the Whitney Warren Collection at the Cooper-Hewitt, National Design Museum, Smithsonian Institution.
20. Charlotte Warren to Stanford White, Thursday (1895), Stanford White Collection, Avery Architectural and Fine Arts Library, Columbia University.
21. Stanford White to Charlotte Warren, October 24, 1895, Stanford White Collection, Avery Architectural and Fine Arts Library, Columbia University.
22. This apartment was most likely used as a studio; at the time Warren lived with his family at 145 Madison Avenue.
23. Whitney Warren to Stanford White, undated, Stanford White Collection, Avery Architectural and Fine Arts Library, Columbia University.
24. The location of this house is not known.
25. Rosalia Hall Wetmore Kent was considered one of the most influential women in western New York. As an early supporter of the Christian Science Church of Boston, she helped found the Christian Science Church in Jamestown for which Charles D. Wetmore designed a picturesque shingle-style church in 1893. Her house had been owned by Alonzo Kent, her second husband's uncle. After his mother's death, Charles D. Wetmore and his half-brother Morgan Bostwick Kent inherited the house, and Wetmore briefly used it from 1917 to 1918 before moving to Long Point on Lake Chautauqua. The Kent house is now the Robert H. Jackson Center.
26. Later, Warren & Wetmore designed a clubhouse for the Iroquois Club at 74 Mt. Auburn Street. The Iroquois Club was founded in 1906 as a waiting club for the Fly Club. The Georgian-style brick clubhouse is now occupied by the Office for the Arts at Harvard. "Iroquois Club, Cambridge, Mass.," *The Architectural Forum* 26 (March 1917): 79; pl. 40.
27. "The New Halls at Harvard Have Quite the Aspect of City Clubs," *The Advocate* (October 17, 1898); Bainbridge Bunting, *Harvard: An Architectural History* (Cambridge, MA: The Belknap Press of Harvard University Press, 1985): 184–85. According to Bunting, Wetmore played a hand in the design of Claverly Hall and Apley Court.
28. Edward Weeks, *My Green Age* (Boston: Little, Brown, 1973): 126–27. Wetmore had two stepdaughters, Lady Martha Thorton and Mrs. Edward Weeks.
29. "Dormitories, Harvard University, Cambridge, Mass.," *The Architectural Review* 10 (January 1901): 11. Also: Warren & Wetmore Collection, Avery Architectural and Fine Arts Library, Columbia University; "The New Halls at Harvard Have Quite the Aspect of City Clubs," *The Advocate*; "Dormitories, Harvard University, Cambridge, Mass.," *The Inland Architect and News Record* 40 (December 1902): 14. Westmorly is now part of Adams House, a Harvard dormitory.
30. "The Enlargement of Harvard," *Harper's Weekly* 53 (December 18, 1909): 17–19; Bunting, *Harvard: An Architectural History*, 181.
31. In 1924 there were forty-five men working in the drafting room. "The Drafting Room Force of Warren & Wetmore, Architects, New York," *Pencil Points* 5 (May 1924): 79. When Morris Lapidus joined the firm in the late 1920s, Warren & Wetmore numbered at two hundred employees.
32. According to Edward Weeks, one of Wetmore's last commissions was designing the interiors of the new Matson liners (1932). It also appears that Wetmore offered legal services out of the offices at 16 East 47th Street, as advertised in *The New York Times* in 1931. By 1938, after his

wife's death, "Wetmore's fortune had drained away as building after building in which he invested passed into bankruptcy." Weeks, *My Green Age*, 319.

33. The Beaux-Arts Institute of Design building at 304 East 44th Street was built in 1928 after the designs of Frederic C. Hirons of Dennision & Hirons. When the institute outgrew its original building at 126 East 75th Street (Jacob Schiff's former stable), it organized a competition—a four-hour *esquisse*—to determine an architect for the new building. Architects Kenneth Murchison and Whitney Warren chaired the planning committee.

34. After the senior partners' departure, the firm was primarily engaged to renovate existing Warren & Wetmore structures.

35. Whitney Warren to Charlotte A. Tooker Warren, Paris, June 20, 1917, Whitney Warren Papers, bMS Am 2113 (246). By the permission of the Houghton Library, Harvard University.

36. Whitney Warren to Charlotte A. Tooker Warren, Paris, September 3, 1915, Whitney Warren Papers, bMS Am 2113 (126). By the permission of the Houghton Library, Harvard University.

37. Whitney Warren to Barrett Wendell, February 7, 1916, Barrett Wendell Papers, bMS Am 1907.1 (1349). By permission of the Houghton Library, Harvard University.

38. This incident led to a lawsuit and found its way into *The New York Times* several days in a row. "Pictures Lead to Suit, *The New York Times* (July 24, 1911): 7.

39. Greenley, "In Memorium, Whitney Warren, 1864–1943," from the archives of the A.I.A., Washington, D.C.

40. Weeks, *My Green Age*, 118, 126.

41. The number of clubs to which the partners belonged fluctuated. According to the Social Register, Wetmore belonged to nine clubs in 1903, including the Knickerbocker, Meadowbrook, Downtown Club, University, Racquet and Tennis, and New York Yacht Club; Warren belonged to six: the Metropolitan, Racquet and Tennis, Tuxedo, Players, New York Yacht Club, and Fencers Club.

42. "Long Swim by Society Man," *The New York Times* (August 8, 1910): 1.

43. Charlotte Warren married William Greenough and had one daughter, Beatrice Goelet Greenough; Gabrielle married Reginald Rives and had two children, Reginald and Lloyd Michael. Whitney Warren Jr., called "Brother," never married. He lived in California for most of his adult life.

44. Basil Woon, *The Paris That's Not in Guide Books* (New York: Brentano's, 1926): 144.

45. Besides inheriting a portion of his father's generous estate of close to $8 million, Warren inherited over $2 million from his uncle Lloyd Phoenix (1841–1926). Phoenix lived at 21 East 33rd Street with his brother Phillips in an "artistic" classical townhouse (1882–84) designed by McKim, Mead & White. Later, Warren & Wetmore removed the stoop and service stair to the house (job # 621).

46. Leslie A. Hyam, "Collection of the Late Whitney Warren," Parke–Bernet Galleries, Public Auction Sale, 1943.

47. "The Architectural Working Library of Whitney Warren," Parke–Bernet Galleries, Public Auction Sale #195, 1940.

48. The Wetmores' house at Long Point was originally built by Ralph Preston, for whom Warren & Wetmore designed a large estate on Long Island in 1904.

49. Whitney Warren as quoted in James Phillip Noffsinger, *The Influence of the École des Beaux Arts on the Architects of the United States* (Washington: Catholic University of America Press, 1955): 37.

50. W. Franckyln Paris, "Lloyd Eliot Warren," *Personalities in American Art* 1 (New York: The Architectural Forum, 1930): 29.

51. Lloyd Warren died at the age of 52 after falling from his apartment window. Suicide was dismissed because Warren was prone to sleepwalking and was wearing his pajamas at the time of his death. "Sleep-Walk Plunge Kills Lloyd Warren," *The New York Times* (October 26, 1922): 1. As noted by Howard Greenley, Warren "sought to minimize the extent of this loyal service, always content to subordinate himself and prompt to disclaim the slightest acknowledgement of the part he played . . . in his brother's conception." (Greenley, "In Memorium, Whitney Warren, 1864–1943," from the archives of the A.I.A., Washington, D.C.)

52. By the 1920s, architectural education in the United States had advanced to the point where it was not necessary to spend years studying at the Ecole. The Fontainebleau School enabled students to experience French methods, however briefly, and study European monuments firsthand. At the school, Warren and Victor Laloux supervised the architectural studies. Laloux's atelier at the Ecole had been favored among American students; alumni included William Adams Delano, Arthur Brown Jr., William Lawrence Bottomley, John W. Cross, Lawrence Grant White, and William Van Alen. "The Fontainebleau School of the Fine Arts," *American Magazine of Arts* (February 1923): 84–87; Isabelle Gournay, "Architecture at the Fontainebleau School of Fine Art, 1929–1939," *Journal of the Society of Architectural Historians* 45 (September 1986): 270–85.

53. "Pageant to Mark Beaux Arts Ball," *The New York Times* (January 29, 1926): 17.

54. Partial building lists from Avery Archives show project numbers in the 1,200s; however, many of the projects listed were never built.

CHAPTER TWO
EARLY PROJECTS: 1898–1904

1. A. D. F. Hamlin and F. S. Lamb, "The New York Architectural Exhibition," *The Architectural Review* 6 (April 1899): 39–53; "New York Yacht Club, 37 West Forty-Fourth Street, New York," *Architecture* 3 (March 1901): 66–75; "Some Recent American Designs," *The Architectural Record* 10 (April 1901): 417–24; "The New York Yacht Club, Warren & Wetmore, Architects," *Architects' and Builders' Magazine* 3 (January 1902): 117–24; Lucy Harvey Syndor, "The Clubhouse of the New York Yacht Club," *The Magazine Antiques* 118 (September 1980): 508–15; Landmarks Preservation Commission, *New York Yacht Club Building, 37 West 44th Street, Manhattan* (New York: Landmarks Preservation Commission, 1979); Robert A. M. Stern, Gregory Gilmartin, and John Massengale, *New York 1900: Metropolitan Architecture and Urbanism, 1890–1915* (New York: Rizzoli, 1983): 238–41; John Rousmaniere, *The Clubhouse at Sea* (New York: New York Yacht Club, 2001).

2. Of those invited, McKim, Mead & White, Carrère & Hastings, and James Lord Brown declined to compete. Although Whitney Warren, Peabody & Stearns, and Howard & Cauldwell were not initially invited to participate, they were later added to the list.

3. Guidelines for the New York Yacht Club Competition and William R. Ware's Report, New York, December 9th, 1898; from the archives of the New York Yacht Club.

4. Whitney Warren's competition entry, December 5th, 1898; from the archives of the New York Yacht Club.

5. Whitney Warren's competition entry, December 5th, 1898.

6. "Current Periodicals," *The Architectural Review* 8 (1901): 72.

7. Warren's collection included over thirty books on the subject. Parke–Bernet Galleries, Inc.,

"The Architectural Working Library of Whitney Warren," 1940, and "The Collection of the Late Whitney Warren," 1943. Warren's collection of ships was exhibited at Avery Library in 1913. "Whitney Warren Exhibition in the Avery Library," *Columbia Alumni News* 4 (March 1928): 413.

8. Whitney Warren, unpublished diary, 52. Redwood Library and Athenaeum, Newport, Rhode Island.

9. Lewis Cass Ledyard, Carter and Ledyard, Counselors at Law, to the Building Committee, November 25th, 1898; from the archives of the New York Yacht Club.

10. Whitney Warren to Stanford White, October 16, 1900, Stanford White Collection, Avery Architectural and Fine Arts Library, Columbia University.

11. Stanford White to Charles D. Wetmore, November 13, 1900, Stanford White Collection, Avery Architectural and Fine Arts Library, Columbia University.

12. Hamlin and Lamb, "The New York Architectural League Exhibition," *The Architectural Review*, 45.

13. "The New Home of N.Y.Y.C.," *The Sun* (January 18, 1901); "N.Y.Y.C's New Home Open," *The New York Times* (July 18, 1901): 8.

14. On December 30, 1899, the first match between Thomas Suffern Tailer and Great Britain's Cecil Bearing was played on the court; the Tuxedo Tennis and Racquet Club later merged with the Tuxedo Club in 1909. "History of Court Tennis" compiled from Allison Danzig, "The Royal & Ancient Game of Tennis," and "History of the Tuxedo Club," *The One Hundred and First Tuxedo Club Gold Racquets Tournament*, February 14–17, 2003 (Tuxedo: The Tuxedo Club, 2003); Warren & Wetmore Collection, Avery Architectural and Fine Arts Library, Columbia University.

15. Warren & Wetmore Collection, Avery Architectural and Fine Arts Library, Columbia University; Jim Zug, "Lost Courts in America," *The Dedans: Newsletter of the United States Court Tennis Association*.

16. Warren & Wetmore Collection, Avery Architectural and Fine Arts Library, Columbia University.

17. Additional projects by the firm in Warren, Pennsylvania, where Wetmore's father was born and raised, included a brick mansion and carriage house for Jerry Crary (1900), the Warren Library (1915–16), and the Warren Theater (1919), located in the Struthers Library Building.

18. Warren & Wetmore Collection, Avery Architectural and Fine Arts Library, Columbia University. The Munroe house has been privately owned since 1976. The Academy of Mount St. Vincent, which occupied the building before 1976, added a classroom annex to the house in the 1950s.

19. Warren & Wetmore Collection, Avery Architectural and Fine Arts Library, Columbia University. The French house was torn down in the 1940s.

20. "High Tide, The Residence of William Miller," *Newport Journal* (July 21, 1900). Warren also worked on the Millers' house, Rock Ledge, in Rhinebeck, New York, designed by Francis L. V. Hoppin (c. 1904–6).

21. Ralph J. Preston married the daughter of Colonel William P. Thompson, a Standard Oil millionaire. In addition to Ivy Hall, he maintained residences in Colorado Springs, Red Bank, New Jersey, and Jamestown, New York, where he was born; he owned Ivy Hall for only two years. After Preston's death in 1919, Wetmore, also from Jamestown, bought Preston's house, Long Point, on Lake Chautauqua; the two men were related through the Hall family. Warren also maintained a friendship with Preston while both were working for the American Clearing House and the Red Cross Commission in Paris

during World War One. *Country Life in America* 25 (March 1914): 2; *Country Life in America* 58 (August 1930): 15; Warren & Wetmore Collection, Avery Architectural and Fine Arts Library, Columbia University; Robert B. MacKay, Anthony K. Baker, and Carol A. Traynor, *Long Island Country Houses and Their Architects, 1860–1940* (New York: W. W. Norton & Co., 1997): 436.

22. Warren & Wetmore Collection, Avery Architectural and Fine Arts Library, Columbia University; Kirby Hill, Garden Club of America Collection, Archives of American Gardens, Smithsonian Institution; MacKay, Baker, and Traynor, *Long Island Country Houses and their Architects, 1860–1940*, 436.

23. A rift developed between McKim, Mead & White and the Mackays as a result of the long, drawn out, expensive project. Warren & Wetmore was most likely a less expensive option because it was a relatively new firm. "The Layout of a Large Estate," *Architectural Record* 16 (December 1904): 531–55; Warren & Wetmore Collection, Avery Architectural and Fine Arts Library, Columbia University; MacKay, Baker, and Traynor, *Long Island Country Houses and Their Architects, 1860–1901*, 434–35.

24. Restoration Committee for W. K. Vanderbilt's "Idle Hour," *William Kissam Vanderbilt's Idle Hour* (Oakdale: Dowling College, 1996); John Foreman and Robbe Pierce Stimson, *The Vanderbilts and the Gilded Age: Architectural Aspirations, 1879–1901* (New York: St. Martin's Press, 1991): 171–92; Warren & Wetmore Collection, Avery Architectural and Fine Arts Library, Columbia University; "Idle Hour Mansion Bought for Club," *The New York Times* (March 29, 1936): 2, 1; MacKay, Baker, and Traynor, *Long Island Country Houses and Their Architects, 1860–1940*, 435.

25. Alva Vanderbilt forced her daughter away from Rutherford so as to marry her to the Duke of Marlborough, events described in Consuelo Vanderbilt Balsan's memoir, *The Glitter and the Gold* (New York: Harper, 1952).

26. Warren & Wetmore Collection, Avery Architectural and Fine Arts Library, Columbia University.

27. The main house became Skywood School for Girls; it was demolished in 1950. The Mount Kisco Country Club now owns several buildings on the estate. Phoebe Whitney and Harriet B. Risley, *Annandale Farm: The Moses Taylor Estate* (New Castle Historical Society, 1986); Warren & Wetmore Collection, Avery Architectural and Fine Arts Library, Columbia University. In 1904, Warren & Wetmore also designed the Moses Taylor Hospital in Lackawanna, New York. Taylor established the hospital to care for employees and their families working in three of the area's industries in which he was an investor—Glen Alden Coal Company, Delaware and Lackawanna Railroad, and Lackawanna Steel Company.

28. Warren & Wetmore Collection, Avery Architectural and Fine Arts Library, Columbia University; Mattie Edwards Hewitt Collection, New York State Historical Association, Cooperstown, New York.

29. "The Fashionable Residential District, No. One," *Real Estate Record and Builder's Guide* 76 (December 16, 1905): 950.

30. An extended discussion of the modern French style can be found in Stern, Gilmartin, and Massengale, *New York 1900*, 325–34.

31. In 1901 and 1902, the average cost of a speculative house was $65,000. "The Fashionable Residential District, No. One," *Real Estate Record and Builder's Guide* 76 (December 16, 1905): 950; Warren & Wetmore Collection, Avery Architectural and Fine Arts Library, Columbia University; Landmarks Preservation Commission, *Upper East Side Historic District Designation Report* (New York: The Commission, 1981): 925–26. The buildings at 832–34 Fifth Avenue were demolished in 1930 to make way for Rosario Candela's fourteen-story apartment building, 834 Fifth Avenue.

32. Number eleven is now the Permanent Mission to the People's Republic of Bulgaria, and number nine has been divided into apartments. New York Landmarks Preservation Commission, *Metropolitan Museum Historic District Designation Report* (New York: The Commission, 1977): 80–81; Christopher Gray, "Streetscapes: 84th Street between Fifth and Madison Avenues," *The New York Times* (September 9, 2001): 11, 9; "Residence, New York," *The Inland Architect and News Record* 42 (November 1903); "9–11 East 84th Street," Warren & Wetmore Architects, 3 East 33rd Street.

33. "Residence, F. K. Pendleton, 7 East 86th Street, New York," *Architecture* 6 (August 1902): 250; Warren & Wetmore Collection, Avery Architectural and Fine Arts Library, Columbia University. This house was demolished in 1960.

34. After Caroline Astor Wilson's death in 1948, the government of India purchased the property and continues to use the building as the Consulate General of India. William Lescaze altered the interiors in 1952. Warren & Wetmore Collection, Avery Architectural and Fine Arts Library, Columbia University; "Residence, M. Orme Wilson, 3 East 64th Street," *Architecture* 10 (July 1904): pl. 55; "Devis approximatif des travaux de Décoration et Ameublements, Monsieur Orme Wilson, Hôtel à New York par H. Nelson, 20 Rue de Chazelles," the New-York Historical Society; "Mansion to House India Diplomats," *The New York Times* (December 12, 1948): 6; Stern, Gilmartin, and Massengale, *New York 1900*, 334–35; Landmarks Preservation Commission, *Upper East Side Historic District Designation Report*, 153.

35. Warren & Wetmore Collection, Avery Architectural and Fine Arts Library, Columbia University; New York Landmarks Preservation Commission, *Metropolitan Museum Historic District Designation Report*, 36–37.

36. *Edey House*: "Residence, Mrs. Fred'k Edey, 10 West 56th St.," *Architecture* 7 (March 1903): pl. 19; Stern, Gilmartin, and Massengale, *New York 1900*, 330, 351; Warren & Wetmore Collection, Avery Architectural and Fine Arts Library, Columbia University; Jean Gorman, "Earthly Delight," *Interiors* 152 (April 1993): 38–45. This house is now a store. *Warren House*: "Residence, G. H. Warren, 924 Fifth Ave., New York," *Architecture* 11 (May 1905): pl. 41. In the late 1940s, this house was demolished to make way for a new apartment building. *Beeckman House*: New York Landmarks Preservation Commission, *The Permanent Mission of Yugoslavia to the United Nations, formerly the R. Livingston Beeckmann House* (New York: The Commission, 1969); Landmarks Preservation Commission, *Upper East Side Historic District Designation Report*, 932. Mrs. Henry White (Emily Vanderbilt Sloane) later purchased the house and eventually sold it to the Federal Peoples Republic of Yugoslavia in 1946. It is now the Permanent Mission of Serbia and Montenegro to the United Nations.

37. Warren & Wetmore Collection, Avery Architectural and Fine Arts Library, Columbia University; "Stable, New York City," *The Inland Architect and News Record* 42 (November 1903): 32.

38. "Personal and Otherwise," *The New York Times* (March 24, 1907): 4, 6.

39. The striking entrance sequence was added later in the design process; early plans for the house placed the main entrance at the street, and the first floor, composed of a large octagonal hall and a double-height dining room with a music gallery above, did not include a porte-cochère.

40. "Personal and Otherwise," *The New York Times*, 4, 6.

41. Edith Wharton and Ogden Codman, Jr., *The Decoration of Houses* (New York: C. Scribner' Sons, 1902; New York: W. W. Norton & Co., 1978): 135.

42. John Jacob Astor VI leased the house from Mrs. Burden after she remarried following James Burden's death in 1932. The Convent of the Sacred Heart bought the house in 1940 and now uses the building for its lower school. Warren & Wetmore Collection, Avery Architectural and Fine Arts Library, Columbia University; "Residence, J. A. Burden, Jr., 7 East 91st Street, New York," *Architecture* 11 (May 1905): pl. 40; Stern, Gilmartin, and Massengale, *New York 1900*, 334, 338; Christopher Gray, "Streetscapes: The Burden Mansion," *The New York Times* (July 10, 1994): 9, 7.

43. John Hartness Brown commissioned the firm's first freestanding office building in Cleveland, Ohio. Brown was a wealthy real estate entrepreneur who reportedly conceived the Euclid Heights residential area. In the design of his six-story building on Euclid Avenue (1901), Warren & Wetmore evoked the image of the great Parisian department store of the nineteenth century. While the pattern of windows and thin steel members created interest, it was the curved corner bay that suggested the stylized quality of the art nouveau. After Brown lost ownership of the building in 1908, it went through a series of renovations under new owners. Eric Johannesen, *Cleveland Architecture, 1876–1976* (Cleveland: The Western Reserve Historical Society, 1979): 68–9.

44. An extended discussion of the development of the high building and skyscraper can be found in Stern, Gilmartin, and Massengale, *New York 1900*, 145–177.

45. Barr Ferree, "The Art of the High Building," *The Architectural Record* 15 (May 1904): 445–66. Also: "A Metropolitan Stand of Building: Mercantile Buildings," *Real Estate Record and Builder's Guide* 73 (June 11, 1904): 1429.

46. Warren's scheme for the Morgan Library is in the collections of the Cooper-Hewitt, National Design Museum, Smithsonian Institution.

47. Henri-Jean Benard of Paris won the competition but was later replaced by John Galen Howard of Howard & Cauldwell. The grand scheme envisioned by Hearst never materialized. Lawrence Biemiller, "A Grand Plan for Berkeley Gone Awry," *The Chronicle of Higher Education* 47 (May 18, 2001): 64; Warren & Wetmore Collection, Avery Architectural and Fine Arts Library, Columbia University.

CHAPTER THREE
THE GRAND CENTRAL YEARS: 1904–1914

1. Reed & Stem's St. Paul office also continued to operate independently. Charles Reed resided in New York to head the railroad design while Alfred Stem oversaw the office and produced buildings in St. Paul, such as the civic auditorium, athletic club, and medical buildings at the University of Minnesota, as well as additional railroad projects in the Midwest. Henry F. Withey and Elsie Rathburn Withey, *Biographical Dictionary of American Architects, Deceased* (Detroit, MI: Omnigraphics, 1994): 498, 570.

2. "Mayor Names Men to Make City Beautiful," *The New York Times* (March 13, 1904): 12; The New York City Improvement Commission, *The Report of the New York City Improvement Commission* (New York: Kalkhoff Company, 1907); Robert A. M. Stern, Gregory Gilmartin, and John Massengale, *New York 1900: Metropolitan Architecture and Urbanism, 1890–1915* (New York: Rizzoli, 1983): 27–34.

3. "The Biggest Bridge on Earth," *The World*

Magazine (March 21, 1909); Warren's more colorful proposals included a magnificent racetrack within city limits and an ice palace, modeled after Berlin's Admiral Ice Palace, with ice dancers imported from Germany. "For the City Beautiful," *The New York Times* (February 9, 1905): 9; "Wants Ice Palace Here," *The New York Times* (April 5, 1914): 4, 2.

4. "For the City Beautiful," *The New York Times*, 9.

5. Wilgus was a self-taught railroad engineer from Buffalo, New York. According to Carl W. Condit's *The Port of New York: A History of the Rail and Terminal System from the Grand Central Electrification to the Present* (Chicago: University of Chicago Press, 1981), Wilgus and Sprague met in 1899. At that time, Sprague, who had already worked on the electrification of the Richmond line—the country's first electrified railroad—as well as lines in Germany and Italy, suggested electrifying a portion of New York Central's lines. Earlier versions of Wilgus's innovative plan from 1901 consisted of partial electrification and steam. Sprague later served on the Commission for Terminal Electrification for the New York Central Railroad.

6. At the time, Wilgus estimated the cost of his proposal would be $43,000,000.

7. At this time, Warren had just completed a bachelors' wing and tennis court building for William K. Vanderbilt at Idle Hour in Oakdale, Long Island. As friends, Vanderbilt and Warren were commonly referred to as cousins, but they were only distantly related through the Kissam family. Vanderbilt's mother was born Maria Kissam.

8. The employment agreement was signed by the various members of Warren & Wetmore: Whitney Warren, Charles D. Wetmore, Lloyd Warren, and John E. Howe. However, Lloyd Warren left the firm in 1905 to head the Society of Beaux-Arts Architects, and John Howe died in 1908. In June 1911, the Associated Architects moved their offices to the terminal building at 70 East 45th Street.

9. John Bacon oversaw the contract work; Clyde Place saw to the mechanics and heating; and the firm Balcom & Darrow were in charge of the structural steel department.

10. The New York Central also acquired all of the property on Park Avenue, running from 50th to 57th Streets, which was also excavated.

11. In 1903, according to *The New York Times*, excavation and demolition were slated to be completed in two and a half years. However, in 1910, only two sections of the work were done. Because the excavation project was so extensive, the construction company—O'Rourke Construction—was continually behind schedule. The firm's contract was canceled in 1907, and the railroad finished up the demolition project using its own men.

12. Each section–or bite—was excavated successively. Then foundations were built, steel framing for the tracks and streets erected, and tracks and third rails laid.

13. Wilgus was successful as a consultant and later worked on the construction of the Holland Tunnel (1927).

14. All of the features of Wilgus's original plan were contained in the Associated Architects' design. According to Wilgus, in describing the project to Stem's new partner, Alfred Fellheimer, for his book *Inception and Creation of the Grand Central Terminal* (1913), "the practical architectural details were ably worked out by Mr. Reed, and . . . the aesthetic treatment of the building is to be credited to Warren & Wetmore." Letter from William Wilgus to A. Fellheimer, February 12, 1913 (Box 1, Folder 1); William J. Wilgus Papers, Manuscripts and Archives Division, The New York Public Library, Astor, Lenox, and Tilden Foundations.

15. Whitney Warren, "Apologia," *Scientific American* 107 (December 7, 1912): 484.

16. "Proposed Station for N.Y. Central R.R.," *The Inland Architect and News Record* 44 (December 1904): 39; "Architectural League of New York Exhibition," *The Inland Architect and News Record* 47 (February 1906): 2–3, pls.; "New York Central Station Building Started," *Real Estate Record and Builder's Guide* 83 (November 28, 1908): 1015–6; "Last Bite for New Grand Central," *Real Estate Record and Builder's Guide* 85 (March 12, 1910): 539; "The New Grand Central Terminal," *Architects' and Builders' Magazine* 11 (November 1910): 45–51; "The New Grand Central Station, New York," *Architects' and Builders' Magazine* 12 (1910–11): 267–271; Robert Anderson Pope, "Grand Central Terminal Station, New York," *Town Planning Review* 2 (April 1911): 55–64; "Monumental Gateway to a Great City," *Scientific American* 107 (December 7, 1912): 484–87, 499–50; "The Architectural View of the Designer," *Evening Post Terminal Supplement* (February 1, 1913): 6; "Grand Central Terminal, New York," *Architecture* 27 (March 1913): 45, 47; pls. 20–29; Theodore Starrett, "The Grand Central Terminal Station," *Architecture and Building* 45 (April 1913): 129–32, 134, 137–54; "The Grand Central Terminal," *Real Estate Record and Builder's Guide* 92 (July 5, 1913): 29–35; John A. Droege, *Passenger Terminals and Trains* (New York: McGraw-Hill, 1916); "The Two Great Railway Stations of New York," *The Builder* 118 (May 21, 1920): 600–1; Condit, *The Port of New York: A History of the Rail and Terminal System from the Grand Central Electrification to the Present*; Stern, Gilmartin and Massengale, *New York 1900*, 34–40; John Belle and Maxinne R. Leighton, *Grand Central: Gateway to a Million Lives* (New York: W. W. Norton & Co., 2000); Kurt C. Schlichting, *Grand Central Terminal: Railroads, Engineering, and Architecture in New York City* (Baltimore: Johns Hopkins University Press, 2001).

17. Whitney Warren, "Apologia," *Scientific American*, 484.

18. Coutan, dean of the Ecole des Beaux-Arts, was well known for his group, *Military France*, on the bridge of Alexander III in Paris and was considered one of the greatest of all modern sculptors. According to *The New York Times*, Whitney Warren's selection of Coutan caused some comment. When interviewed at his Paris studio at 72 rue du Cherche-Midi about visiting the United States, Coutan replied, "I have no such desire. From what I have learned pictorially of the characteristics of your country, especially with reference to the standards of art, I do not think that it would interest me. In fact, I should wish rather to avoid it. I fear that the sight of some of your architecture would distress me." "Jules Coutan," *The New York Times* (February 24, 1939): 24.

19. Starrett, "The Grand Central Terminal Station," *Architecture and Building*, 132.

20. "The New York Central's Station," *The American Architect and Building News* 86 (December 31, 1904): 105.

21. "Stairways Eliminated from the Grand Central Terminal," *Real Estate Record and Builder's Guide* 86 (July 26, 1910): 108.

22. According to *The New York Times*, the idea of ramps evolved from ancient times when builders and armies used ramps to haul heavy artillery, wagons, and building materials. "First Great Stairless Railway Terminal in History," *The New York Times* (February 2, 1913): 9, 5. The main concourse contained one sweeping set of steps, modeled after Garnier's grand stair at the Paris Opera House. According to John Belle and Maxinne R. Leighton, coauthors of *Grand Central: Gateway to a Million Lives*, a 1911 design for the concourse included a large skylight and two symmetrical single stairs to the east and west leading to the upper galleries, ele-

vators, and a proposed office building above. When the office building was abandoned, so was the east stair. Beyer Blinder Belle used plans of Warren's intended stair to support their argument to add an east stair in the terminal's revitalization.

23. "The New Grand Central Station, New York," *Architects' and Builders' Magazine*, 267.

24. Warren not only collected Helleu's work but also had a portrait of Helleu by John Singer Sargent in his collection. Helleu and Sargent were close friends, and Sargent often painted the French artist. According to John Belle and Maxinne R. Leighton, Helleu was responsible for the idea of illuminating the stars and Hewlett detailed the drawings of the zodiac. From below, the ceiling appears in reverse, as though the artists were working above the ceiling when they painted it.

25. Salières also executed the sculptural ornament for Warren's tomb for John Paul Jones at the Naval Academy in Annapolis, Maryland in 1912 as well as for private houses, including William K. Vanderbilt Sr.'s tennis court building at Idle Hour.

26. "The Grand Central Terminal," *Real Estate Record and Builder's Guide*, 32.

27. New York Landmarks Preservation Commission, *Grand Central Terminal Interiors* (New York: The Commission, 1980): 13.

28. "The Two Great Railway Stations of New York," *The Builder*, 601.

29. Since Wetmore was formally trained as a lawyer, he had the ability to draw up legal documents. "Supreme Court, New York County, Allen H. Stem against Whitney Warren and Charles D. Wetmore, Trial before Mr. Justice Delehanty at Special Term, Part 4, January 27– March 31, 1916," (Box 2, Folder 110, 48); William J. Wilgus Papers, Manuscripts and Archives Division, The New York Public Library, Astor, Lenox, and Tilden Foundations.

30. "Holland's Letter: Buildings in N.Y. City that are Looked Upon as Monuments to the Genius of the Architects," *Wall Street Journal* (March 7, 1911): 1.

31. "Supreme Court, New York County, Allen H. Stem against Whitney Warren and Charles D. Wetmore, Trial before Mr. Justice Delehanty at Special Term, Part 4, January 27–March 31, 1916," (Box 2, Folder 110, 52); William J. Wilgus Papers, Manuscripts and Archives Division, The New York Public Library, Astor, Lenox, and Tilden Foundations.

32. Letter from William J. Wilgus to W. J. Reed, Scarsdale, July 16, 1916 (Box 1, Folder 1); William J. Wilgus Papers, Manuscripts and Archives Division, The New York Public Library, Astor, Lenox, and Tilden Foundations. In the following years, Wilgus wrote articles about the inception and creation of the terminal. In 1919 he also wrote to Henry Rutgers Marshall of the Century Association to make him aware of his claim of Warren & Wetmore's unethical conduct in the profession of architecture.

33. "Supreme Court, New York County, Allen H. Stem against Whitney Warren and Charles D. Wetmore, Trial before Mr. Justice Delehanty at Special Term, Part 4, January 27–March 31, 1916," (Box 2, Folder 110); William J. Wilgus Papers, Manuscripts and Archives Division, The New York Public Library, Astor, Lenox, and Tilden Foundations.

34. Warren wrote to his wife in 1916 that the "Grand Central suit has been decided against Warren and Wetmore which means we must appeal—the Judge was very severe on us. . . . Charlie accredited him with too much decency or intelligence or honesty—he promptly handed us one!!! It is life—I had hoped to get some money—these years of waiting and having disposed of a godly portion of it!! Enfin. It will all come out all right." This was the only mention

of the lawsuit in Warren's letters from the years 1914–1919. Whitney Warren to Charlotte A. Tooker Warren, Paris, 12 August 1916. Whitney Warren Papers, bMS Am 2113 (181). By permission of the Houghton Library, Harvard University.

35. Letter from Harold Swain to William J. Wilgus, November 7, 1921 (Box 1, Folder 1); William J. Wilgus Papers, Manuscripts and Archives Division, The New York Public Library, Astor, Lenox, and Tilden Foundations.

36. When the terminal was completed in 1913, seven buildings within the air-rights district had or were being constructed: the Vanderbilt Avenue Building, the Biltmore Hotel, the Yale Club, the Vanderbilt Concourse Building, the Post Office, Grand Central Palace, and 466 Lexington.

37. Warren, in revising elevations of the terminal building's entrance facade, noted to "put a soffit decorated as in P. O. Building" above the great windows. From notations on drawing at the New-York Historical Society.

38. "Post Office and General-Office Building, New York Central R. R., New York, N.Y.," *The American Architect and Building News* 90 (November 24, 1906): pls.; Historic American Buildings Survey, *Grand Central Post Office Annex*.

39. The original Grand Central Palace operated as a temporary terminal during the construction period. "Grand Central Palace, Lexington Ave. and 46th St., New York," *Architecture* 24 (August 1911): pls. 83–4; "Grand Central Palace, Lexington Avenue & 46th Street, New York," *The Architectural Yearbook* 1 (1912): 375; W. Parker Chase, *New York, the Wonder City*, 1932 (New York: New York Bound, 1983): 246; Christopher Gray, "Streetscapes," *The New York Times* (March 2, 1997): 9, 5; "Adams Express Company Building," *Architecture and Building* 44 (August 1912): 330. The Grand Central Palace was superseded by the Coliseum at Columbus Circle in the 1950s. The Waldorf-Astoria (1929–31), designed by Schultze & Weaver, replaced the Adams Express Building, powerhouse, and Railroad Y.M.C.A.; however, the sublevel platforms were kept, enabling guests to move directly from trains into the hotel.

40. "The New Grand Central Railway Terminal Approached by a Bridge over 42nd Street, at Park Avenue," *Architectural Record* 32 (November 1912): 483–85; "The Park Avenue Viaduct, New York," *Architecture and Building* 51 (May 1919): 44, pls. 86–88; "The Park Avenue Improvement in New York," *The American Architect* 65 (May 28, 1919): 756–58; Landmarks Preservation Commission, *Pershing Square Viaduct (Park Avenue Viaduct), Park Avenue from 40th Street to Grand Central Terminal* (New York: The Commission, 1980).

41. "A Modern Railway Terminal Hotel," *Real Estate Record and Builder's Guide* 93 (January 10, 1914): 59–64; "The Biltmore Hotel, New York," *The American Architect* 105 (February 11, 1914): 53–57; Montgomery Schuyler, "The Biltmore Hotel, Madison Avenue, New York," *The Brickbuilder* 23 (February 1914): 37–40; Theodore Starrett, "The Biltmore Hotel Building," *Architecture and Building* 46 (February 1914): 48–49; Walter S. Schneider, "The Hotel Biltmore: The Newest Addition to New York's Palatial Hotels," *Architectural Record* 35 (March 1914): 221–45; Stern, Gilmartin, and Massengale, *New York 1900*, 270–72.

42. The Biltmore Corporation took out a forty-two-year lease on the building. Canadian-born Bowman caught the attention of hotel proprietor Gustav Baumann when working at Holland House. When the Biltmore was constructed, Bowman informally superintended the building, and on its opening, was named the vice-president of the company. Soon after, Baumann died

and Bowman was named president. He went on to buy additional hotels and to build many more throughout the country. "John M'E. Bowman, Hotel Builder, Dies," *The New York Times* (October 28, 1931): 12.

43. The Biltmore was a hotly debated issue during the Grand Central trial. The Associated Architects had begun working on the Biltmore's design before Charles Reed's death in 1911, and the hotel, as built, conformed substantially to those plans. During the trial, it was initially found that Reed & Stem was entitled to its share of the fee, calculated at 3 percent of the final cost of the building (for preliminary and working plans). Through its appeals, Warren & Wetmore reduced this amount to 1 percent, which covered work done on the preliminary plans. "Stem Against Whitney Warren and Charles D. Wetmore, Reference before Charles L. Hoffman, Esq., June 23, 1920 to April 8, 1921," (Box 2, Folder 110, 13–14); William J. Wilgus Papers, Manuscripts and Archives Division, The New York Public Library, Astor, Lenox, and Tilden Foundations.

44. Starrett, "The Biltmore Hotel Building," *Architecture and Building*, 50.

45. According to the *Real Estate Record and Builder's Guide*, New York Central's president William H. Newman, Whitney Warren, and other prominent businessmen leased these apartments.

46. Schuyler, "The Biltmore Hotel, Madison Avenue, New York," *The Brickbuilder*, 37.

47. "Open Big Biltmore on New Year's Eve," *The New York Times* (December 26, 1913): 12; Starrett, "The Biltmore Hotel Building," *Architecture and Building*, 67.

48. J. D. Salinger, *The Catcher in the Rye* (New York: Little Brown, 1951; New York: Little Brown, 1991): 106. In 1981 developers stripped the Biltmore down to its steel skeleton and reconstructed it as a glass and granite clad office building for Bank of America. Preservation groups attempted but failed to save several of the building's more significant spaces, including the famous palm court, from destruction.

49. Warren & Wetmore and Reed & Stem designed stations at Ludlow, Yonkers, Glenwood, Ossining, Mt. Vernon, Bronxville, Scarsdale, Hartsdale, White Plains, Fordham, Hastings, Newburgh, Watertown, Catskill, Hyde Park, and Poughkeepsie.

50. The accounting provided for the Grand Central trial showed that profits for the suburban stations were as low as $130.04 (Glenwood) or $183.90 (Yonkers). In many cases, the cost of the stations exceeded payment. "Stem Against Whitney Warren and Charles D. Wetmore, Reference before Charles L. Hoffman, Esq., June 23, 1920 to April 8, 1921," (Box 2, Folder 110, 78–80); William J. Wilgus Papers, Manuscripts and Archives Division, The New York Public Library, Astor, Lenox, and Tilden Foundations.

51. "Station and Office Building of the Michigan Central Railroad at Detroit, Mich.," *Architecture and Building* 47 (February 1915): 53–60; Harold Eberlein, "Recent Railways Stations in American Cities," *Architectural Record* 36 (August 1914): 119–21; Droege, *Passenger Terminals and Trains*, 78–82.

52. Eberlein, "Recent Railways Stations in American Cities," *Architectural Record*, 119.

53. The upper stories of the Detroit station remained empty for most of the seventy-five years the building was open; the interiors of the top five floors were never completed. The station has stood empty since the 1980s but is currently being considered for redevelopment as police headquarters.

54. Compared to the terminals built, the firm also executed an equivalent number of designs that were never realized. Warren & Wetmore's schemes for stations in Denver, New Orleans, Dallas, Birmingham, and Montreal presented a

range of styles and approaches. While the Denver and Dallas terminals were classically inspired, the proposed New Orleans station was a low-lying Spanish-baroque building with a double-height concourse embellished with floridly carved ornament, ribbed vaulting, and exuberant cartouches. Warren & Wetmore Collection, Avery Architectural and Fine Arts Library, Columbia University.

55. Around this time, Warren & Wetmore designed a Tudor-style house outside Toronto, in Scarborough, for Donald D. Mann (1853–1934), named Fallingbrook. Mann, who was knighted in 1911, was then vice-president of the Canadian Northern Railways. As designed, the terminal structure could support six additional stories. "The Fort Garry Terminal: A Union Station at Winnipeg, Manitoba," *The American Architect* 95 (February 10, 1909): 46–50; Droege, *Passenger Terminals and Trains*, 84–87.

56. The Houston Belt & Terminal Railway Company was the consolidation of four railroads. The building was originally designed with three floors; however, soon after it was completed, Warren & Wetmore added two additional floors. In the 1960s the waiting room was partitioned into offices, and the last train departed in 1974. In 1999 the building was restored as the main entrance to Enron Field (now Minute Maid Park).

57. According to Stern, Gilmartin, and Massengale, *New York 1900*, 252–53, Astor House, New York's first grand hotel, offered bathrooms on every floor—a great innovation—in 1936. The Fifth Avenue Hotel introduced the first passenger elevator in the city.

58. In a period when society wives traveled especially to Paris for current fashion, such pageantry did not seem so far-fetched. Warren's wife Charlotte was often featured in the society columns for her attire. On her return from one Parisian trip, she declared only a portion of her purchases—$1,500 worth of gowns, hats, jewelry, and laces—which was valued at $12,000. Mrs. Warren was indicted and fined $8,000.

59. It was rumored that Hyde and Warren's effervescent daughter Charlotte were briefly engaged. Patricia Beard, *After the Ball* (New York: Harper Collins, 2003); "A New Day of Elegance for Sherry's," *The New York Times* (July 24, 1966): 56.

60. "C. D. Wetmore Funeral Today at St. Thomas," *New York Herald Tribune* (May 10, 1941): 8.

61. Charles D. Wetmore, "The Development of the Modern Hotel," *The Architectural Review* 2 (April 1913): 37–39.

62. Walter Hopkins, "Architectural Design for Hotel Interiors," *Architectural Forum* 39 (November 1923): 205–9.

63. "The Belmont," *New York Herald* (April 29, 1906): magazine, 4; H. W. Frohne, "The Hotel Belmont," *Architectural Record* 20 (July 1906): 63–70; "The Hotel Belmont," *Architecture and Building* 38 (May 1906): 319–35; Stern, Gilmartin, and Massengale, New York 1900, 268, 270. According to the *New York Herald*, F. G. Colton of Warren & Wetmore worked closely with Bates on the design of the hotel. The Belmont was demolished in 1939. Warren also designed a large French mansion on 92nd Street and Fifth Avenue for Belmont's brother, Perry Belmont; this house was never built.

64. Hopkins, "Architectural Design for Hotel Interiors," *Architectural Forum*, 205.

65. Frohne, "The Hotel Belmont," *Architectural Record*, 67.

66. Warren & Wetmore also designed an office building for the Goelets at 8–14 East 47th Street in 1912. At the Ritz, the firm designed apartments for S. J. Hesslein and Frank W. Storrs. The hotel was first sold to Harvard University in 1941 and, later, the Astor estate in 1943; the hotel was demolished and replaced with an office building in 1950. "Ritz-Carlton Hotel and

Carlton House, Madison Ave.," *Architecture* 23 (January 1911): pls. 7–8; "The Ritz-Carlton Hotel, 46th Street and Madison Ave., New York City," *New York Architect* 5 (January 1911): pls.; "Ritz-Carlton Hotel and the Carlton House," *Architects' and Builders' Magazine* 43 (February 1911): 196–208; "The Ritz Carlton Hotel, New York," *The American Architect* 99 (February 1, 1911): 44–48; "Ritz-Carlton Hotel," *Architectural Yearbook* 1 (1912): 363–65; "Ritz-Carlton Hotel, New York City," *Architectural Review* 11 (April 1913): 109–11; Matlack Price, "Great Modern Hotels of America," *Arts and Decoration* 21 (July 1924): 39–41, 52; Stern, Gilmartin, and Massengale, *New York 1900*, 262–3, 267.

67. "The Ritz Carlton Hotel, New York," *The American Architect*, 46.

68. *Reminiscences of Lawrence Grant White*, 1956, on page 111 in the CUOHROC.

69. In 1925 Walton H. Marshall and his associates, Charles D. Wetmore, Edmund L. Baylies, and William Astor Chanler, purchased the hotel. In 1967 it was converted to apartments with offices on the lower six floors. "The Vanderbilt Hotel," *Architecture and Building* 43 (February 1911): 211–14; "Vanderbilt Hotel, Park Ave., New York," *Architectural Yearbook* 1 (1912): 357–61; "Hotel Vanderbilt, New York," *The Brickbuilder* 21 (March 1912): 71–74, pls. 35–36; "The Vanderbilt Hotel, New York," *The American Architect* 101 (February 14, 1912): 69–73; "The Vanderbilt Hotel," *Architecture and Building* 44 (May/April 1912): 150–52; Walton H. Marshall, "The Vanderbilt Hotel," *Architectural Review* 11 (April 1913): 66–70; William Hagerman Graves, "The Use of Tile in the Interior Finish and Decoration of Hotels," *The Architectural Review* 2 (April 1913): 46–47; Stern, Gilmartin, and Massengale, *New York 1900*, 272.

70. Landmarks Preservation Commission, *(Former) Della Robbia Bar in the (Former) Vanderbilt Hotel* (New York: The Commission, 1994): 2.

71. After Mrs. Vanderbilt moved out of the fifteen-room penthouse duplex, it was occupied by the Women's City Club and subsequently by the celebrated tenor Enrico Caruso and his family.

72. "Hotel Vanderbilt, New York," *The Brickbuilder*, 74.

73. "The Vanderbilt Hotel, New York," *The American Architect*, 71. Articles on the Della Robbia Restaurant, part of which was named a New York City interior landmark in 1994, include: Samuel Howe, "Della Robbia Room, Hotel Vanderbilt, New York," *The Brickbuilder* 21 (February 1912): 43–46; Landmarks Preservation Commission, *(Former) Della Robbia Bar in the (Former) Vanderbilt Hotel*.

74. Montreal-born architect Frederick Garfield Robb, who had joined Warren & Wetmore in 1910, oversaw the Ritz construction. Canadian law required the firm to have a local representative.

75. "Ritz-Carlton Hotel, Montreal," *Architecture* 27 (March 1913): 46–52; "The Ritz-Carlton Hotel, Montreal, Canada," *The Brickbuilder* 22 (March 1913): pls. 33–34; "Ritz-Carlton Hotel, Montreal, Canada," *The Architectural Review* 19 (April 1913): 112–13; Adrian Waller, *No Ordinary Hotel: The Ritz-Carlton's First Seventy-Five Years* (Montreal: Véhicule Press, 1989).

76. "Ritz-Carlton Hotel, Philadelphia, PA.," *The Architectural Review* 11 (April 1913): 134–35; "The Ritz-Carlton Hotel, Philadelphia, PA.," *Architectural Record* 34 (September 1913): 213–14; "The New Ritz Carlton Hotel, Philadelphia, PA," *American Architect* 107 (April 14, 1915): pls.

77. One of Bing & Bing's first ventures was 903 Park Avenue. They would go on to develop apartment buildings in collaboration with Emery Roth. "Tallest Apartment House Going up on Park Avenue," *The New York Times* (June 9, 1912): 21; "Apartments, Park Ave. and 79th Street, New York," *Architecture* 28 (July 1913): 152–3; Stern, Gilmartin, and Massengale, *New York 1900*, 357–58; Christopher Gray, "Streetscapes: 903 Park Avenue," *The New York Times* (May 12, 2002): 11, 7.

78. After Vanderbilt's death in 1920, the guesthouse was turned into an apartment building and held offices for Juilliard. In 1939 it was turned into a broadcasting studio for CBS radio and substantially renovated, inside and outside. In recent years, the modern facade addition was stripped away. "New Radio Studios of Modern Design," *The New York Times* (February 18, 1940): 11, 1–2; Rachelle Garbarine, "A Mansion Will Wake Up to Find It's 1908 Again," *The New York Times* (October 20, 1996): 39; Warren & Wetmore Collection, Avery Architectural and Fine Arts Library, Columbia University.

79. The Bertron house and Carrère & Hastings's adjacent house for Edwin Gould were demolished in the mid-1950s and replaced by an eighteen-story apartment building. The Brookman house, subsequently owned by George D. Widener, was demolished in 1974 and replaced by an extension to the Frick Collection. Landmarks Preservation Commission, *Upper East Side Historic District Designation Report* (New York: The Commission, 1981): 462.

80. *Guggenheim outbuildings*: Warren & Wetmore Collection, Avery Architectural and Fine Arts Library, Columbia University. The buildings are now part of the Village Club of Sand's Point. *Eagle's Nest*: Suffolk County Vanderbilt Museum, Centerport, New York; Robert B. MacKay, Anthony K. Baker, and Carol A. Traynor, *Long Island Country Houses and their Architects, 1860–1940* (New York: W. W. Norton & Co., 1997): 436–39.

81. Stanford White to Whitney Warren, January 6, 1906, Stanford White Collection, Avery Architectural and Fine Arts Library, Columbia University.

82. At the same time, Warren redid some of the decoration in the drawing room. He also painted over Edward Simmons's ceiling murals in the reception room. Nina Gray and Pamela Herrick, "Decoration in the Gilded Age: The Frederick W. Vanderbilt Mansion, Hyde Park, New York," *Studies in the Decorative Arts* 10 (Fall-Winter 2002–2003): 98–141. Frederick Vanderbilt (1856–1938) was William K. Vanderbilt Sr.'s younger brother.

83. "The Chelsea Improvement," *Real Estate Record and Builder's Guide* 84 (September 18, 1909): 510; "The Chelsea Section Improvement: A Municipal Enterprise," *Architects' and Builders' Magazine* 42 (February 1910): 165–73; Kevin Bone, ed., *The New York Waterfront: Evolution and Building Culture of the Port and Harbor* (New York: Monacelli Press, 1997): 71–74, 198–201; Stern, Gilmartin, and Massengale, *New York 1900*, 49–50. The last of the Chelsea Piers was torn down in 1991, despite preservation efforts.

84. "The Chelsea Improvement," *Real Estate Record and Builder's Guide*, 510.

85. The Seamen's Church Institute was founded in 1844 when the Episcopal Church of our Savior was organized in a floating chapel moored at Pike Street in the East River for the seamen. Baylies' new building was constructed from funds raised by many of the institute's prominent members—both J. P. Morgan and John D. Rockefeller were major contributors. Due to the building's popularity, a thirteen-story addition, also designed by Warren & Wetmore, was erected in 1926, providing accommodation for 500,000 men a year. The institute also improved the neighboring Jeannette Park in 1921, and the firm designed a bandstand in memorial to the seamen who served in World War One. Although the building has been demolished, the sixty-foot Titanic Memorial Lighthouse now stands at the entrance to the South Street Seaport. "Model Hotel for Seamen, Costing $500,000," *The New York Times* (March 5, 1911): 8, 1; "Sailors' Club Begins in Tears for Titanic," *The New York Times* (April 17, 1912): 16; "Seamen's Church Institute of New York," *Architecture and Building* 45 (August 1913): 334; "Seamen's Church Institute to Have $2,400,000 Annex," *Real Estate Record and Builder's Guide* 117 (February 27, 1926): 11; Leah Robinson Rousmaniere, *Anchored within the Veil: A Pictorial History of the Seamen's Church Institute* (New York: The Seamen's Church Institute of New York and New Jersey, 1995).

86. The Windsor Arcade was eventually replaced by John B. Snook's store for W. & J. Sloane (1912) and Warren & Wetmore's bank building for S. W. Straus (1921). In the Windsor Arcade, Warren & Wetmore designed a banking room for the Windsor Trust Company, of which Charles D. Wetmore was a director along with August Belmont, James Burden, Robert Goelet, and Cornelius Vanderbilt. The wood-paneled space contained tellers booths and an elaborately carved door enframement around the entrance to the vault.

87. "New Fifth Avenue Building," *Real Estate Record and Builder's Guide* 80 (October 19, 1907): 609; "Building for Dreicer & Co., Fifth Avenue, New York," *New York Architect* 5 (September 1911); 515–19; "Building of Dreicer & Co., Fifth Avenue, New York," *Architectural Yearbook* 1 (1912): 371–73; C. Matlack Price, "A Renaissance in Commercial Architecture," *The Architectural Record* 31 (May 1912): 453–54; "Shop Building, Fifth Ave. and 46th St., New York," *Architecture* 25 (June 1912); Birch Burdette Long, "The Use of Color in Architecture," *The Brickbuilder* 23 (June 1914): 125–29; Rawson W. Haddon, "Some Recent Salesroom Interiors," *Architecture* 36 (July 1917) 125–29; Stern, Gilmartin, and Massengale, *New York 1900*, 200.

88. "Store of Theodore B. Starr, Inc. New York, New York," *New York Architect* 5 (September 1911); 521–25; Private Showroom, Store of Theodore B. Starr, Inc., New York," *Architectural Yearbook* 1 (1912): 367–69; Stern, Gilmartin, and Massengale, New York 1900, 200.

89. Francis S. Swales, "Architecture in the United States—The Commercial Buildings—The Shops," *Architectural Review* 25 (February 1909): 85.

90. Warren & Wetmore Collection, Avery Architectural and Fine Arts Library, Columbia University. Also: "Hudson City Savings Institution, Hudson City, N.Y.," *The American Architect* 92 (May 4, 1910): pls.

91. Green-Wood Cemetery was one of the first rural cemeteries in the country; it was established by Henry J. Pierrepont in 1838. Warren & Wetmore also designed a gatehouse at the cemetery's 20th Street entrance. While it did not design any vaults at Green-Wood, the firm did design mausoleums for William B. Hornblower and William H. Newman at Woodlawn Cemetery and a crypt for John Paul Jones in Annapolis, Maryland. Warren & Wetmore's chapel was recently restored by Platt Byard Dovell White. "Mortuary Chapel, Greenwood Cemetery, Brooklyn, N.Y.," *Architecture and Building* 45 (May 1913): 182.

CHAPTER FOUR
INVENTORS OF THE MODERN CITYSCAPE:
1914–1922

1. Whitney Warren, "The Destruction of the Monuments of France," *The Architectural Review* 6 (April 1916): 53–57.

2. In 1917 Warren was made an officer of the

Legion of Honor; however, he felt the honor was undeserved, because he had never served in the army.

3. Whitney Warren to Charlotte A. Tooker Warren, Paris, November 2, 1914, Whitney Warren Papers, bMS Am 2113 (31). By permission of the Houghton Library, Harvard University.

4. The Waldorf-Astoria replaced Warren & Wetmore's YMCA, powerhouse, and Adams Express Building—all projects related to the terminal that Schultze had supervised.

5. "Apartments, 340–50 Park Avenue, New York," *Architecture* 35 (April 1917): 71, pl. 67. Both 320–30 and 340–50 Park Avenue were replaced by office buildings in 1959.

6. Louis C. Stone, "400 Park Avenue—A Venture in Change," *American Architect and Architecture* 149 (December 1936): 59. Also: Robert A. M. Stern, Gregory Gilmartin, and Thomas Mellins, *New York 1930: Architecture and Urbanism between the Two World Wars* (New York: Rizzoli, 1988): 395, 400. In 1936 Walker & Gillette renovated the building, dividing the twenty-room layout into one apartment with five rooms and three apartments with six rooms, and added central air conditioning. In 1955, it was demolished.

7. "Apartment House, 420 Park Avenue, New York, N.Y.," *The Architectural Forum* 26 (March 1917): pls. 42–43; "Three Block Fronts of Tall Apartments Going up on Park Avenue to Meet Demand," *The New York Times* (October 31, 1915): 7, 1; "Remarkable Record in this Season's Apartment Rentals," *The New York Times* (July 2, 1916): 3, 2; "The History of 420–30 Park Ave.," *The New York Times* (August 26, 2001): 11, 10. This building was reconstructed and reclad as an office building for the Bank of Montreal in 1953–55.

8. "270 Park Avenue: The Largest of Apartment-Houses," *Architecture* 37 (May 1918): 143, pls. 78–81; "Apartment House, No. 270 Park Avenue, New York City," *Architecture and Building* 50 (May 1918): pls. 83–85; "Avignon Restaurant, 270 Park Avenue, New York City," *Architecture and Building* 50 (December 1918): pl. 165; Foster Ware, "Profiles: Maker of Castles," *New Yorker* 3 (July 2, 1927): 19–20; Stern, Gilmartin, and Mellins, *New York 1930*, 417. In 1957, this building (also known as the Marqueray Apartment Hotel) was replaced by a fifty-two-story office for the Union Carbide and Carbon Corporation. Warren & Wetmore had originally designed a pair of thirty-one story cooperative office buildings, known as the Park–Madison Building, for the site, which was never realized. "Plans for Thirty-One Story Grand Central Building Ready," *Real Estate Record and Builder's Guide* 105 (May 29, 1920): 707–8.

9. "270 Park Avenue: The Largest of Apartment-Houses," *Architecture*, 143.

10. "Apartment House, 925 Fifth Avenue, New York," *Architecture* 37 (January 1918): pls. 1–4; Landmarks Preservation Commission, *Upper East Side Historic District Designation Report* (New York: The Commission, 1981): 950; Stern, Gilmartin, and Mellins, *New York 1930*, 384.

11. "Combination Ownership Home to Cost $4,000,000," *The New York Times* (January 17, 1920): 5; "Apartment House, 290 Park Avenue, New York," *Architecture and Building* 53 (April 1921): 29, pls. 45–46; "Apartment House, 290 Park Avenue, New York," *Architecture and Building* 54 (April 1922): 37, pls. 51–53; Stern, Gilmartin, and Mellins, *New York 1930*, 390–92, 417; W. Parker Chase, *New York, the Wonder City, 1932* (New York: New York Bound, 1983): 277. The firm also designed interiors for tenants Henry F. Du Pont, James H. Wainwright, and John T. Terry as well as a branch office for the Columbia Trust Company. This building was replaced by an office building in 1960.

12. In 1919 Louis Sherry closed his 44th Street establishment, claiming he could not operate under Prohibition. Two years later he opened Sherry's at 300 Park Avenue with the Du Pont Hotel Group, which became almost as famous as its predecessor. The building was replaced by an office building in 1953. "Apartment House, 300 Park Avenue, New York," *Architecture and Building* 54 (April 1922): 38, pls. 58–61; Stern, Gilmartin, and Mellins, *New York 1930*, 390, 392; Chase, *New York, the Wonder City, 1932*, 277.

13. "Hotel Chatham, Vanderbilt Ave., New York," *Architecture* 36 (December 1917): pls. 207–10; "Hotel Chatham," *Architecture and Building* 49 (December 1917): 111, pls. 171–72; Stern, Gilmartin, and Mellins, *New York 1930*, 202.

14. Warren & Wetmore designed the interior finishes of S. W. Straus's apartment at the Ambassador. The hotel was demolished in 1964. "Contract Awarded for Palatial Hotel on Park Avenue," *Real Estate Record and Builder's Guide* 104 (August 23, 1919): 250; "Hotel Ambassador, Park Avenue and Fifty-First Street, New York City," *Architecture and Building* 52 (August 1920): pl. 98; "Rentals in New Ambassador Hotel Reach Record Figures," *Real Estate Record and Builder's Guide* 105 (February 14, 1920): 204; "Zoning Setbacks Used as Gardens," *The American Architect* 117 (June 30, 1920): 829; "Hotel Ambassador, New York," *Architecture and Building* 53 (June 1921): 45–6; pls. 78–81; "The Ambassador—A Homelike Hotel," *Decorative Furnisher* 40 (June 1921): 59–60; "The Ambassador Hotel, Park Avenue, New York," *The American Architect* 119 (June 22, 1921): 644–47; pls.; Stern, Gilmartin, and Mellins, *New York 1930*, 201–3.

15. At the same time the Commodore was constructed, Warren & Wetmore also designed and built the Commodore-Biltmore Garage at 323 East 44th Street (1919). It was reclad in glass and renovated by Der Scutt in 1980. It is currently the Grand Hyatt Hotel. "The Commodore—A New Hotel on Pershing Square, New York," *The American Architect* 115 (March 5, 1919): 337–38, pls. 69–76; "Reactions of the War on Taste as Seen in New York's Two Newest Hotels," *Good Furniture* 12 (March 1919): 131–148; "The Hotel Commodore, New York," *Architecture* 39 (April 1919): 98–99, pls. 47–51; Charles Warren Hastings, "Hotel Commodore, New York," *Architecture and Building* 51 (April 1919): 30–35, pls. 57–71; "Hotel Commodore, New York," *The Architectural Review* 8 (1919): 69–75, pls. 40–48; "The Commodore-Biltmore Garage," *Architecture and Building* 51 (April 1919): 36; pl. 72; Robert A. M. Stern, Gregory Gilmartin, and John Massengale, *New York 1900: Metropolitan Architecture and Urbanism, 1890–1915* (New York: Rizzoli, 1983): 272.

16. Edith Wharton and Ogden Codman, Jr., *The Decoration of Houses* (New York: C. Scribner' Sons, 1902; New York: W.W. Norton, 1978): xi.

17. Born in Palermo, Italy, John B. Smeraldi (né Giovanni Battista Smeraldi) moved to the United States in 1899 and forged a career in decorative and architectural painting, particularly in the Renaissance styles then popular. His work appears in hotels as well as several courthouses in California, where he lived. He is also credited with having painted the Blue Room in the White House.

18. *Hotel McAlpin*: "Annex to Hotel McAlpin," *Architecture and Building* 50 (August 1918): 53–54, pls. 139–41; *Plaza*: "Hotel Plaza Addition," *Architecture and Building* 54 (February 1922): pls. 15–17. The Plaza is currently undergoing a renovation to convert the hotel into condominiums; 150 hotel rooms will remain.

19. "Westchester-Biltmore Country Club, Rye, New York," *Architecture and Building* 54 (July 1922): 67–68, pls. 103–7; "Westchester Biltmore Country Club Completed," *The New York Times* (May 21, 1922): 112.

20. "Providence-Biltmore Hotel, Providence, R.I.," *Architecture and Building* 54 (July 1922): 68–69, pls. 108–112; Historic American Buildings Survey, *Providence-Biltmore Hotel* (Philadelphia: Department of the Interior).

21. "Bowman Buys Cuban Hotel," *The New York Times* (October 30, 1919): 25.

22. Initially, Count James Pourtales of Silesia developed the Broadmoor property and built a small hotel and casino on the site. When the new Broadmoor was constructed, the casino was moved across the lake and used as a golf club. "Broadmoor Hotel, Colorado Springs, Colo.," *Architecture and Building* 50 (June 1918): pl. 104; "The Broadmoor Hotel, Colorado Springs, Col.," *Architectural Review* 8 (April 1919): 93–98, pls. 56–58; "The Broadmoor Hotel, Colorado Springs, Colorado," *The Western Architect* 30 (April 1921): pl. 13; J. J. Kramer, *The Last of the Grand Hotels* (New York: Van Nostrand Reinhold Company, 1978): 116–20; Brian McGinty, *The Palace Inns: A Connoisseur's Guide to Historic American Hotels* (Harrisburg, PA: Stackpole Books, 1978): 115–25.

23. Long considered a white elephant, the renovated hotel reopens in 2005 with ninety-three rooms and restored public areas. "Condado-Vanderbilt Hotel, Porto Rico," *Architecture and Building* 52 (July 1920): 67, pls. 80–82.

24. "Atlantic City Plan to Cost $20,000,000," *The New York Times* (September 30, 1919): 16.

25. "The Ritz Carlton Hotel, Atlantic City, N. J.," *Architecture and Building* 53 (September 1921): 71–72, pls. 132–38. The Ritz now operates as condominiums.

26. The syndicate was also responsible for the eponymous Park Avenue establishment operated by the Ambassador. While the steel skeleton of the hotel still exists, the original hotel has been replaced by what is now the Tropicana Hotel and Casino. "Hotel Ambassador, Atlantic City, N. J.," *Architecture and Building* 52 (August 1920): 73–74, pls. 84–88; "Addition to the Hotel Ambassador, Atlantic City, N. J.," *The American Architect* 118 (September 8, 1920): 314–15.

27. "Shelburne Hotel Addition, Atlantic City, N. J.," *Architecture and Building* 54 (November 1922): pls. 184–87; Historic American Buildings Survey, *The Shelburne Hotel* (Philadelphia: Department of the Interior). The Shelburne and St. Charles Hotel have been replaced by the Bally Complex and Showboat Casino.

28. While the firm was working in Houston, it also designed a house for Texas Company's first vice-president, T. A. Donoghue, at 17 Courtlandt Place (1915–16). "Building for the Texas Co., Houston, Tex.," *Architecture and Building* 47 (August 1915): 302–3.

29. "Goelet Building, 402 Fifth Avenue, New York," *Architecture and Building* 47 (October 1915): 76–77; Christopher Gray, "Streetscapes: The 1914 Stewart Building," *The New York Times* (July 22, 1990): 10, 6.

30. "Terra Cotta and Stucco Finished Building at 37th St. and 5th Ave., New York," *Architecture and Building* 47 (October 1915): 373; Christopher Gray, "Streetscapes: Readers' Questions," *The New York Times* (February 6, 2005): 11, 10.

31. *Equitable Trust Building*: "Equitable Trust Building, Madison Avenue, New York," *The American Architect* 114 (November 13, 1918): pls. 147–50; "Equitable Trust Building, New York City," *Architecture and Building* 50 (July 1918): pls. 129–35; Chase, *New York, the Wonder City, 1932*, 244. *Marlin Rockwell Building*: Stores at street level included clothier F. R. Tripler. "Contracts Let for Large Buildings in Mid-Town Section," *Real Estate Record and Builder's Guide* 104 (July 19, 1919): 85; "Marlin Rockwell Building, 45th to 46th Streets and Madison

Avenue, New York City," *Architecture and Building* 52 (October 1920): 120–21. *Vanderbilt Concourse Building*: "Vanderbilt Concourse Offices on East 45th Street, New York," *Architecture and Building* 47 (April 1915): 149–50, 151. The December 1925 issue of *Arts and Decoration* showed a series of images of Thomas Hastings's rooftop apartment at 52 Vanderbilt Avenue, "entirely planned by himself."

32. "The All America Cables Building, New York City," *Architectural Review* 11 (October 1920): 109–11; "All America Cables Building," *Architecture and Building* 52 (February 1920): 26, pls. 17–18.

33. "S. W. Straus & Co. Moves Into Uptown Financial Center," *Real Estate Record and Builder's Guide* 107 (June 4, 1921): 713.

34. Born in Bologna, Italy, Leo Lentelli came to the United States in 1903. His work also includes *Golden Sprays*, two eleven-foot nudes from the 1939 New York World's Fair and sculptural decorations for Rockefeller Center and Saint John the Divine in New York City.

35. Offices occupied the upper floors of the building, and five shops fronted the street. "Work Begun on Bank Building for S. W. Straus & Co.," *Real Estate Record and Builder's Guide* 106 (September 25, 1920): 427; "S. W. Straus & Co. Moves Into Uptown Financial Center," *Real Estate Record and Builder's Guide*, 713; "Creating a New Investment Center in New York," *The American Architect* 119 (June 22, 1921): 639–43, pls.; "Banking-House, S. W. Straus & Co., Fifth Avenue and 46th Street, New York," *Architecture* 44 (August 1921): pls. 116–19; "Banking House of S. W. Straus & Co.," *Architecture and Building* 53 (August 1921): 65, pls. 125–31.

36. "Two Large Office Buildings for Upper Mid-Town Sites," *Real Estate Record and Builder's Guide* 105 (February 21, 1920): 241; "New Heckscher Building on 5th Ave. to Cost $10,000,000," *Real Estate Record and Builder's Guide* 106 (August 21, 1920): 250; "The Heckscher Building, Fifth Avenue and 57th Street, New York," *Architecture* 44 (September 1921): pl.; "Heckscher Building, New York," *Architectural Forum* 35 (October 1921): 151, pls. 47–49; "Heckscher Building, New York," *Architecture and Building* 54 (February 1922): 17–18, pls. 19–21; "Heckscher Building, New York," *The American Architect* 136 (July 20, 1929): 105; John Burchard and Albert Bush-Brown, *The Architecture of America: A Social and Cultural History* (Boston: Little, Brown, 1966): 349; Christopher Gray, "Streetscapes: The Crown Building," *The New York Times* (February 3, 1991): 10, 6; Stern, Gilmartin, and Mellins, *New York 1930*, 590.

37. Before constructing his twenty-five-story building, Heckscher, who had bought the corner property in 1913, commissioned H. Edwards Ficken to build a three-story office and shop on the site, pulling down large houses that once belonged to Charles C. Morse and William C. Whitney. The Whitney house, designed by George E. Harney in 1875, was originally commissioned by Frederick and Adele Stevens; it was the first important freestanding mansion in the fashionable residential district.

38. The weathervane was removed and melted down for military use during the Second World War.

39. "Heckscher Building, New York," *Architecture and Building*, 17.

40. George Harold Edgell, quoted in Stern, Gilmartin, and Mellins, *New York 1930*, 590.

CHAPTER FIVE
LATE PROJECTS: 1922–1931

1. "Masterpiece of Modern Architecture for Murray Hill," *Real Estate Record and Builder's Guide* 115 (April 11, 1925): 9; "The Tower Building, 200 Madison Avenue, New York City," *Architecture and Building* 58 (July 1926): 80–81, pls. 137–42; Robert A. M. Stern, Gregory Gilmartin, and Thomas Mellins, *New York 1930: Architecture and Urbanism between the Two World Wars* (New York: Rizzoli, 1988): 590.

2. "Another Notable Structure Started in Terminal Zone," *Real Estate Record and Builder's Guide* 110 (August 26, 1922): 265; "Park Lexington Building, New York City," *Architecture and Building* 55 (September 1923): 90, pls. 188–89; W. Parker Chase, *New York, the Wonder City, 1932* (New York: New York Bound, 1983): 246.

3. Brandt's atelier created ironwork for private clients and homes as well as for large-scale projects, including *L'Oasis* at the 1925 Exposition des Arts Décoratif et Industrials Modernes in Paris, the Municipal Theater in Nancy, the Mollien staircase at the Louvre, and the Au Bon Marché department stores.

4. Steinway & Sons had found the 57th and 58th Street sites by 1916. However, the 1916 zoning regulations prohibited commercial buildings on 58th Street. This regulation was later amended. In 1925 the Fifth Avenue Association awarded Steinway Hall its highest honor—the gold medal. Steinway Hall was designated a New York City landmark in 2001. "New Uptown Fine Arts Center is Rapidly Being Created," *Real Estate Record and Builder's Guide* 112 (October 6, 1923): 1923; "Steinway Building, New York City," *Architecture and Building* 57 (August 1925): 69–71, pls. 170–74; W. L. Hopkins, "The Steinway Building, New York," *The Architectural Record* 58 (September 1925): 201–10; "1925 Annual Architectural Awards," *Architecture* 53 (February 1926): 55; Landmarks Preservation Commission, *Steinway Hall, 109–113 West 57th Street, Manhattan* (New York: The Commission, 2001); Stern, Gilmartin, and Mellins, *New York 1930*, 358–59.

5. "Steinway Building, New York City," *Architecture and Building*, 69.

6. "Aeolian Company to Build New Home on Fifth Avenue," *Real Estate Record and Builder's Guide* 115 (April 4, 1925): 7; "Aeolian Building, Fifth Avenue, New York," *The American Architect* 131 (February 5, 1927): 153; "Aeolian Co. Gives Golden Key to City," *The New York Times* (February 24, 1927): 11; "The New Aeolian Building, New York City," *Architecture and Building* 59 (May 1927): 146–47, pls. 91–93; "The Aeolian Building, 689 Fifth Avenue, New York," *The Architect* 8 (June 1927): 335–345; Lewis Mumford, "The Skyline: New Faces on the Avenue," *The New Yorker* 15 (September 8, 1939): 63–64; Landmarks Preservation Commission, *The Aeolian Building* (New York: The Commission, 2002); Carter B. Horsley, "The Aeolian Building: A Bit of Paris on 5th Ave.," *The New York Times* (January 14, 1979): 8, 4; Christopher Gray, "Streetscapes: The Aeolian Building," *The New York Times* (March 23, 2003): 11, 5.

7. The 1912 Aeolian Building replaced the West Presbyterian Church. Oval niches above the side entrances featured bronze busts—Gertrude Vanderbilt Whitney's *Apollo* and Sylvain Salières's *Calliope*. "The New Aeolian Hall," *Architectural Record* 32 (October 1912): 530–51; "Business Growing Rapidly in Forty-Second Street," *The New York Times* (June 25, 1911): 8, 2; "Aeolian Hall Opening," *The New York Times* (October 13, 1912): 8, 2.

8. Charles A. Gould died in 1926 during the construction of the building. When the building was complete in January 1927, it was sold at auction to Gould's daughter, Celia Gould Milne. The Milne Security and Realty Co. owned the building until 1944, when Elizabeth Arden acquired it. In 1929, when Elizabeth Arden was leasing space on the ground floor, a new black marble storefront by Mott Schmidt was added.

9. "Aeolian Co. Gives Golden Key to City," *The New York Times*, 11.

10. "Fifth Avenue Association Makes Annual Medal Awards," *Real Estate Record and Builder's Guide* 118 (December 18, 1926): 7.

11. "Towering Office Building to Replace Academy of Music," *Real Estate Record and Builder's Guide* 117 (April 10, 1926): 7, 9; "Consolidated Gas Company's Building, New York City," *Architecture and Building* 60 (December 1928): 376, 394–95; "Editorially Speaking," *The Architect* 12 (August 1929): 495–97, 513–31; Chase, *New York, the Wonder City, 1932*, 199; Stern, Gilmartin, and Mellins, *New York 1930*, 590.
Warren & Wetmore had previously designed elegant branch offices for the company at 212–18 West 57th Street (1916) and Audubon Avenue and 166th Street (1924). *57th Street*: "New 57th Street Building," *The New York Times* (March 4, 1917): 54; "Consolidated Gas Company Building, West 57th Street, New York," *The Architectural Forum* 28 (March 1918): pls. 33–37. *166th Street*: "Branch House for Consolidated Gas and United Electric," *Real Estate Record and Builder's Guide* 114 (November 29, 1924): 9; "District Office Building of the Consolidated Gas Company, New York City," *Architecture and Building* 57 (October 1925): 87–88.

12. The company's holdings consisted of a twelve-story midblock building and a nineteen-story building designed by Henry J. Hardenbergh in 1919 built around it.

13. T-Square, "The Sky Line: A Glory Regained—New Towers—Glimpses into the Near Future," *The New Yorker* 4 (February 16, 1929): 71; "Editorially Speaking," *The Architect*, 495.

14. "Editorially Speaking," *The Architect*, 497.

15. Before building the Empire Trust and Knabe Building, Kramer commissioned Cross & Cross to design a thirteen-story building for Brentano's at One East 47th Street in 1925. "New Knabe Building in Fifth Avenue to Cost $2,500,000," *Real Estate Record and Builder's Guide* 119 (March 19, 1927): 9; "The Empire Trust Building, New York City," *Architecture and Building* 60 (May 1928): 140, 150–54.

16. "Park Avenue Traffic to Flow Through 35-Story Building," *The New York Times* (September 18, 1927): 1; "To Span Park Avenue with Monumental Building," *Real Estate Record and Builder's Guide* 120 (September 24, 1927): 7–8; "34-Story New York Central Office Building Part of Traffic Improvements," *New York Central Lines Magazine* 8 (October 1927): "Mr. Murchison of New York Says," *The Architect* 10 (April 1928): 115–16; "Bison Heads Adorn the New Building in New York," *New York Central Lines Magazine* 9 (May 1928): 38; "Giant Clock Nears Completion," *The New York Times* (May 13, 1928): 31; C. W. Y. Currie, "Unusual Structural Features in New York Central Skyscraper," *The American Architect* 134 (July 5, 1928): 59–61; "New York Central Building Has 'Cellar' on 15th Floor," *The New York Times* (February 17, 1929): 169; "The New York Central Building, New York City," *Architecture and Building* 56 (May 1929): 138, 153–56, 163; "The New York Central Building Spans Park Avenue," *Through the Ages* 8 (May 1930): 22–26; Chase, *New York, the Wonder City, 1932*, 247; John Burchard and Albert Bush-Brown, *The Architecture of America: A Social and Cultural History* (Boston: Little, Brown, 1966): 270–72; Landmarks Preservation Commission, *New York Central Building* (New York: The Commission, 1987); Stern, Gilmartin, and Mellins, *New York 1930*, 590–594; Christopher Gray, "Streetscapes: 230 Park Avenue," *The New York Times* (September 15, 1996): 9, 5.

17. These plans required extensive collaboration between the city and railroad; negotiations

began in 1919. Once both parties had reached an agreement, legislation was passed to make way for the new building. In return for the building space, the railroad granted the city's desire for easements over the two parcels of land owned by the railroad between 45th and 46th Streets, where the wings of the building are now located, and an extension of Vanderbilt Avenue. These easements gave rise to the shape and form of the building.

18. At this time, Park Avenue's median was reduced from 46th to 57th Street to provide an additional thirty-six feet of roadway.

19. "New York: A City of Clocks," *The New York Times* (May 6, 1928): 131. Educated at the Beaux-Art, McCartan (1879–1947) also executed the Eugene Field Memorial in Lincoln Park, Chicago, and the statue of Diana at the Metropolitan Museum of Art.

20. These details included the winged helmet of Mercury, God of Commerce, mallet and fasces representing development and power, a pendulum supporting the wheels of Progress, and scrolls of Wisdom.

21. While the New York Central occupied offices at 230 Park Avenue, most of the building was intended to be leased.

22. T-Square, "The Sky Line: One Silver Lining—Madison Mixture—And Contents Noted," *The New Yorker* 5 (June 1, 1929): 71.

23. Lewis Mumford, "From a City Notebook," *The New Republic* 60 (September 18, 1929): 125.

24. Harry F. Cunningham, "Architecture," *The American Year Book 1928* (New York: The American Year Book Corporation, 1929): 814.

25. "Beauty of New Office Building in New York is Appreciated by Observer," *New York Central Lines Magazine* 9 (May 1928): 38.

26. T-Square, "The Skyline: Lexington Gothic and Fifth Avenue Modernity," *The New Yorker* 5 (November 16, 1929): 51–2; R. W. Sexton, "The Architect Becomes A Sales Counselor," *The American Architect* 136 (December 1929): 46–51; "Stewart & Company's Store, New York City," *Architecture and Building* 61 (December 1929): 362–80; "Nickel Silver in Stewart & Co.'s Store, New York City," *The Metal Arts* 3 (January 1930): 11, 35; "Store Building for Stewart & Co., New York," *The Architectural Forum* 52 (February 1930): 231–233; James B. Newman, "A Modern Store," *The Architectural Forum* 53 (November 1930): 571–94; T-Square, "The Skyline: Views in Reverse, East Side Tower, Prophecy, Nudes and Commerce," *The New Yorker* 6 (October 18, 1930): 93–95; Office of Metropolitan History, *The Bonwit Teller Building with Notes on Previous Locations* (New York: Office of Metropolitan History, 1978); Stern, Gilmartin, and Mellins, *New York 1930*, 316, 319–21.

27. "Stewart & Company's Store, New York City," *Architecture and Building*, 362; T-Square, "The Skyline: Lexington Gothic and Fifth Avenue Modernity," *The New Yorker* 5, 52. In the late 1920s, the firm also acted as supervising architects for the Lincoln Building (1930) by J. E. R. Carpenter and the Fulton-Flatbush Building, also carried out in a stripped classical style.

28. Sexton, "The Architect Becomes A Sales Counselor," *The American Architect*, 48.

29. One of the leading architectural sculptors of the time, René Paul Chambellan, was also responsible, with Lee Lawrie, for the well-known statue of Atlas in front of Rockefeller Center and the decorative sculpture in Sloan & Robertson's Chanin Building on 42nd Street. Developer Donald Trump demolished the Stewart Building (then known as Bonwit Teller) in 1980 to construct a sixty-two-story bronze-colored glass apartment tower. At that time, he promised the Metropolitan Museum the white stone bas-relief sculptures on the facade; however, they were ultimately smashed because, according to a vice-president of the Trump Organization,

"the merit of these stones was not great enough to justify the effort to save them." Robert D. McFadden, "Developer Scraps Bonwit Sculptures," *The New York Times* (June 6, 1980): 1.

30. "Deal on to Lease Stewart & Co. Store," *The New York Times* (March 27, 1930): 3.

31. Jacques Carlu (1890–1976), Professor of Advanced Design at M.I.T., also designed interiors for T. Eaton Department Stores in Toronto and Montreal. Eugene Schoen (1880–1957), a designer specializing in modern interiors and furniture, executed the decor for the Center Theater at Rockefeller Center (1932). J. Franklin Whitman Jr. was a specialist in industrial design.

32. Newman, "A Modern Store," *The Architectural Forum*, 572.

33. Originally, the height limit of buildings on upper Fifth Avenue, set by the 1916 zoning resolution, stood at 150 feet. Civic groups and homeowners unhappy with the generous height allotment effectively reduced the measure in court to 75 feet in 1921. However, real estate investors and landowners expeditiously reversed the decision in New York's Court of Appeals in 1923, reinstating the 150-foot limit.

34. Advertisement for 1020 Fifth Avenue, *The New York Times*, 1925. The firm also designed the interior finishes for Samuel O. Allen's apartment at 1020 Fifth Avenue. "Apartment House, 1020 Fifth Avenue, New York City," *Architecture and Building* 57 (November 1925): 99–100; Andrew Alpern, *Apartments for the Affluent* (New York: McGraw-Hill, 1975): 120–21; New York Landmarks Preservation Commission, *Metropolitan Museum Historic District Designation Report* (New York: The Commission, 1977): 96–97; Stern, Gilmartin, and Mellins, *New York 1930*, 388–89.

35. "Unique Fifth Avenue Duplex Nearing Completion," *Real Estate Record and Builder's Guide* 120 (September 19, 1927): 9; Stern, Gilmartin, and Mellins, *New York 1930*, 389; Andrew Alpern, *The New York Apartment Houses of Rosario Candela and James Carpenter* (New York: Acanthus Press, 2001): 72–73.

36. "Fifth Avenue Home of Gary to be Razed," *The New York Times* (September 3, 1926): 1; "$1,800,000 Apartment to Occupy Judge Gary Site," *Real Estate Record and Builder's Guide* 120 (December 10, 1927): 7; Alpern, *The New York Apartment Houses of Rosario Candela and James Carpenter*, 48–49.

37. Both Richmond Shreve and William Lamb had been partners at Carrère & Hastings. In 1924, they left to form their own practice. Dorothy Draper also consulted on the interior decorations.

38. "$5,000,000 Apartment House on Clark Mansion Site," *Real Estate Record and Builder's Guide* 129 (October 22, 1927): 9; Pent-House, "New Apartments: Filling a Gap—Park Avenue Still Undaunted—Quiet Magnificence," *The New Yorker* 4 (February 16, 1929); "Apartment at 960 Fifth Avenue, New York City," *The Architectural Record* 67 (March 1930): 244; Stern, Gilmartin, and Mellins, *New York 1930*, 389; David Netto, "960 Fifth Avenue," *The Classicist* 3 (1996–97): 35–41; Alpern, *The New York Apartment Houses of Rosario Candela and James Carpenter*, 62–63.

39. "$5,000,000 Apartment House on Clark Mansion Site," *Real Estate Record and Builder's Guide*, 9.

40. "Another Big Apartment for Upper Fifth Avenue," *The New York Times* (April 1, 1926): 44; "Apartments to be Erected on the Site of the Former Whitney Warren House, 1041 Fifth Avenue, Warren & Wetmore, Architects," *The New York Times* (April 4, 1926): 11, 2; "Lloyd Warren House," *New York Architect* 4 (July 1910): 3–9; 13–25. Warren & Wetmore had

altered two row houses (c. 1905) for Warren by removing the front steps and altering the stairs. Lloyd Warren's double-height living room and dining room contained panels by Robert Winthrop Chanler.

41. Warren & Wetmore also served as consulting architects for a number of important hotels, including the Château Laurier in Ottawa (Ross & McFarlane) and Vancouver Hotel (Francis S. Swales) for the Canadian National Railways, the Château Frontenac in Quebec City for the Canadian Pacific Railways, Dayton-Biltmore in Ohio (Frederick J. Hughes), and Chamberlain-Vanderbilt Hotel in Old Point Comfort, Virginia. Plans for the McConkey Hotel in Toronto, the Ritz-Carlton in Chicago and Rio de Janeiro, and hotels in Bar Harbor, Mexico, Winnipeg, Houston, and Havana never materialized.

42. Beresford, who had worked for the Supervising Architect of the Treasury and the Superintendent of the Capitol, acted as supervising architect on site. A streambed ran below the site, causing the hotel's construction to continue for two and a half years because its foundations had to be burrowed deep underground.

43. "The Mayflower Hotel, Washington, D.C.," *Architecture and Building* 57 (April 1925): 32, 35, pl. 83; C. Stanley Taylor and Vincent K. Buss, eds., *Hotel Planning and Outfitting* (Chicago: Albert–Pick–Barth Companies, 1928): 183. In the mid-1980s the Mayflower underwent a large restoration in which the original lobby was uncovered, skylights in the Palm Court reopened, and murals restored.

44. The Mid Ocean Club in Tucker's Town later occupied Warren & Wetmore's Bermuda Golf Club. However, in 1972, the club dismantled the building and constructed a new building adjacent to the site of the old club, a portion of which still serves as a maintenance building.

45. The three largest hotels in Bermuda were the Bermudiana, the Hamilton, and the Princess. While the firm was working in Bermuda, it also designed a building for Butterfield Bank in Hamilton. "Hotel Bermudiana, Hamilton, Bermuda," *Architecture and Building* 57 (April 1925): 31, pls. 79–80.

46. "New Hotel for Kingston," *The New York Times* (December 23, 1927): 35.

47. Apparently, the architects did not visit the construction site before embarking on the project. During the final phase of construction, the structure began to sink into the swampy ground that was characteristic of the Waikiki area. A retired engineer, called onto the project, recommended placing large girders under the building, using jacks between the girders and sinking columns to prop the building. While the solution worked, it raised the cost of the hotel substantially. Over one thousand guests attended the elaborate soirée and pageant celebrating the opening of the hotel, despite the fact that the *Malalo* did not actually arrive in Hawaii until ten months after the hotel's opening. Colin Wark, "The Royal Hawaiian," *Town & Country* 92 (March 1937): 73–74, 110; Brian McGinty, "Where Trade Winds Blow: The Moana and the Royal Hawaiian, Honolulu," *The Palace Inns: A Connoisseur's Guide to Historic American Hotels* (Harrisburg: Stackpole Books, 1978): 84–94; Stan Cohen, *The Pink Palace: Royal Hawaiian, Waikiki* (Missoula, Montana: Pictorial Histories Publishing Company, 1986).

48. Morgan continued to take a personal interest in the resort and retained his majority investment throughout his life. J. J. Kramer, "The Homestead, Hot Springs, Virginia," *The Last of the Grand Hotels* (New York: Van Nostrand Reinhold, 1978): 60–64.

49. The firm also designed alterations and additions to both the National Theater in Washington, D.C. in 1923 and the Warren Theater in Warren,

Pennsylvania, in 1919. Warren & Wetmore later served as supervising architects for the extravagant Michigan Theater and office building in Detroit (1926) and the Paramount Theater and office building in New York at 1501 Broadway (1926), both by C.W. and George L. Rapp.

50. The organizers of the theater corporation included Otto Kahn, John Jacob Astor, Edmund Baylies, August Belmont, W. B. Osgood Field, James H. Hyde, Clarence H. Mackay, J. Pierpont Morgan, William K. Vanderbilt, Cornelius Vanderbilt, Henry Walters, and Orme Wilson.

51. On March 19, 1911, *The New York Times* announced that Warren & Wetmore had been selected to design the new home of the New Theater, which was to move to a site on 44th Street adjoining the Hotel Astor, after the Central Park West location proved unsuccessful. The plan never materialized.

52. Renamed the St. James in 1932, the Erlanger was designated a New York City interior and exterior-landmark in 1987. "The Erlanger Theatre, New York City," *Architecture and Building* 59 (September 1927): 286, 312, pls. 189–90; Landmarks Preservation Commission, *St. James Theater (originally Erlanger Theater)* (New York: the Commission, 1987); "St. James Theater," *Interior Design* 58 (September 1987): 286–7.

53. "Erlanger Theater: Buffalo, N.Y.," *Marquee* 4 (2nd quarter, 1972): 20.

54. The Berkeley-Carteret, completed in 1925, filled a large city lot and, like the Westchester-Biltmore, was composed of a central block with four wings extending off the building at obtuse angles. While a central tower capped the spare brick structure, Warren & Wetmore's architectural decoration and ornamentation were kept to a minimum. "The Berkeley-Carteret Hotel, Asbury Park, N. J.," *Architecture and Building* 57 (October 1925): 88, pls. 214–16.

55. Plans for the convention hall from 1923 consisted of a red brick building with terra-cotta trim and a picturesque tower. Asbury Partners are currently restoring the convention hall, theater, power plant, and carousel building. "Paramount Theatre and Conventional Hall, Asbury Park, N. J., *Architecture and Building* 62 (August 1930): 244–45, 249.

56. "$1,500,000 Casino for Asbury Park's Boardwalk," *The New York Times* (May 20, 1928): 154; "Casino Building, Asbury Park, N. J.," *Architecture and Building* 62 (August 1930): 250.

57. Vanderbilt left Eagle's Nest to Suffolk Country upon his death in 1944. The house, grounds, and museum are now the Vanderbilt Museum. Augusta Owen Patterson, "Rambling Spanish House on Long Island," *Town & Country* 83 (October 15, 1928): 44–49; "The Vanderbilt Museum," *Town & Country* 92 (December 1937): 81–83, 169; Lisa and Donald Sclare, *Beaux-Arts Estates: A Guide to the Architecture of Long Island* (New York: Viking Press, 1979): 185–89; Archives, Suffolk County Vanderbilt Museum, Centerport, Long Island; Robert B. King, *Vanderbilt Homes* (New York: Rizzoli, 1989): 148–58; Robert B. MacKay, Anthony K. Baker, and Carol A. Traynor, *Long Island Country Houses and Their Architects, 1860–1940* (New York: W. W. Norton & Co., 1997): 436–38.

58. Ronald Pearce worked at Warren & Wetmore for a number of years. By 1940, he had his own practice at 11 East 40th Street. A close friend of Warren, Pearce was also an usher at Warren's funeral service in 1943.

59. Letter from Ronald H. Pearce to William K. Vanderbilt, June 6, 1923, in the archives of the Suffolk County Vanderbilt Museum, Centerport, Long Island.

60. Letter from Whitney Warren to William K. Vanderbilt, April 24th, 1930, in the archives of the Suffolk Country Vanderbilt Museum.

Apparently, the firm had commissioned Henri Courtais to do work in one of the bedrooms without Vanderbilt's approval. Previously, at Vanderbilt's apartment at 651 Park Avenue, the firm had commissioned murals by Allyn Cox in the card room without his knowledge.

61. Ronald H. Pearce, "The Deepdale Golf and Country Club, Great Neck, Long Island," *The Architectural Record* 60 (December 1926): 517–26. Also: MacKay, Baker, and Traynor, *Long Island Country Houses and Their Architects, 1860–1940*, 438–39.

62. Warren & Wetmore Collection, Avery Architectural and Fine Arts Library, Columbia University; Frank W. Skinner, "The Structure of Indoor Tennis Courts," *Architectural Forum* 49 (August 1928): 270–74; MacKay, Baker, and Traynor, *Long Island Country Houses and Their Architects, 1860–1940*, 439.

63. John Foreman and Robbe Pierce Stimson, *The Vanderbilts and the Gilded Age: Architectural Aspirations, 1879–1901* (New York: St. Martin's Press, 1991): 119–21.

64. Whitney Warren to Charlotte A. Tooker Warren, Paris, June 12, 1915. Whitney Warren Papers, bMS Am 2113 (103). By permission of the Houghton Library, Harvard University. While Warren mentions this scheme to his wife, it appears that it was Wetmore who first suggested it to Warren. Warren, entrenched in the wartime situation in France, was concerned that Wetmore's proposition would compromise his philanthropic motives in Europe. He wrote, "I am the only American over here working for the cause, who has absolutely nothing to pull out of it excepting the satisfaction of having rendered what little service one could to humanity in general and I very much want to keep right along this road." However, after some consideration, Warren felt they could "undertake the matter . . . at the request and sanction of the French government," noting that "there is sure to be a certain amount of criticism, but that is always the lot of anybody who attempts to do anything." Whitney Warren to Charles D. Wetmore, Paris, June 6, 1915. Whitney Warren Papers, bMS Am 2113 (100). By permission of the Houghton Library, Harvard University.

65. Whitney Warren, "To the Editor: $600,000 for Louvain Library," *The New York Times* (February 17, 1924): 8, 16.

66. The site chosen for the library was originally intended for the Palais de Justice or the Magistrates Court. "La Nouvelle Bibliothèque de Louvain," *L'Illustration* 15 (July 23, 1921); "Design for the Library at Louvain," *The Architects' Journal* 54 (August 24, 1921): 219; "To Rebuild the Library at Louvain," *Architecture* 45 (March 1922): 73–77; Glen C. Quiett, "Rebuilding the Library at Louvain," *The American Magazine of Art* 14 (March 1923): 140–43; Rexford Newcomb, "The New Library at the University of Louvain," *The Western Architect* 32 (April 1923): 47–48; Pierre de Soete, *The Louvain Library Controversy: The Misadventures of an American Artist or "Furore Teutonico Diruta, Dono Americano Restituta"* (Concord, New Hampshire: Rumford Press, 1929); Ian C. MacCallum, "*Diruta Teutonica Furore,*" *Journal of the A.I.A.* 10 (October and November 1948): 170–78, 202–208; Chris Coppens, Mark Derez, and Jan Roegiers, eds., *Leuven University Library: 1425–2000* (Leuven: University Press, 2005).

67. Butler's committee inaugurated a $1 million drive in 1923. Seven hundred colleges, universities, and institutions of learning in the United States contributed money toward the library.

68. Hoover's American Commission for Relief in Belgium raised $300,000; his Commission for Relief in Belgium's Educational Foundation raised an additional $350,000.

69. Lessing Williams, Autobiographical Statement: Education and Training, Box One, Lessing

Williams Collection, Avery Architectural and Fine Arts Library, Columbia University. When work was suspended on the library in 1924, Williams returned to the United States. He later became a leading church designer in the Gothic tradition.

70. Quoted in Quiett, "Rebuilding the Library at Louvain," *The American Magazine of Art*, 141.

71. Quiett, "Rebuilding the Library at Louvain," *The American Magazine of Art*, 143.

72. Newcomb, "The New Library at the University of Louvain," *The Western Architect*, 47.

73. Lessing Williams, Autobiographical Statement: Education and Training, Box One, Lessing Williams Collection, Avery Architectural and Fine Arts Library, Columbia University.

74. After a German attack on the library in 1940, Henry Lacoste (1885–1968) redesigned the interior finishes in the reading room.

75. The gold leaf helmet on Notre Dame des Victoires was created from a five-dollar gold piece given to Warren by an American mother during one of his fundraising lectures for the library at the University of Virginia. The piece was among her son's personal effects, found after he was killed during the war.

76. On the gables there was an eagle (United States), lion (Belgium), unicorn (England), cock (France), she-wolf (Italy), and dragon (Japan); on the rear gables, Serbia and Montenegro (eagle), Romania (lion), Russia (bear), and Portugal (griffon). In the wrought-iron vases set into the balustrade were additional symbols of the Allies: the lily (France), chrysanthemum (Japan), maple leaf (Canada), and rose (York), all executed by Louvain sculptor Jozef van Uyvanck (1884–1967). A figure of Cardinal Mercier by Pierre de Soete was incorporated into the side of the building.

77. MacCallum, "*Diruta Teutonica Furore,*" *Journal of the A.I.A.*, 203.

78. At the building's inauguration on July 4, 1928, the issue of the inscription was still unsolved. A wood balustrade covered in plaster of Paris was installed for the dedication. Warren, Hoover (then campaigning for the presidency), and the king and queen of Belgium (embarrassed by the controversy) were absent.

79. The lower court had based its decision on the Belgian law protecting architects' plans. The upper court, however, contended that that law was intended to prevent the pirating of plans, not to allow an architect to impose details on the building's owner.

80. "Foresees New Riots Over Louvain Decision," *The New York Times* (March 9, 1932): 19. Warren was ordered by the court to pay for all of the proceedings from the beginning of the trial ($39,500).

81. Warren's local representative, Pierre De Soete, was questioned in Morren's second balustrade smashing. He maintained that neither he nor Warren gave Morren any sort of encouragement to smash the balustrade. The words *Furore Teutonico Diruta* were eventually incorporated into a war memorial at Dinant, despite protests from Berlin; in 1940 German forces destroyed the monument.

82. William L. Shirer, *Berlin Diary: A Journal of a Foreign Correspondent, 1934–41* (Baltimore: Johns Hopkins Press, 2002): 356.

83. "Whitney Warren Dies; Designed Grand Central," *New York Herald Tribune* (January 25, 1943): 8.

BIBLIOGRAPHY

Alpern, Andrew. *Apartments for the Affluent*. New York: McGraw-Hill, 1975.

———. *The New York Apartment Houses of Rosario Candela and James Carpenter*. New York: Acanthus Press, 2001.

Auchincloss, Louis. *The Vanderbilt Era: Profiles of a Gilded Age*. New York: Charles Scribner's Sons, 1989.

Bacon, Mardges. *Ernest Flagg: Beaux-Arts Architect and Urban Reformer*. New York: The Architectural History Foundation, 1986.

Baker, Paul R. *Stanny: The Gilded Life of Stanford White*. New York: Free Press, 1989.

Beals, Allen E. "The New York Hotel and Its Mission," *Real Estate Record and Guide* 87 (May 13, 1911): 898.

Beard, Patricia. *After the Ball*. New York: Harper Collins, 2003.

Belle, John, and Maxinne R. Leighton. *Grand Central: Gateway to a Million Lives*. New York: W. W. Norton & Company, 2000.

Bennett, Arnold. *Those United States*. London: Martin Secker, 1912.

———. *Paris Nights*. New York: George H. Doran Company, 1913.

Boyd, John Taylor, Jr. "The New York Zoning Resolution and Its Influence upon Design." *Architectural Record* 48 (September 1920): 192–217.

Brooklyn Museum. *The American Renaissance: 1876–1917*. New York: Pantheon Books, 1979.

Brown, Frank Chouteau. "The Decoration of Hotel Rooms and Suites." *The Architectural Review* 2 (April 1913).

Burchard, John, and Albert Bush-Brown. *The Architecture of America: A Social and Cultural History*. Boston: Little, Brown, 1966.

Bunting, Bainbridge. *Harvard: An Architectural History*. Cambridge, Mass.: The Belknap Press of Harvard University Press, 1985.

Cable, Mary. *Top Drawer: American High Society from the Gilded Age to the Roaring Twenties*. New York: Atheneum, 1984.

Chase, W. Parker. *New York, the Wonder City, 1932*. New York: New York Bound, 1983.

Cleveland, Amory. *Who Killed Society?* New York: Harper & Brothers, 1960.

Condit, Carl W. *The Port of New York: A History of the Rail and Terminal System from the Grand Central Electrification to the Present*. Chicago: University of Chicago Press, 1981.

De Penanrun, David, Roux, and Delaire. *Les Architects: Élèves de l'École des Beaux-Arts*. Paris: Librarie de la Construction Moderne, 1907.

De Soete, Pierre. *The Louvain Library Controversy: The Misadventures of an American Artist*. Concord, N. H.: Rumford Press, 1929.

Drexler, Arthur. *The Architecture of the Ecole des Beaux-Arts*. Cambridge, Mass.: MIT Press, 1977.

Dorsey, Hebe. *The Belle Epoque in the Paris Herald*. London: Thames & Hudson, 1986.

Droege, John Albert. *Passenger Terminals and Trains*. New York: McGraw-Hill, 1916.

Edgell, George Harold. *American Architecture of To-Day*. New York: Scribner's, 1928.

Foreman, John, and Robbe Pierce Stimson. *The Vanderbilts and the Gilded Age: Architectural Aspirations, 1879–1901*. New York: St. Martin's Press, 1991.

Gayle, Margot, and Michele Cohen. *The Art Commission and the Municipal Art Society Guide to Manhattan's Outdoor Sculpture*. New York: Prentice Hall Press, 1988.

Graves, William Hagerman. "The Use of Tile in the Interior Finish and Decoration of Hotels." *The Architectural Review* 2 (April 1913): 44–48.

Gregory, Alexis. *The Golden Age of Travel, 1880–1939*. New York: Rizzoli, 1990.

Groth, Paul. *Living Downtown: The History of Residential Hotels in the United States*. Berkeley: University of California Press, 1994.

Havemeyer, Harry W. *Along the Great South Bay: From Oakdale to Babylon, the Story of a Summer Spa, 1840–1940*. Mattituck, N. Y.: Amereon House, 1996.

Hopkins, Walter. "Architectural Design for Hotel Interiors." *Architectural Forum* 39 (November 1923): 205–9.

James, Henry. *The American Scene*. 1907. Reprint, New York: Scribner's Sons, 1946.

Kidney, Walter C. *The Architecture of Choice: Eclecticism in America 1880–1930*. New York: Braziller, 1974.

Kramer, J. J. *The Last of the Grand Hotels*. New York: Van Nostrand Reinhold, 1978.

Lorne, Francis. "The New Architecture of a Flamboyant Civilization." *Arts and Decoration* 24 (November 1925): 58–59, 90.

MacKay, Robert B., Anthony K. Baker, and Carol A. Traynor. *Long Island Country Houses and Their Architects, 1860–1940*. New York: W. W. Norton and Company, 1997.

McGinty, Brian. *The Palace Inns: A Connoisseur's Guide to Historic American Hotels*. Harrisburg, Pa.: Stackpole, 1978.

Meeks, Carroll L. V. *The Railroad Station: An Architectural History*. New Haven, Conn.: Yale University Press, 1956.

Middleton, William D. *Grand Central: The World's Greatest Railway Terminal*. San Marino, Calif.: Golden West Books, 1977.

"Monumental Gateway to a Great City: Completing the Grand Central Terminal, New York." *Scientific American* 107 (December 7, 1912): 484–87, 499–500.

Nevins, Deborah, ed. *Grand Central Terminal: A City within a City*. New York: Municipal Art Society, 1982.

"New York's Hotels, Old and New." *The American Architect* 68 (July 14, 1920): 43–44.

Noffsinger, James Phillip. *The Influence of the École des Beaux Arts on the Architects of the United States*. Washington, D.C.: Catholic University of America Press, 1955.

Oliver, Richard, ed. *The Making of an Architect, 1881–1981: Columbia University in the City of New York*. New York: Rizzoli, 1981.

Pennoyer, Peter, and Anne Walker. *The Architecture of Delano & Aldrich*. New York: W. W. Norton & Co., 2003.

Pevsner, Nikolaus. *A History of Building Types*. London: Thames & Hudson, 1976.

Price, Matlock. "Great Modern Hotels of America." *Arts and Decoration* 21 (July 1924): 39–52.

Rousmaniere, John. *The Clubhouse at Sea*. New York: New York Yacht Club, 2001.

Schlichting, Kurt C. *Grand Central Terminal: Railroads, Engineering, and Architecture in New York City*. Baltimore: Johns Hopkins University Press, 2001.

Sclare, Lisa, and Donald Sclare. *Beaux-Arts Estates: A Guide to the Architecture of Long Island*. New York: Viking Press, 1979.

Shaver, Peter D. *The National Register of Historic Places in New York State*. New York: Rizzoli, 1993.

Sorel, Cécile. *An Autobiography*. London: Staples Press Limited, 1953.

———. *Les Belle Heures de ma Vie*. Monaco: Éditions du Rocher, 1946.

Stein, Susan R., ed. *The Architecture of Richard Morris Hunt*. Chicago: University of Chicago Press, 1986.

Stern, Robert A. M., Gregory Gilmartin, and John Massengale. *New York 1900: Metropolitan Architecture and Urbanism, 1890–1915*. New York: Rizzoli, 1983.

———, Gregory Gilmartin, and Thomas Mellins. *New York 1930: Architecture and Urbanism between the Two World Wars*. New York: Rizzoli, 1988.

———, Thomas Mellins, and David Fishman. *New York 1960: Architecture and Urbanism between the Second World War and the Bicentennial*. New York: Monacelli Press, 1995.

Strouse, Jean. *Morgan: American Financier*. New York: Perennial, 1999.

Swales, Francis S. "The Railway Hotel: Its Function, Planning, and Service Equipment." *The Architectural Review* 2 (April 1913): 54–57.

Tallmadge, Thomas E. *The Story of Architecture in America*. New York: W. W. Norton & Company, 1936.

Weeks, Edward. *My Green Age*. Boston: Little, Brown, 1973.

Wetmore, Charles D. "The Development of the Modern Hotel." *The Architectural Review* 2 (April 1913): 37–39.

Wharton, Edith, and Ogden Codman, Jr. *The Decoration of Houses*. 1902. Reprint, New York: W. W. Norton & Company, 1978.

White, Samuel G. *The Houses of McKim, Mead & White*. New York: Rizzoli, 1998.

White, Samuel G., and Elizabeth White. *McKim, Mead & White: The Masterworks*. New York: Rizzoli, 2003.

Wilson, Richard Guy. *McKim, Mead & White, Architects*. New York: Rizzoli, 1983.

Woon, Basil. *The Paris That's Not in Guide Books*. New York: Brentano's, 1926.

UNPUBLISHED SOURCES

Centre Historique des Archives Nationales, Archives, École Nationale Superieure des Beaux-Arts, Paris, France.

George B. Corsa Hotel Collection, The New-York Historical Society, New York City.

Lessing Williams Collection, Avery Architectural and Fine Arts Library, Columbia University.

Archives, New York Yacht Club, New York City.

Spinzia, Raymond E., and Judith A. Spinzia. *Long Island's Prominent North Shore Families: Their Estates and Their Country Houses*. Nassau County Museum, Long Island Studies Institute, Hempstead, Long Island, 1997.

Stanford White Collection, Avery Architectural and Fine Arts Library, Columbia University.

Suffolk County Vanderbilt Museum, reference and archives, Centerport, New York.

ACKNOWLEDGMENTS

Letters of Mary Whitney Phoenix to her daughter, Mary Caroline Phoenix Warren, 1875–76, Newport Historical Society, Newport, Rhode Island.

Warren & Wetmore Collection, Avery Architectural and Fine Arts Library, Columbia University.

A list of the Works of Warren & Wetmore presented to Avery Library by P. M. Corry in memory of Whitney Warren and Charles D. Wetmore, 1952.

William Wilgus Papers, Manuscripts and Archives Division, The New York Public Library, Astor, Lenox, and Tilden Foundations.

Whitney Warren Papers, Houghton Library, Harvard University.

Whitney Warren, unpublished diaries, Redwood Library and Athenaeum, Newport, Rhode Island.

Whitney Warren Collection, Cooper-Hewitt, National Design Museum, New York.

ARTICLES AND LECTURES BY WHITNEY WARREN

État de la cathedrale de Reims après le bombardement par les Allemands. Lecture given at the Institute de France, October 3, 1914. Paris: Typ. de Firmin-Didot et cie, 1914.

The Testimony of an American Citizen in France, 1914–15. A Lecture at the Ritz Hotel, December 9, 1915 for the Benefit of the Secours National of France. New York: Cheltenham Press, privately printed, 1915.

On the Neutrality of the United States. Speech made before the American Club, Paris, June 10, 1915. Paris: La Renaissance, 1915.

Our Friend, France. Lecture given at the Harvard Club under the auspices of the Cercle Francais, February 1, 1916.

American Charity in France: What has been done and what remains to be done? Lecture given in Boston, February 4, 1916. New York, 1916.

The Duty of the Neutrals. A Lecture given at the Ateneo, Madrid, Spain, January 10, 1917. New York: s.n., 1917.

The Question of Alsace and Lorraine. Lecture given at Aeolian Hall, New York, March 14, 1917. New York: 1917.

The Just Claims of Italy: The Question of the Trenton, of Trieste and of the Adriatic. 1917.

L'immense Effort de l'Italie. Roma: Direzione della Nuova Antologia, 1917.

Fiume and d'Annunzio. Lecture given on November 4, 1919 in Paris.

The Role of the Italian Navy in the Great War. Lecture given at the Colony Club, New York, January 22, 1920. New York, 1920.

Montenegro, the Crime of the Peace Conference. New York: Brentano's, 1922.

"The Vicious Circle." Why Is the Treasury Worse than Empty and Confidence Absolutely Lacking? New York: W. Warren, 1931–32.

Among the firms that shaped New York during the first decades of the twentieth century, Warren & Wetmore was one of the most important and prolific. Under the leadership of Virgil Conway, the MTA and Beyer Blinder Belle executed an awe-inspiring and meticulous rehabilitation of Grand Central Terminal, which recovered the beauty of this New York landmark and highlighted the creativity of Warren & Wetmore's work. While many books have been written about the firm's role in the design of Grand Central, none has examined Warren & Wetmore's impressive body of work as a whole. Any study of a New York-based architectural firm starts with a firm foundation of scholarship, such as that established by the four volume series by Robert A. M. Stern and his coauthors. Both *New York 1900: Metropolitan Architecture and Urbanism, 1890–1915* by Robert A. M. Stern, Gregory Gilmartin, and John Massengale and *New York 1930: Architecture and Urbanism between the Two World Wars* by Robert A. M. Stern, Gregory Gilmartin, and Thomas Mellins provided us with a solid picture of the context of Warren & Wetmore's world. Recent publications, such as John Belle and Maxinne R. Leighton's *Grand Central: Gateway to a Million Lives* and Kurt C. Schlichting's *Grand Central Terminal: Railroads, Engineering, and Architecture in New York City*, provided an excellent starting point for our research.

Among the many people and organizations who shared recollections and information or supported our work, we are grateful to Louis Auchincloss; Paul R. Baker; at Le Parker Meridien, Victoria Barr; Patricia Beard; John Belle; at the New York Yacht Club, Sam Croll and Michael Levitt; Andrew Dolkart; at the University Club, John Dorman; Whitney Ellsworth; Patricia Fenoff; at the Century Association Archives Foundation, Russell Flinchum; John Foreman; at the Centre Historique des Archives Nationales, Nadine Gastaldi; Ray Gastil; Gregory Gilmartin; John Goelet; Christopher Gray; William Irvine; Thomas Jayne; Maxinne R. Leighton; Aleks Matviak; Rob McLean; at the Mid Ocean Club, Bryan J. Mewett; Joseph and Nazee Moinian; Henry W. Munroe; Alan Pergament; at the Ritz-Carlton Montreal, Paola Pillot; Henry Hope Reed; John Rousmaniere; Michael Rives; Brian Sichol; Christian Sonne; at the New York State Historical Association, Shelley Stocking; W. Barry Thomson; Jack Turpin; Elsie Wilson Thompson; William Wetmore; at the Sheraton, Waikiki, B. J. Whitman; and Mrs. Orme Wilson, Jr. Information provided by local historical societies, libraries, and hotels designed by the firm was integral to our effort to piece together a picture of the partners and their work and helped us compile our catalogue raisonné.

We are indebted to the following people and organizations for giving us access to the firm's buildings: at the Convent of the Sacred Heart, Craig MacPherson; Mr. and Mrs. Richard Gordon; at Metro North, Marjorie Anders; at the Myopia Hunt Club, Penny Patronzio; G. C. Rapaille; at Steinway & Sons, Leo Spellman; at the Suffolk County Vanderbilt Museum, Carol Sperandeo; at the Tuxedo Club, Kenneth W. Adams; at the University Library, Louvain, Mark Derez; George H. Warren; George H. Warren Jr.; at the Westchester Country Club, David B. Prentiss.

We must thank Director Gerald Beasley, Curator of Drawings and Archives Janet Parks, and Julie Tozer at Columbia University's Avery Architectural and Fine Arts Library for all of their help. We are also grateful to Floramae McCarron-Cates, Assistant Curator Drawings, Prints and Graphic Design, Cooper-Hewitt, National Design Museum; Florence Ogg, Director of Exhibits and Collections, Suffolk Country Vanderbilt Museum; Melanie Bower and Marguerite Lavin at the Museum of the City of New York; Lynda M. Bronaugh, Redwood Library & Athenæum, Newport, Rhode Island; Sandra Markham, New-York Historical Society; Marie Barbot-Cooper, Library of Congress, and the staff of the Houghton Library at Harvard University.

Finally, we are especially grateful to Robert A. M. Stern for his encouragement and guidance; Jonathan Wallen, assisted by Lester Ali, for the beautiful photography; Abigail Sturges for her book design; and our editor, Nancy Green, at W. W. Norton & Company, for making this book possible.

INDEX

Numbers in *italics* refer to illustrations.